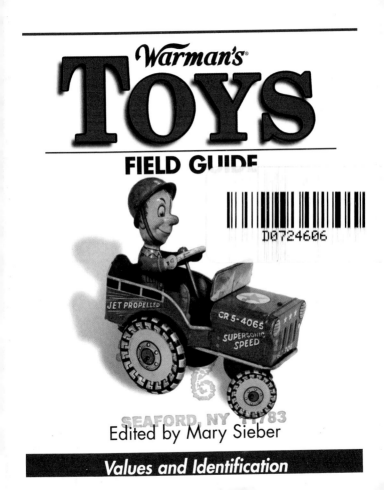

Warman's
TOYS
FIELD GUIDE

JET PROPELLED

CR 5-4065

SUPERSONIC SPEED

SEAFORD, NY 11783

Edited by Mary Sieber

Values and Identification

©2004 by Krause Publications

Published by

kp **krause publications**
An imprint of F+W Publications, Inc.

700 East State Street • Iola, WI 54990-0001
715-445-2214 • 888-457-2873
www.krause.com
Our toll-free number to place an order or obtain
a free catalog is (800) 258-0929.

Library of Congress Catalog Number: 2004101587

ISBN: 0-87349-817-8

Edited by Mary Sieber

Designed by Kay Sanders

Printed in the United States of America

Contents

Introduction

Since I was a kid, my dad and I have attended weekend toy shows. While we both scour dealers' tables for new additions to my dad's toy collection, it was my special task to root through the bargain boxes on the floor. After all, you never know what you'll find until you dig in. There's a little bit of everything in those oft-overlooked boxes, and through the years I have uncovered some fabulous toys.

One such bargain box led to a remarkable discovery. I pulled out a Corgi Batmobile. Its paint was chipped and dull, the scratched windshield had a section missing, and its plastic Batman figure was long lost. I had to have it. That Batmobile began a toy collection beyond my childhood playthings. I'm sure that most collectors also have vivid stories recalling the discovery of the one special piece that started their collections.

There has never been a better time to be a toy collector. Toys of all vintages and varieties are readily available through auction houses, toy shows, online auctions, garage sales, and classified ads. No matter where you look, education and experience are valuable tools that help unearth collectible toys. Appreciation for the hobby as a whole often leads us down collecting avenues we hadn't previously considered—I wasn't searching for Corgi Batmobiles that day, I just liked Batman.

This book is a lot like those bargain boxes—there's a little bit of everything, and it's all worth digging through. Whether your tastes drift toward action figures, farm toys, games, space toys, or vehicles, you can make discoveries in Fisher-Price, PEZ, tin wind-ups, model kits, or a host of other areas. Enjoy!

Karen O'Brien, Editor
O'Brien's Collecting Toys
Toys & Prices

Common Abbreviations

Common abbreviations found throughout this book are listed below. In some sections more detailed abbreviations or additional comments are noted. If no abbreviation is listed by the price, assume the toy is mint-in-package condition.

MIP or MIP (Mint in Box, Mint in Package, C10):
Just like new, in the original package, preferably still sealed. Boxes may have been opened, but any packages inside (as with model kits) remain unopened. Blister cards should be intact, undamaged, and unopened. Factory-sealed boxes should be unopened and often command higher prices.

MNP or MNB (Mint No Package, Mint No Box, C10):
This describes a toy typically produced in the 1960s
or later in mint condition, but missing its original
package. This may also include a prototype or one-of-
a-kind toy. A toy outside its original package is often
referred to as "loose."

NM (Near Mint, C9):
A toy that appears like new in overall appearance but
exhibits very minor wear and does not have the
original box. An exception would be a toy that came
in kit form. A kit in near mint condition would be
expected to have the original box, but the box would
display some wear.

EX (Excellent, C8):
A toy that is complete and has been played with. Signs of
minor wear may be evident, but the toy is very clean
and well cared for.

VG (Very Good, C6):
A toy that obviously has been played with and shows
general overall wear. Paint chipping is readily
apparent. In metal toys, some minor rust may be
evident. In sets, some minor pieces may be missing.

GD or G (Good, C4):
A toy with evidence of heavy play, dents, chips, and
possibly moderate rust. The toy may be missing
a major replaceable component, such as a battery
compartment door, or may be in need of repair. In
sets, several pieces may be missing.

Action Figures

By Tom Bartsch

If you had to pick one of the most expansive, diverse and fastest-growing markets in the toy industry, you don't need to look any further than action figures.

When action figures first burst on the scene in 1964 with the introduction of G.I. Joe, boys finally had an answer to fashion dolls and Barbie. Once Joe hit the scene, the floodgates started to open on the male-oriented action figure genre.

Super Power Rangers by Kenner. Left to right: Firestorm, 1985, and Parademon, 1985. Each $35 MIP.

Using the foundations of comic books, TV series and movies, action figures had all the ammunition they needed to entice a buying public. The background stories were already laid out – all kids had to do was re-enact what they were watching and reading.

The figures produced today are a far cry from the same-body, different face scheme used by many companies in years past. With technologies like RealScan, a laser scan of the actor or actress from a film or TV series is scanned from head to toe, figures become eerily life-like.

The action figure market is vast and fickle at the same time. Action figure aficionados are a unique breed. Some will collect anything and everything, while others are fanatic about little-known properties and will scoop every related collectible they can find.

If you need an overall rule of thumb of which figures carry a higher price tag, check their release date. Most figures from the 1960s through the mid-1970s will make you a very happy person if you have one.

Tom Bartsch is editor of Toy Shop *magazine and associate editor of* Toy Cars & Models, *both published by Krause Publications, Iola, Wis.*

Action Figures

Batman & Robin (Kenner, 1997-98)

12" Figures

	NM	MIP
Batgirl, 1997-98, Kenner	$15	$35
Batman, 1997-98, Kenner	$13	$25
Batman and Poison Ivy, Kenner, 2-pack, cloth outfits	$20	$40
Ice Battle Batman (WB Exclusive), 1997-98, Kenner, includes Batarang and Bat Laser	$10	$25
Mr. Freeze, 1997-98, Kenner	$10	$20
Robin, 1997-98, Kenner	$13	$23
Ultimate Batman, 1997-98, Kenner	$8	$20
Ultimate Robin, 1997-98, Kenner	$8	$20

5" Figures

Bane, 1997, Kenner, Series 1, w/double-attack axe and colossal crusher gauntlet	$3	$8
Batgirl, 1997, Kenner, on the right w/battle blade blaster and strike scythe	$3	$5
Batman, Ambush Attack, 1998, Kenner, Series 2, w/Arsenal Cape and Restraint Rockets	$3	$8
Batman, Battle Board with Ring, 1997-98, Kenner	$3	$8
Batman, Heat Scan, 1997, Kenner, Series 1, w/opti-scope launcher and laser ray emitters	$3	$8
Batman, Hover Attack, 1997, Kenner, Series 1, w/Blasting battle sled and sickle shields	$3	$8
Batman, Ice Blade, 1997-98, Kenner	$3	$8
Batman, Ice Blade with Ring, 1997-98, Kenner	$3	$13

Batman & Robin—Ice Battle Batman (WB Exclusive), Kenner, $50 MIP.

	NM	MIP
Batman, Laser Cape with Ring, 1997-98, Kenner	$3	$8
Batman, Mail Away from Fuji, 1997-98, Kenner	$23	$40
Batman, Neon Armor, 1997-98, Kenner	$3	$8
Batman, Neon Armor with Ring, 1997-98, Kenner	$3	$13
Batman, Rotoblade with ring, 1997-98, Kenner	$3	$13
Batman, Sky Assault with ring, 1997-98, Kenner	$3	$13
Batman, Snow Tracker, 1997-98, Kenner	$3	$8
Batman, Thermal Shield with ring, 1998, Kenner, Series 2, w/Heatblast cape and flying disc blaster	$3	$13
Batman, Wing Blast, 1997-98, Kenner	$3	$8
Batman, Wing Blast with Ring, 1997-98, Kenner	$3	$13
Bruce Wayne, Battle Gear, 1997, Kenner, Series 1, w/ice block armor suit and cryo claw shooter	$3	$8
Frostbite, 1997-98, Kenner	$3	$8
Jungle Venom Poison Ivy, 1997, Kenner, on the left, Series 1, w/toxic spray venom cannon and entanglement vines	$3	$5
Mr. Freeze, Ultimate Armor with Ring, 1997, Kenner, Series 2, w/freeze-on missile	$5	$13
Robin, Attack Wing with Ring, 1998, Kenner, Series 2, w/vertical assault cape	$3	$8
Robin, Blade Blast, 1998, Kenner, Series 2, w/rapid deploy vine slicers and blasting battle spear	$3	$8

Batman & Robin—Ultimate Batman, Kenner, $40 MIP.

	NM	MIP
Robin, Iceboard, 1997-98, Kenner	$3	$5
Robin, Razor Skate, 1997, Kenner, Series 1, w/chopping blade launcher and ice battle armor	$3	$5
Robin, Talon Strike, 1998, Kenner, Series 2, w/twin capture claws and roto blade	$3	$5
Robin, Talon Strike with Ring, 1997-98, Kenner	$3	$13
Robin, Triple Strike, 1997-98, Kenner	$3	$5
Robin, Triple Strike with Ring, 1997-98, Kenner	$3	$13

Accessories

	NM	MIP
Batmobile, 1998, Kenner	$8	$20
Batmobile, Sonic, 1998, Kenner	$8	$15
Ice Fortress, 1998, Kenner	$5	$8
Ice Hammer, 1998, Kenner	$10	$20
Iceglow Bathammer, 1997, Kenner	$25	$50
Jet Blade, 1998, Kenner	$8	$20
NightSphere, 1998, Kenner	$10	$25

Deluxe Figures, 1997

	NM	MIP
Batgirl with Icestrike Cycle, 1997, Kenner, w/snow assault mode and razor wheel launcher	$10	$20
Batman, 1998, Kenner	$5	$10
Batman, Blast Wing, 1997, Kenner, w/ice chopper hover pack and freeze-seeker missile	$5	$8
Batman, Rooftop Pursuit, 1997, Kenner	$5	$8
Mr. Freeze, Ice Terror, 1997, Kenner	$5	$8
Robin, 1998, Kenner	$5	$10
Robin, Blast Wing, 1997, Kenner	$5	$8

Batman: The Animated Series—Batcycle, Kenner, $20 MIP.

	NM	MIP

Robin, Glacier Battle, 1997, Kenner, Tandem Assault
  Snow Skiff and Stinger Missile.................$5...........................$13
Robin, Redbird Cycle, 1997, Kenner, w/Night strike
  missile and ice slice blades. ....$10...........................$20

Figures
Aerial Combat Batman, 1997, Kenner..............$10...........................$20
Mr. Freeze, Iceblast, 1997, Kenner, Series 1, w/Ice ray
  cannon and rocket thrusters ....$7...........................$12
Mr. Freeze, Jet Wing with Ring, 1998, Kenner, Series 2,
  w/Glacier assault wing and ice blaster.....$10...........................$20

Two Pack Figures, 1998
Batman vs Poison Ivy, 1998, Kenner ....$20...........................$40
A Cold Night At Gotham, 1998, Kenner ....$5...........................$10
Brain vs. Brawn, 1998, Kenner,
  Batman and Bane.....................................$5...........................$10
Challengers Of The Night, 1998, Kenner ....$10...........................$15
Cryo Freeze Chamber, 1998, Kenner................$3............................$8
Guardians Of Gotham, 1998, Kenner,
  Batman and Robin....................................$5...........................$10
Night Hunter Robin vs. Evil Entrapment
  Poison Ivy, 1998, Kenner ....$5............................$8
Wayne Manor Batcave, 1998, Kenner...............$23...........................$53

Batman: The Animated Series (Kenner, 1992-95)
Accessories
AeroBat, 1992, Kenner ....$150...........................$30
B.A.T.V. Vehicle, 1992, Kenner ....$10...........................$20
Batcave, 1993, Kenner, play set ....$50...........................$125

Batman: The Animated Series—Dick Grayson/Robin, Kenner, $15 MIP.

	NM	MIP
Batcycle, 1992, Kenner, w/Batman figure	$10	$20
Batcycle, 1992, Kenner, with Nightwing	$10	$20
Batmobile, 1992, Kenner	$10	$65
Bat-Signal Jet, 1992, Kenner	$10	$20
Crime Stalker, 1992, Kenner	$10	$20
Hoverbat Vehicle, 1992, Kenner	$5	$15
Ice Hammer, 1994, Kenner	$10	$15
Joker Mobile, 1992, Kenner	$6	$20
Robin Dragster, 1992, Kenner, very rare	$75	$325
Street Jet, 1993, Kenner	$15	$25
Turbo Batplane, 1992, Kenner	$6	$20

Figures

	NM	MIP
Anti-Freeze Batman, 1994, Kenner, Series 3, w/Firing Shield and Blaster	$4	$10
Bane, 1995, Kenner, Series 4, w/"Body Slam" action and venom tube	$5	$10
Battle-Helmet Batman, 1995, Kenner, Mail order figure	$20	$35
Bola Trap Robin, 1994, Kenner, Series 3	$7	$12
Bruce Wayne, 1993, Kenner, Series 2	$5	$10
Catwoman, 1993, Kenner, Series 2, w/Whipping arm action and Claw Hook	$7	$25
Clay Face, 1994, Kenner, Series 3	$5	$20
Combat Belt Batman, 1992, Kenner, Series 1	$15	$40
Cyber Gear Batman, 1995, Kenner, Series 4	$15	$25

	NM	MIP
Dick Grayson/Robin, 1994, Kenner, Series 3	$5	$15
Glider Robin, 1995, Kenner, Series 4, w/Winged Jet Pack and Firing Claw	$10	$20
Ground Assault Batman, 1994, Kenner, Deluxe figure w/Motorized turbo-powered ground jet	$5	$10
High-Wire Batman, 1994, Kenner, Deluxe figure w/Quick Escape Cable Wire and Cable-Riding Action	$15	$30
Infrared Batman, 1993, Kenner, Series 2 w/Launching Bat-Signal Disks	$5	$10
Joker, 1993, Kenner, Series 2 w/Laughing gas spray gun	$7	$15
Killer Croc, 1994, Kenner, Series 3 w/Power punch arm and pet crocodile	$8	$15
Knight Star Batman, 1994, Kenner, Series 3 w/Star Blade Rocket Launcher	$4	$10
Lightning Strike Batman, 1994, Kenner, Series 3 w/Transforming Cape Glider	$4	$10
Manbat, 1993, Kenner, Series 2	$7	$25
Mech-Wing Batman, 1994, Kenner, deluxe figure w/Mechanized Soaring Wings and pop-out wing action	$4	$10
Mr. Freeze, 1994, Kenner, Series 3 w/Firing Ice Blaster	$8	$15
Ninja Robin, 1993, Kenner, Series 2 w/chopping arm action and ninja weapons	$8	$15
Penguin, 1992, Kenner, Series 1	$12	$85
Poison Ivy, 1994, Kenner, Series 3, w/crossbow and Venus Flytrap weapon	$20	$30

	NM	MIP

Power Vision Batman, 1994, Kenner, Deluxe figure w/electric light up
eyes, firing missile......................................$8.....................$15

Radar Scope Batman, 1995, Kenner,
Series 4..$15.....................$25

Rapid Attack Batman, 1994, Kenner, Series 3
w/Escape Hook and Utility Belt ....$15.....................$25

Riddler, 1992, Kenner, Series 1 w/Question
mark launcher...................................$10.....................$40

Robin, 1992, Kenner, Series 1 with
Turbo Glider......................................$8.....................$15

Scarecrow, 1993, Kenner, Series 2...................$7.....................$20

Sky Dive Batman, 1993, Kenner, Series 2
w/working parachute...............................$5.....................$10

Tornado Batman, 1994, Kenner, Series 3
w/Whirling Weapon ....$15.....................$25

Turbojet Batman, 1992, Kenner, Series 1 w/Firing Wrist Rocket &
Pivoting Engines ....$7.....................$15

Two Face, 1992, Kenner, Series 1 ....$7.....................$25

Ultimate Batman (16"), 1994, Kenner ....$25.....................$75

Multi-Packs

Ninja Batman and Robin, 1994, Kenner, w/Duo-power
Ninja weapons.....................................$10.....................$20

Best of the West (Marx, 1965-75)

Accessories

Buckboard with Horse and Harness, 1967-75, Marx, #4424, with
Thunderbolt.......................................$100.....................$225

Buckskin Horse, 1967, Marx, #2036, for 12" figures, head nods and
neck bends...$125.....................$60

Circle X Ranch Play set, 1967, Marx, #5275, 22 pieces,
cardboard, rare.....................................$325.....................$170

Best of the West—Daniel Boone, Marx, $200 MIP.

	NM	MIP

Comanche Horse, 1967, Marx, #1861, for 12" figures,
head and leg articulation ....$125..........................$60

Covered Wagon, 1967-75, Marx, #4434,
with horse and harness..............................$100..........................$225

Flame Horse, 1966, Marx, #2081, for 12" figures,
legs in trotting pose ....$140..........................$65

Fort Apache Play set, 1967, Marx, #1875, scaled
for 12" figures ....$400..........................$200

Pancho Pony, 1967, Marx, #1061, for 7-1/2" figures,
brown with off-white mane and tail. Includes
black plastic saddle and bridle ....$50..........................$75

Storm Cloud Horse, 1967, Marx, #2071, originally "Pinto,"
brown w/white spots ....$125..........................$60

Thunderbolt Horse, 1965-75, Marx, #2061, most common horse
produced, black version rarest..................$75..........................$125

Thundercolt Horse, 1967-69, Marx, #2031a, for use
with ranch and corral sets ....$25..........................$50

Figures

Bill Buck, 1967, Marx, #1868, Fort Apache
Fighters Series..$300..........................$475

Captain Tom Maddox, 1967, Marx, #1865, Fort Apache Fighters, blue
body, brown hair......................................$175..........................$80

Chief Cherokee, 1965, Marx, included headdress,
rifle, spear, Bowie knife, ceremonial mask,
pipe and more..$150..........................$200

Daniel Boone, 1965, Marx, #2060,
limited articulation ....$100..........................$200

Davy Crockett, 1960s, Marx ....$175..........................$250

Fighting Eagle, 1967, Marx, #1864, fully poseable,
includes spear, Bowie knife, hatchet, bear claw necklace,
pouch and more..$150..........................$225

Best of the West by Marx. Left to right: Best of the West Johnny West, $150 MIP; Johnny West Covered Wagon with Horse & Harness, $225 MIP.

	NM	MIP
General Custer, 1967, Marx, #1866, blue molded uniform, with yellow and dark blue plastic accessories	$100	$200
Geronimo, 1967, Marx, #1863, with tan molded buckskin uniform, darker brown, yellow and medium brown plastic accessories including Bowie knife, headband, mask, spear, rifle and more	$100	$150
Geronimo and Pinto, 1967-75, Marx, #2087, mail-order set	$150	$200
Geronimo w/Storm Cloud, 1967-75, Marx, figure and horse in colored box	$175	$90
Jamie West, 1967, Marx, #1062A, body molded in caramel, light blue, or black in Canada	$50	$100
Jane West, 1966, Marx, #2067, included white plastic clothes and accessories	$60	$120
Jane West w/Flame, 1967-75, Marx, mail-order figure and horse	$175	$90
Janice West, 1967, Marx, #1067b, turquoise body, short black hair	$50	$100
Jay West, 1967, Marx, #1062b, caramel body, blonde hair	$50	$100
Jed Gibson, 1957, Marx, #2057c, African-American cavalry soldier, teal body, rare	$950	$425
Johnny West, 1965, Marx, #2062, straight hands in 1965, curved hands 1966-75, caramel body, brown hair	$75	$150
Johnny West w/Thunderbolt, 1967-75, Marx, #2062, mail-order figure and horse	$175	$90
Johnny West with Comanche, 1967, Marx, fully jointed	$80	$125
Josie West, 1967, Marx, #1067a, turquoise body, blonde hair	$50	$100

Buck Rogers—Draconian Guard, Mego, $80 MIP.

	NM	MIP

Princess Wildflower, 1974, Marx, #2097, included 22
   accessories and gear..............................$100.......................$175
Sam Cobra, 1972, Marx, #2072, black molded-plastic
   clothing and accessories.....................$100.......................$200
Sam Cobra w/Thunderbolt, 1975, Marx, #4959075,
   mail-order figure and horse...................$200.......................$90
Sheriff Garrett, 1973, Marx, #2085, blue-molded clothing
   with white and blue plastic clothing
   and accessories included.......................$150 ....**NP** $200
Sheriff Garrett w/horse, 1967-75, Marx, mail-order figure and horse,
   rare ....$300.......................$150
Zeb Zachary, 1967-69, Marx, #1862, Fort Apache Fighters,
   blue body, black hair ....$200.......................$300

Buck Rogers (Mego, 1979)

12" Figures
Buck Rogers, 1979, Mego..................................$30...............$60
Doctor Huer, 1979, Mego ....$30...............$60
Draco, 1979, Mego ....$30...............$60
Draconian Guard, 1979, Mego, With brown
   and silver uniform.....................................$30...............$60
Killer Kane, 1979, Mego ....$30...............$60
Tiger Man, 1979, Mego, with tattooed face and head and
   tiger-skin vest and clothing....................$30...............$125
Twiki, 1979, Mego ....$30...............$60

3-3/4" Figures
Ardella, 1979, Mego ....$6...............$15
Buck Rogers, 1979, Mego..................................$35...............$60
Doctor Huer, 1979, Mego ....$6...............$20

*Captain Action by Playing Mantis. Left to right: Lone Ranger; Tonto.
Each $25 MIP. Photo courtesy Playing Mantis.*

	NM	MIP
Draco, 1979, Mego	$6	$20
Draconian Guard, 1979, Meg	$10	$20
Killer Kane, 1979, Mego	$6	$15
Tiger Man, 1979, Mego	$10	$25
Twiki, 1979, Mego	$20	$45
Wilma Deering, 1979, Mego	$12	$25

3-3/4" Play Sets

	NM	MIP
Star Fighter Command Center, 1979, Mego	$35	$100

3-3/4" Vehicles

	NM	MIP
Draconian Marauder, 1979, Mego	$25	$50
Land Rover, 1979, Mego	$20	$40
Laserscope Fighter, 1979, Mego	$20	$40
Star Fighter, 1979, Mego	$25	$50
Star Searcher, 1979, Mego	$30	$60

Captain Action (Ideal, 1966-68)

12" Figures

	NM	MIP
Captain Action, 1967, Ideal, parachute offer on box	$275	$700
Captain Action, 1966, 1966, Ideal, with red-shirted Lone Ranger on box	$200	$500
Captain Action, 1966, 1966, Ideal, with blue-shirted Lone Ranger on box	$200	$500
Captain Action, 1966, 1966, Ideal, photo box	$300	$900
Dr. Evil, 1967, 1967, Ideal, photo box	$250	$450
Dr. Evil, Lab Set Display Box, 1968, Ideal	$1000	$3000

	NM	MIP

Dr. Evil, Mailer box version of lab set, 1968,
Ideal...$1000 ....$2500

9" Figures

Action Boy, 1967, 1967, Ideal ....$275.......................$900
Action Boy, 1968,1968, Ideal, with
space suit...$350 ....$1100

Accessories

Action Cave Carrying Case, 1967, 1967,
Ideal, vinyl ....$400........................$700
Directional Communicator Set, 1966, 1966,
Ideal..$110........................$300
Dr. Evil Sanctuary, 1967, 1967,
Ideal...$2500 ....$3500
Jet Mortar, 1966, 1966, Ideal ....$110........................$300
Parachute Pack, 1966, 1966, Ideal ....$100........................$225
Power Pack, 1966, 1966, Ideal ....$125........................$250
Quick Change Chamber, 1967, 1967, Ideal,
Sears Exclusive, cardboard ....$750........................$900
Silver Streak Amphibian, 1967, 1967,
Ideal..$800 ....$1200
Silver Streak Garage, 1966-68, Ideal, Sears Exclusive,
with Silver Streak Vehicle...................$1500 ....$2000
Survival Kit, 1967, 1967, Ideal,
twenty pieces....................................$125........................$275
Vinyl Headquarters Carrying Case, 1967, 1967,
Ideal, Sears Exclusive ....$200........................$500
Weapons Arsenal, 1966, 1966, Ideal, ten pieces
....$110........................$225

Action Boy Costumes

Aqualad, 1967, 1967, Ideal ....$300........................$900

	NM	MIP

Robin, 1967, 1967, Ideal, included gloves, Batarangs, boots,
uniform, face mask, suction cups for climbing buildings
....$300 ....$1200

Superboy, 1967, 1967, Ideal...........................$300 ....$1000

Captain Action Costumes

Aquaman, 1966, 1966, Ideal ....$160.......................... $600

Aquaman, 1967, 1967, Ideal,
with flasher ring ....$180..........................$950

Batman, 1966, 1966, Ideal ....$225.......................... $700

Batman, 1967, 1967, Ideal,
with flasher ring ....$250 ....$1100

Buck Rogers, 1967, 1967, Ideal,
with flasher ring ....$450 ....$2700

Captain America, 1966, 1966,
Ideal...$220.......................... $900

Captain America, 1967, 1967, Ideal,
with flasher ring ....$225 ....$1200

Flash Gordon, 1966, 1966, Ideal, white spacesuit
with helmet, boots, space pistol, belt and mask
....$200.......................... $600

Flash Gordon, 1967, 1967, Ideal,
with flasher ring ....$225..........................$800

Green Hornet, 1967, 1967, Ideal,
with flasher ring ....$2000 ....$7500

Lone Ranger, 1966, 1966,
Ideal, red shirt ....$200.......................... $700

Lone Ranger, 1967, 1967, Ideal, blue shirt, flasher ring

Phantom, 1966, 1966, Ideal, includes uniform, boots, bayonet,
rifle, two pistols and a mask...................$200.......................... $750

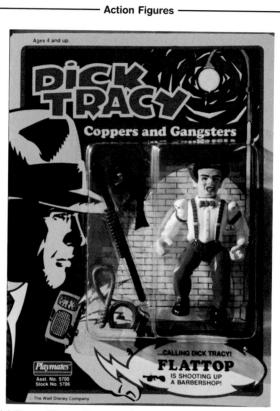

Dick Tracy—Flattop, Playmates, $12 MIP.

	NM	MIP

Phantom, 1967, 1967, Ideal,
    with flasher ring ....$250..........................$900
Sgt. Fury, 1966, 1966, Ideal..........................$200..........................$800
Spider-Man, 1967, 1967, Ideal,
    with flasher ring ....$550 ....$8000
Steve Canyon, 1966, 1966, Ideal....................$200..........................$700
Steve Canyon, 1967, 1967, Ideal, with flasher ring,
    includes jumpsuit uniform, helmet,
    pistol, pack, ring and mask ....$225..........................$850
Superman, 1966, 1966, Ideal ....$200..........................$700
Superman, 1967, 1967, Ideal,
    with flasher ring ....$225......................$1100
Tonto, 1967, 1967, Ideal,
    with flasher ring ....$375 ....$1100

Dick Tracy (Playmates, 1990)

Figures, Large

Breathless Mahoney, 1990, based on the movie, shown
    here with the Dick Tracy figure................$25..........................$50
Dick Tracy, 1990, shown here
    with "Breathless" ....$25..........................$50
Al "Big Boy" Caprice, 1990 ....$8..........................$15
Blank, The, 1990...$50..........................$150
Brow, The, 1990 ....$6..........................$12
Dick Tracy, 1990 ....$8..........................$15
Flattop, 1990, Playmates, includes Tommy gun
    and bullwhip...$6..........................$12
Influence, 1990..$6..........................$12
Itchy, 1990..$8..........................$15

Dick Tracy—The Blank, Playmates, $150 MIP.

	NM	MIP
Lips Manlis, 1990	$6	$12
Mumbles, 1990	$6	$12
Pruneface, 1990	$6	$12
Rodent, The, 1990	$8	$15
Sam Catchem, 1990	$6	$12
Shoulders, 1990	$6	$12
Steve the Tramp, 1990	$6	$12

Doctor Who (Denys Fisher, 1976)

Figures

Cyberman, 1976, Denys Fisher, very 1930s-looking robotic figure from the BBC-TV series. Called "The Threat from the Outerworld" on the box. ....$250....................$600

Dalek, 1976 ....$250....................$600

Doctor Who (4th), 1976 ....$100....................$225

Giant Robot, 1976, Denys Fisher, gray plastic robot from the BBC-TV series ....$165....................$375

K-9, 1976, Palitoy, looking much like today's toy robot dogs, this Talking K-9 could say a variety of phrases by pressing the control panel on his back. ....$150....................$300

Leela, 1976, Denys Fisher. ....$200....................$400

Vehicles

Tardis play set, 1976, Denys Fisher, plastic model of the time-traveling police call box as seen in the popular BBC-TV series. ....$150....................$300

Lone Ranger Rides Again (Gabriel, 1979)

Figures

Butch Cavendish, 1979, Gabriel, figure shown here with Smoke, Butch's horse. ....$40....................$75

Legend of Lone Ranger by Gabriel. Left to right: Silver, $30 MIP;
Lone Ranger, $30 MIP.

	NM	MIP
Dan Reid, 1979, Gabriel	$25	$60
Little Bear with Hawk, 1979, Gabriel	$25	$60
Lone Ranger, 1979, Gabriel, figure includes revolvers, hat, mask, scarf. Shown here with Silver.	$20	$60
Red Sleeves, 1979, Gabriel	$25	$60
Tonto, 1979, Gabriel, includes buckskin cloth outfit. Shown here with Scout. The horses in this series were fully poseable and included stands	$20	$60

Masters of the Universe (Mattel, 1981-1988)

12" Figures (Italian)

	NM	MIP
Megator, 1987	$300	$1000
Tylus, 1987	$400	$1200

Accessories

	NM	MIP
Battle Bones Carrying Case, 1984	$10	$20
Battle Cat, 1982	$15	$50
Battle Cat with Battle Armor He-Man, 1984	$50	$125
Battle Cat with He-Man, 1982	$50	$150
Beam Blaster and Artillery, 1987	$25	$60
Bionatops, 1987, Mattel, creature	$25	$45
He-Man and Wind Raider, 1982, Mattel	$10	$25
Jet Sled, 1986	$5	$15
Mantisaur, 1986	$15	$25
Megalaser, 1986. While this weapon didn't fire any projectiles, it had a blast-effect action and fit warriors in the series.	$5	$15
Monstroid Creature (The Evil Horde), 1986, Mattel. Creature grabs warriors in pincers and whirls them around.	$30	$75

Masters of the Universe—Zodac, Mattel, $50 MIP.

	NM	MIP
Night Stalker, 1984	$15	$30
Night Stalker with Jitsu, 1984	$40	$75
Panthor, 1983	$25	$50
Panthor with Battle Armor Skeletor, 1984	$35	$125
Panthor with Skeletor, 1983	$40	$150
Ring of caps for Thunder Punch He-Man, 1985, Mattel	$2	$6
Road Ripper w/Battle Armor He-Man, 1984, Mattel	$20	$40
Screech, 1983	$15	$40
Screech with Skeletor, 1983	$40	$70
Screech w/Battle Armor Skeletor, 1984, Mattel	$20	$40
Slime Vat, 1986, Mattel	$2	$6
Stilt Stalkers, 1986	$5	$20
Stridor Armored Horse, 1984	$10	$30
Stridor with Fisto, 1984	$30	$75
Weapons Pak, 1984, included laser guns, body armor, battle axe, shield, sword and more	$5	$15
Zoar, 1983	$15	$30
Zoar with Teela, 1983	$40	$120

Figures

	NM	MIP
Battle Armor He-Man, 1984	$15	$40
Battle Armor Skeletor, 1984	$15	$40
Beast Man, 1982	$25	$70
Blade, 1987	$25	$70
Blast-Attack, 1987, limbs actually fly off the figure during battle	$20	$40
Buzz-Off, 1984	$25	$40

Masters of the Universe—Stratos, blue wings, Mattel, $75 MIP.

	NM	MIP
Buzz-Saw Hordak (The Evil Horde), 1987	$15	$40
Clamp Champ, 1987	$15	$45
Clawful, 1984	$20	$45
Dragon Blaster Skeletor, 1985	$25	$75
Dragon Blaster Skeletor, 1985, Mattel	$20	$40
Dragstor (The Evil Horde), 1986, Mattel. Ripcord (like the SST's series) makes this "transforming evil warrior vehicle" pursue the good guys.	$15	$40
Evil-Lyn, 1983	$25	$50
EXtendar, 1986, with extending arms, legs, head and torso	$15	$35
Faker, 1983, Mattel	$30	$120
Faker II, 1987	$20	$70
Fisto, 1984	$10	$40
Flying Fists He-Man, 1986	$25	$75
Grizzlor (The Evil Horde), 1985	$15	$40
Grizzlor, black, 1985	$75	$150
Gwildor, 1987, figure from Masters of the Universe movie	$15	$75
He-Man, original, 1982, 1983	$40	$130
Hordak (The Evil Horde), 1985	$20	$40
Horde Trooper, 1986	$20	$40
Hurricane Hordak, 1986	$15	$60
Jitsu, 1984	$20	$45
King Hiss (Snake Men), 1986	$20	$45
King Randor, 1987, with scepter and mini comic book	$30	$75
Kobra Kahn (Snake Men), 1984, 1986	$10	$35
Leech (The Evil Horde), 1985	$10	$35

	NM	MIP
Man-At-Arms, 1982, Mattel	$20`	$40
Man-E-Faces, 1983	$25	$50
Man-E-Faces, five extra weapons, 1983	$75	$175
Mantenna (The Evil Horde), 1985	$25	$40
Mekaneck, 1983	$20	$40
Mer-Man, 1982	$25	$50
Modulok (The Evil Horde), 1985	$15	$35
Mosquitor (The Evil Horde), 1987	$25	$45
Moss Man, 1985	$10	$40
Multi-Bot (The Evil Horde), 1986	$20	$40
Ninjor, 1987	$35	$80
Orko, 1984	$20	$50
Prince Adam, 1984	$20	$60
Ram-Man, 1983	$20	$60
Rattlor (Snake Men), 1986, with translucent plastic "snake staff" and mini comic book	$10	$35
Rattler, red neck, 1986	$10	$30
Rio Blast, 1986, Mattel, an "old West" warrior with hidden weapons. Includes comic book.	$25	$40
Roboto, 1985	$15	$35
Rokkon (Comet Warrior), 1986	$15	$35
Rotar (Energy Zoids), 1987	$35	$70
Saurod, 1987, figure from Masters of the Universe movie	$30	$70
Scare Glow, 1987	$35	$75
Skeletor, original, 1982, 1983	$35	$110
Snake Face (Snake Men), 1987	$25	$45
Snout Spout, 1986	$15	$40
Sorceress, 1987	$25	$70
Sssqueeze (Snake Men), 1987, Mattel, traps warriors in "slither-hold" grip. Includes serpent.	$25	$45

	NM	MIP
Stinkor, 1985	$15	$35
Stonedar (Comet Warriors), 1986	$15	$35
Stratos, blue wings, 1982, Mattel	$25	$75
Stratos, red wings, 1982	$25	$75
Sy-klone, 1985	$20	$40
Teela, 1982	$25	$65
Terror Claws Skeletor, 1986	$25	$75
Thunder Punch He-Man, 1985, Mattel	$15	$35
Thunder Punch He-Man, 1985	$25	$60
Trap Jaw, 1983	$30	$85
Tri-Klops, 1983	$30	$40
Tung Lashor (Snake Men), 1986	$10	$45
Twistoid (Energy Zoids), 1987	$30	$75
Two-Bad, 1985	$10	$30
Webstor, 1984	$10	$30
Whiplash, 1984	$10	$25
Zodac, 1982, Mattel	$25	$50

Giftsets

	NM	MIP
Battle for Eternia, 1983, Mattel, Skeletor, Panthor, Man-E-Faces	$25	$45
Battle for Eternia, 1984, Mattel	$30	$60
Evil Horde, 1986, Mattel, Hordak, Leech, Mantenna	$40	$60
Evil Warriors, 1983, Mattel, Skeletor, Beast Man, Faker	$25	$45
Evil Warriors, 1984, Mattel, Battle Armor Skeletor, Webstor, Mer-Man	$30	$60
Evil Warriors, 1985, Mattel, Stinkor, Webstor, Whiplash	$40	$60

Mighty Morphin Power Rangers—Blue Ranger, Bandai, $6 MIP.

	NM	MIP
Flying Fist He-Man and Terror Claws Skeletor, 1986, Mattel	$50	$100
Heroic Warriors, 1983, Mattel, He-Man, Teela, Ram-Man	$25	$45
Heroic Warriors, 1984, Mattel, Battle Armor He-Man, Man-At-Arms, Man E-Faces	$30	$60
Heroic Warriors, 1985, Mattel, Mekaneck, Buzz-Off, Moss-Man	$40	$60
Jet Sled w/He-Man, 1986, Mattel	$25	$50
Mantisaur w/Hordak, 1986, Mattel	$15	$35

Mighty Morphin Power Rangers (Bandai, 1993-95)

3" Figures

	NM	MIP
Black Ranger, 1995, Bandai	$5	$15
Blue Ranger, 1995 Bandai	$5	$15
Pink Ranger, 1995, Bandai	$5	$15
Red Ranger, 1995, Bandai	$5	$15
Yellow Ranger, 1995, Bandai	$5	$15

5" Figures With Thunder Bikes

	NM	MIP
Black Ranger, 1995, Bandai	$6	$15
Blue Ranger, 1995 Bandai	$6	$15
Pink Ranger, 1995, Bandai	$6	$15
Red Ranger, 1995, Bandai	$6	$15
Yellow Ranger, 1995, Bandai	$6	$15

8" Aliens, 1993

	NM	MIP
Baboo, 1993, Bandai	$10	$20
Bones, 1993, Bandai	$10	$20
Finster, 1993, Bandai	$10	$20
Goldar, 1993 Bandai	$10	$20
King Sphinx, 1993, Bandai	$10	$20

Mighty Morphin Power Rangers—Black Ranger, Bandai, 1998, $6 MIP.

	NM	MIP
Putty Patrol, 1993, Bandai	$10	$20
Squatt, 1993, Bandai	$10	$20

8" Figures, 1993

Black Ranger, 1993, Bandai	$7	$20
Blue Ranger, 1993 Bandai	$7	$20
Pink Ranger, 1993 Bandai	$10	$20
Red Ranger, 1993 Bandai	$5	$20
Yellow Ranger, 1993, Bandai	$10	$20

8" Movie Figures, 1995

Black Ranger, 1995, Bandai, metallic	$6	$15
Blue Ranger, 1995, Bandai, metallic	$6	$15
Pink Ranger, 1995, Bandai, metallic	$6	$15
Red Ranger, 1996, Bandai, metallic	$6	$15
White Ranger, 1995, Bandai, metallic	$6	$15
Yellow Ranger, 1995, Bandai, metallic	$6	$15

Planet of the Apes (Mego, 1973-75)

8" Figures

Astronaut, 1973, Mego, boxed	$50	$250
Astronaut, 1975, Mego, carded	$50	$100
Astronaut Burke, 1975, Mego, carded	$50	$100
Astronaut Burke, 1975, Mego, boxed	$50	$250
Astronaut Verdon, 1975, Mego, boxed	$50	$250
Astronaut Verdon, 1975, Mego, carded	$50	$125
Cornelius, 1973, Mego, boxed	$40	$200
Cornelius, 1975, Mego, carded	$40	$100
Dr. Zaius, 1973, Mego, boxed	$40	$200
Dr. Zaius, 1975, Mego, carded	$40	$100
Galen, 1975, Mego, carded	$40	$100

Six Million Dollar Man—Maskatron, Kenner, $150 MIP.

	NM	MIP
Galen, 1975, Mego, boxed	$40	$200
General Urko, 1975, Mego, boxed	$50	$250
General Urko, 1975, Mego, carded	$50	$250
General Ursus, 1975, Mego, boxed	$50	$250
General Ursus, 1975, Mego, carded	$50	$250
Soldier Ape, 1973, Mego, boxed	$50	$250
Soldier Ape, 1975, Mego, carded	$50	$200
Zira, 1973, Mego, boxed	$30	$200
Zira, 1975, Mego, carded	$30	$100

Accessories

	NM	MIP
Action Stallion, 1975, Mego, brown, motorized, remote-controlled	$50	$100
Battering Ram, 1975, Mego, boxed	$20	$40
Dr. Zaius' Throne, 1975, Mego, boxed	$20	$40
Jail, 1975, Mego, boxed	$20	$40

Play Sets

	NM	MIP
Forbidden Zone Trap, 1975, Mego, boxed	$90	$200
Fortress, 1975, Mego, boxed	$85	$200
Treehouse, 1975, Mego, boxed	$75	$200
Village, 1975, Mego, boxed	$85	$200

Vehicles

	NM	MIP
Catapult and Wagon, 1975, Mego, boxed	$75	$150

Six Million Dollar Man (Kenner, 1975-78)

Accessories

	NM	MIP
Backpack Radio, 1975-78, Kenner	$10	$25
Bionic Cycle, 1975-78, Kenner	$10	$20
Bionic Mission Vehicle, 1975-78, Kenner	$25	$25

	NM	MIP
Bionic Transport, 1975-78, Kenner	$10	$45
Bionic Video Center, 1975-78, Kenner	$35	$100
Critical Assignment Arms, 1975-78, Kenner	$15	$45
Official Assignment Legs, 1975-78, Kenner	$15	$45
Dual Launch Drag Set with 4" Steve Austin Bionic Bigfoot figure, 1975-78, Kenner	$45	$80
Flight Suit, 1975-78, Kenner	$15	$30
Mission Control Center, 1975-78, Kenner	$25	$75
Mission to Mars Space Suit, 1975-78, Kenner	$15	$30
OSI Headquarters, 1975-78, Kenner	$30	$70
OSI Undercover Blue Denims, 1975-78, Kenner	$15	$30
Porta-Communicator, 1975-78, Kenner	$20	$50
Tower & Cycle Set, 1975-78, Kenner	$25	$50
Venus Space Probe, 1975-78, Kenner	$125	$275

Figures

	NM	MIP
Bionic Bigfoot, 1975-78, Kenner. Must have the chestplate to be complete.	$75	$175
Maskatron, 1975-78, Kenner	$40	$150
Oscar Goldman, 1975-78, Kenner. Wearing familiar checked jacket and carrying exploding briefcase, should Steve Austin's secrets fall into the wrong hands.	$50	$100
Steve Austin, 1975-78, Kenner	$50	$100
Steve Austin with biosonic arm, 1975-78	$75	$300
Steve Austin with engine block, 1975-78	$50	$150
Steve Austin with girder, 1975-78	$60	$200

Spawn (McFarlane, 1994-Present)

Series 01, 1994 (Todd Toys Packaging)

	NM	MIP
Clown, clown head, 1994	$6	$20
Medieval Spawn, black armor, 1994	$5	$25
Overtkill, dark green, 1994	$5	$15
Spawn, Diamond Exclusive, 1994	$45	$120
Tremor, dark green costume, 1994	$5	$15
Violator, 1994, McFarlane	$5	$20

Series 02, 1995

Angela, 1995, McFarlane	$5	$25
Bedrock, blue, 1995, McFarlane, With firing missiles	$10	$25
Chapel, blue/black pants, 1995, McFarlane. Includes gun and jagged-edge sword	$6	$20
Commando Spawn, 1995, McFarlane. Black and red uniform, includes weapons and headset	$7	$20
Malebolgia, 1995, McFarlane, highly-detailed figure	$30	$60
Pilot Spawn, black costume, 1995, McFarlane, black uniform with red highlights, includes jet pack and dagger	$8	$20

Series 03, 1995

Cosmic Angela, No. 62 Spawn and No. 9 Curse of Spawn, Diamond Exclusive, 1997, McFarlane	$25	$100
Curse, The, McFarlane Collector's Club Exclusive, 1997, McFarlane	$5	$15
Vertebreaker, gray or black body, exclusive available through various stores, 1996, McFarlane	$5	$15

Spawn (Series 7)—Sam and Twitch, McFarlane Toys, $15 MIP. Photo courtesy McFarlane Toys

Series 04, 1996

	NM	MIP
Clown II, black guns, 1996, McFarlane	$6	$20
Cy-Gor, gold trim, 1996, McFarlane	$4	$15
EXo-Skeleton Spawn, black and gray exo-skeleton, 1996, McFarlane	$5	$20
Maxx, The, with black Isz, 1996, McFarlane	$15	$40
Shadowhawk, black with silver trim, 1996, McFarlane	$4	$15

Series 05, 1996

Nuclear Spawn, green skin, 1996, McFarlane	$3	$10
Overtkill II, flesh colored with gray trim, 1996, McFarlane	$5	$15
Tremor II, purple with green bloob, 1996, McFarlane	$3	$10
Vandalizer, FAO Schwarz Exclusive, 1996, McFarlane	$10	$25
Viking Spawn, 1996, McFarlane	$5	$25
Widow Maker, purple and rose outfit, gray body, 1996, McFarlane	$8	$20

Series 06, 1996

Alien Spawn, black with white, 1996, McFarlane	$5	$15
Battleclad Spawn, black costume, 1996, McFarlane	$5	$20
Freak, The, tan flesh, 1995, McFarlane	$5	$15
Sansker, brown and tan, 1996, McFarlane	$5	$15
Superpatriot, silver arms and legs, 1996, McFarlane	$3	$10

Manga Spawn (Series 10)—Samurai Spawn, McFarlane Toys, $8 MIP.

	NM	MIP

Tiffany the Amazon, McFarlane Collector's Club
    Exclusive, 1998 .... $8 .... $25

Series 07, 1997

Crutch, green goatee, 1977, McFarlane .... $5 .... $15

Mangler, The, 1997, McFarlane, figure includes
    skull-topped staff .... $5 .... $15

No-Body, 1997, McFarlane. Detailed robotic figure containing smaller
    "No-Body" inside .... $5 .... $15

Sam and Twitch, 1997, McFarlane, Sam with donut and pistol,
    Twitch with rifle .... $5 .... $15

Scourge, 1997, McFarlane .... $5 .... $15

Spawn III, with owl and bat, 1997, McFarlane ... $8 .... $25

Zombie Spawn, tan skin with red tunic, 1997, McFarlane. Figure
    includes chainsaw and large machine-gun rifle.
    .... $3 .... $10

Series 08, 1997

Curse of the Spawn, 1997 .... $5 .... $15

Gate keeper, 1997 .... $4 .... $15

Grave Digger, 1997 .... $4 .... $12

Renegade, tan flesh, 1997 .... $4 .... $12

Rotarr, 1997 .... $4 .... $12

Sabre, 1997 .... $4 .... $12

Series 09, 1997

Goddess, The, 1997 .... $4 .... $12

Manga Clown, 1997 .... $4 .... $12

Manga Curse, 1997 .... $4 .... $12

Manga Ninja Spawn, 1997 .... $4 .... $12

Manga Spawn, 1997 .... $5 .... $15

Manga Violator, 1997 .... $4 .... $12

Series 10, Manga 2, 1998

	NM	MIP
Cybertooth, 1998, McFarlane	$4	$15
Manga Cyber Violator, 1998, McFarlane	$4	$8
Manga Dead Spawn, 1998, McFarlane	$4	$8
Manga Freak, 1998, McFarlane	$4	$8
Manga Overtkill, 1998, McFarlane	$4	$8
Manga Samurai Spawn, 1998, McFarlane	$4	$8

Series 11, Dark Ages, 1998

Horrid, The, 1998, McFarlane. Two figures; one winged human-type (larger) and the other a small skeletal figure with weapon.	$3	$8
Ogre, The, 1998, McFarlane. Large Ogre figure controlled by smaller figure riding on shoulders. Also includes war club.	$5	$15
Raider, The, 1998, McFarlane. Centaur figure with battle armor, double-edged pike/axe, string of defeated skulls.	$3	$8
Skull Queen, The, 1998, McFarlane. Figure includes battle axes, flying skeletal warrior	$4	$12
Spawn The Black Knight, 1998, McFarlane	$5	$15
Spellcaster, The, 1998, McFarlane. Includes battle axe, shield, and helmet.	$4	$15

Series 12, 1998

BottomLine, 1998, McFarlane	$5	$15
Creech, The, 1998, McFarlane	$5	$20
Cy-Gor II, 1998, McFarlane, Deluxe boxed figure	$5	$25

	NM	MIP
Heap, The, 1998, McFarlane	$5	$15
Re-Animated Spawn, 1998, McFarlane	$5	$15
Spawn IV, 1998, McFarlane	$5	$15
TopGun, 1998, McFarlane	$5	$15

Series 13, Curse of the Spawn, 1999

	NM	MIP
Curse of the Spawn II, 1999, McFarlane	$5	$10
Desiccator, 1999, McFarlane, Deluxe boxed figure	$7	$12
Hatchet, 1999, McFarlane	$5	$10
Medusa, 1999, McFarlane	$5	$10
Priest and Mr. Obersmith, 1999, McFarlane	$5	$10
Raenius, 1999, McFarlane	$5	$10
Zeus, 1999, McFarlane	$5	$10

Series 14, Dark Ages 2, 1999

	NM	MIP
Iguantus and Tuskadon, 1999	$5	$15
Mandarin Spawn the Scarlet Edge, 1999. A double-edged sword that is twice the size of the figure.	$5	$15
Necromancer, 1999	$5	$15
Spawn the Black Heart, 1999	$5	$15
Tormentor, 1999	$5	$15
Viper King, 1999	$5	$15

Series 15, Techno Spawn, 1999

	NM	MIP
Code Red, 1999	$5	$15
Cyber Spawn, 1999	$5	$15
Gray Thunder, 1999	$3	$10
Iron Express, 1999	$3	$10
Steel Trap, 1999	$3	$10
Warzone, 1999	$3	$10

Star Trek—Gorn, 1975, Mego, $180 MIP. Photo courtesy Corey LeChat

Series 16, Nitro Riders, 2000

	NM	MIP
Spawn: After Burner, 2000, 5-1/4" figure and 9x4-1/4" cycle	$3	$10
Spawn: Exlipse 5000, 2000, 5-1/2" figure and 9-1/2x5-1/2" cycle	$3	$10
Spawn: Flash Point, 2000, 5-1/4" figure and 9x4-1/2" cycle	$3	$10
Spawn: Green Vapor, 2000, 5-1/4" figure and 9-1/2x5-1/2" cycle	$3	$10

Star Trek (Mego, 1974-80)

Carded Figures

Andorian, 1976, Mego	$300	$650
Captain Kirk, 1974, Mego	$25	$50
Cheron, 1975, Mego, black and white face and uniform	$85	$175
Dr. McCoy, 1974, Mego, medical tricorder pack	$35	$75
Gorn, 1975, Mego	$80	$180
Klingon, 1974, Mego, black boots, brown plastic body armor, brown tunic	$25	$50
Lt. Uhura, 1974, Mego	$50	$135
Mr. Spock, 1974, Mego	$25	$50
Mugato, 1976, Mego	$275	$500
Neptunian, 1975, Mego	$100	$225
Romulan, 1976, Mego	$600	$1000
Scotty, 1974, Mego	$35	$80
Talos, 1976, Mego	$275	$500
The Keeper, 1975, Mego	$75	$175

Star Trek: The Motion Picture—Mr. Spock, Mego, $35 MIP.

Play Sets

	NM	MIP
Mission to Gamma VI, 1974-80 Mego	$300	$700
U.S.S. Enterprise Bridge, 1974-80 Mego	$100	$275

Star Trek: The Motion Picture (Mego, 1979-81)

12" Boxed Figures

Arcturian, 1979, Mego	$40	$125
Captain Kirk, 1979, Mego	$40	$75
Decker, 1979, Mego	$45	$115
Ilia, 1979, Mego	$40	$75
Klingon, 1979, Mego	$40	$125
Mr. Spock, 1979, Mego	$40	$75

3-3/4" Carded Figures

Acturian, 1980, Mego, Series 2, light tan uniform	$75	$150
Betelgeusian, 1980, Mego, Series 2	$75	$150
Captain Kirk, 1979, Mego, Series 1	$12	$35
Decker, 1979, Mego, Series 1	$12	$35
Dr. McCoy, 1979, Mego, Series 1, white shirt, gray pants	$12	$35
Ilia, 1979, Mego, Series 1	$10	$20
Klingon, 1980, Mego, Series 2	$75	$150
Megarite, 1980, Mego, Series 2	$75	$150
Mr. Spock, 1979, Mego, Series 1, dark gray uniform as seen in movie	$12	$35
Rigellian, 1980, Mego, Series 2	$75	$150
Scotty, 1979, Mego, Series 1	$12	$35
Zatanite, 1980, Mego, Series 2	$75	$150

Star Trek: The Next Generation—Jean-Luc Picard, Galoob, $15 MIP.

Play Sets

	NM	MIP
U.S.S. Enterprise Bridge, 1980, Mego	$45	$105

Star Trek: The Next Generation (Galoob, 1988-89)

Accessories

	NM	MIP
Enterprise, 1989, Galoob, die-cast vehicle	$10	$35
Ferengi Fighter, 1989, Galoob, vehicle	$15	$50
Galileo Shuttle, 1989, Galoob, vehicle	$15	$50
Phaser, 1989, Galoob, role playing toy	$20	$40

Series 1 Figures

	NM	MIP
Data, blue face, 1988, Galoob	$70	$100
Data, brown face, 1988, Galoob	$30	$50
Data, flesh face, 1988, Galoob	$15	$30
Data, spotted face, 1988, Galoob	$15	$30
Geordi La Forge, 1988 Galoob	$5	$15
Jean-Luc Picard, 1988, Galoob	$5	$15
Lt. Worf, 1988, Galoob	$5	$15
Tasha Yar, 1988, Galoob	$10	$25
William Riker, 1988, Galoob	$5	$15

Series 2 Figures

	NM	MIP
Antican, 1989, Galoob	$35	$75
Ferengi, 1989, Galoob	$35	$75
Q, 1989, Galoob	$35	$75
Selay, 1989, Galoob	$35	$75

*Super Powers by Kenner. Left to right: Steppenwolf on card, 1985,
$75 MIP; Mantis, $30 MIP.*

Super Powers (Kenner, 1984-86)

5" Figures

	NM	MIP
Aquaman, 1984, Kenner	$15	$45
Batman, 1984, Kenner	$35	$75
Braniac, 1984, Kenner, chrome plastic figure, includes free mini comic book	$15	$30
Clark Kent, mail-in figure, 1986, Kenner	$50	$75
Cyborg, 1986, Kenner	$150	$300
Cyclotron, 1986, Kenner	$35	$75
Darkseid, 1985, Kenner, gray and blue figure with "Power Action Raging Motion"	$5	$15
Desaad, 1985, Kenner	$10	$30
Dr. Fate, 1985, Kenner	$35	$80
Firestorm, 1985, Kenner	$15	$35
Flash, 1984, Kenner, figure has power action legs that simulate the Flash's lightning-speed running style	$10	$25
Golden Pharaoh, 1986, Kenner	$50	$125
Green Arrow, 1985, Kenner, with bow	$25	$55
Green Lantern, 1984, Kenner, with lantern	$30	$60
Hawkman, 1984, Kenner	$25	$65
Joker, 1984, Kennre	$15	$30
Kalibak, 1985, Kenner	$5	$15
Lex Luthor, 1984, Kenner, has "Power Action Nuclear Punch"	$5	$15
Mantis, 1985, Kenner, figure has "Power Action Pincer Thrust" and includes a free comic book	$10	$30
Martian Manhunter, 1985, Kenner	$15	$45

Super Powers by Kenner. Top row, left to right: Penguin, 1984, $40 MIP; Mr. Freeze, 1986, $65 MIP. Bottom row, left to right: Cyclotron, 1986, $75 MIP; Green Lantern, 1984, $60 MIP.

	NM	MIP
Mister Miracle, 1986, Kenner	$60	$145
Mr. Freeze, 1986, Kenner	$25	$65
Orion, 1986, Kenner, with "Power Action Astro Punch"	$25	$65
Parademon, 1985, Kenner, includes mini-comic book	$15	$35
Penguin, 1984, Kenner	$20	$40
Plastic Man, 1986, Kenner	$65	$150
Red Tornado, 1985, Kenner	$65	$85
Robin, 1984, Kenner	$25	$50
Samurai, 1986, Kenner	$45	$95
Shazam (Captain Marvel), 1986, Kenner, bright-colored figure, very "cartoony" look	$25	$65
Steppenwolf, in mail-in bag, 1985, Kenner	$15	$20
Steppenwolf, on card, 1985, Kenner	$15	$75
Superman, 1984, Kenner	$20	$35
Tyr, 1986, Kenner, with yellow attached "Power Action Rocket Launcher"	$40	$75
Wonder Woman, 1984, Kenner	$15	$40

Teenage Mutant Ninja Turtles (Playmates, 1988-92)

Series 01, 1988

	NM	MIP
April O'Neil, no stripe, 1988, Playmates	$50	$1000
Bebop, 1988, Playmates	$3	$8
Donatello, 1988 Playmates	$8	$20
Leonardo, 1988, Playmates	$8	$20
Michaelangelo, 1988, Playmates	$8	$20
Raphael, 1988, Playmates	$8	$20
Shredder, 1988, Playmates	$8	$20
Splinter, 1988, Playmates	$8	$20

Teenage Mutant Ninja Turtles — Leo the Sewer Samurai, Playmates, $15 MIP.

Series 02, 1989

	NM	MIP
Ace Duck, hat off, 1989, Playmates	$5	$40
Genghis Frog, black belt, bagged weapons, 1989, Playmates	$5	$30

Series 03, 1989

Casey Jones, 1989, Playmates	$5	$15
General Traag, 1989, Playmates	$5	$15
Leatherhead, 1989, Playmates	$25	$50
Metalhead, 1989, Playmates, carded	$5	$15

Series 04, 1990

Mondo Gecko, 1990, Playmates	$5	$15
Muckman and Joe Eyeball, 1990, Playmates	$5	$15
Scumbag, 1990, Playmates	$5	$15
Wingnut & Screwloose, 1990, Playmates	$5	$15

Series 05, 1990

Fugitoid, 1990, Playmates	$5	$15
Slash, purple belt, red "S," 1990, Playmates	$25	$75
Triceraton, 1990, Playmates	$5	$15

Series 06, 1990

Mutagen Man, 1990, Playmates	$5	$15
Napoleon Bonafrog, 1990, Playmates	$5	$15
Panda Khan, 1990, Playmates	$5	$15

Series 07, 1991

April O'Neil, 1991, Playmates	$25	$125
Ray Fillet, purple body, red "V," 1991, Playmates purple torso, red V	$10	$25

Teenage Mutant Ninja Turtles — Michaelangelo, Playmates, $20 MIP.

Series 08, 1991

	NM	MIP
Don The Undercover Turtle, 1991, Playmates	$5	$15
Leo the Sewer Samurai, 1991, Playmates	$5	$15
Mike the Sewer Surfer, 1991, Playmates	$5	$15
Ralph the Space Cadet, 1991, Playmates	$5	$15

Series 09, 1991

Chrome Dome, 1991, Playmates, carded	$5	$15
Dirt Bag, 1991, Playmates, carded	$5	$15
Ground Chuck, 1991, Playmates	$5	$15
Storage Shell Leo, 1991, Playmates	$5	$15

Series 10, 1991

Grand Slam Ralph, 1991, Playmates	$5	$15
Hose 'em Down Don, 1991, Playmates	$5	$15
Lieutenant Leo, 1991, Playmates	$5	$15

Series 11, 1992

Rahzer, red nose, 1992, Playmates	$7	$25
Skateboard'n Mike, 1992, Playmates	$5	$15
Super Shredder, 1992, Playmates	$5	$15
Tokka, brown trim, 1992, Playmates	$9	$25

Series 12, 1992

Movie Don, 1992, Playmates	$5	$15
Movie Leo, 1992, Playmates	$5	$15
Movie Mike, 1992, Playmates	$5	$15
Movie Raph, 1992, Playmates	$5	$15
Movie Splinter, with tooth, 1992, Playmates	$25	$75

Teenage Mutant Ninja Turtles — Mike the Sewer Surfer, Playmates,
$15 MIP.

Transformers (Kenner, 1984-1995)
Generation 1, Series 1, 1984

	NM	MIP
Bluestreak, blue, 1984 Kenner	$100	$350
Brawn, 1984 Kenner	$10	$40
Bumblebee, red, 1984 Kenner	$40	$100
Cliffjumper, yellow, 1984 Kenner	$20	$50
Hound, 1984 Kenner	$100	$275
Jazz, 1984 Kenner	$75	$250
Megatron, 1984 Kenner, Deception Leader turns from handgun to robot	$100	$300

Generation 1, Series 2, 1985

Blaster, 1985 Kenner	$20	$50
Bombshell, 1985 Kenner	$8	$25
Bumblebee with Minispy, yellow, 1985 Kenner	$20	$50
Cliffjumper with Minispy, red, 1985 Kenner	$20	$50
Grapple, 1985 Kenner	$50	$125
Hoist, 1985 Kenner	$50	$125
Inferno, 1985 Kenner	$40	$100
Kickback, 1985 Kenner	$8	$25
Optimus Prime, 1985 Kenner	$75	$250
Red Alert, 1985 Kenner	$60	$175
Shrapnel, 1985 Kenner	$8	$25
Smokescreen, 1985 Kenner	$50	$150
Tracks, 1985 Kenner	$60	$175
Whirl, 1985 Kenner	$50	$150

Generation 1, Series 3, 1986

Beachcomber with patch, 1986 Kenner	$8	$20
Blurr, 1986 Kenner	$30	$80

Transformers—Nightbeat, Generation 1, Series 5, Kenner, 1988, $60 MIP.

	NM	MIP
Broadside, 1986 Kenner	$20	$60
Groove, 1986 Kenner	$10	$30
Hubcap, 1986 Kenner	$5	$15
Octane, 1986 Kenner	$30	$75
Rampage, metal body, 1986 Kenner	$20	$75
Sandstorm, metal or plastic toes, 1986 Kenner	$50	$150
Springer, metal or plastic front, 1986 Kenner	$50	$100
Tantrum with poster, plastic body, 1986 Kenner	$30	$80
Tantrum, metal body, 1986 Kenner	$40	$100
Wreck-gar with poster, 1986 Kenner	$30	$80

Generation 1, Series 3, 1987

Headstrong, plastic body, 1987 Kenner	$30	$80

Generation 1, Series 4, 1987

Air Raid with decoy, 1987 Kenner	$10	$35
Brainstorm, 1987 Kenner	$20	$50
Chromedome, 1987 Kenner	$30	$75
Crosshairs, 1987 Kenner	$50	$150
Cyclonus, , 1987 Kenner	$50	$130
Fortess Maximus, 1987 Kenner	$300	$900
Grotusque, 1987 Kenner	$20	$45
Hot Rod, 1987 Kenner	$100	$300
Kup, 1987 Kenner	$50	$150
Lightspeed with decoy, 1987 Kenner	$8	$2
Pointblank, 1987 Kenner	$30	$70
Scourge, 1987 Kenner	$50	$130
Slugslinger, 1987 Kenner	$30	$80

Transformers—Lightspeed with decoy, Generation 1, Series 4, Kenner, 1987, $25 MIP.

	NM	MIP
Snapdragon, 1987 Kenner	$20	$55
Triggerhappy, 1987 Kenner	$30	$80

Generation 1, Series 5, 1988

Bomb-burst, clear insert, 1988 Kenner	$20	$60
Cloudburst, clear insert, 1988 Kenner	$20	$50
Darkwing, 1988 Kenner	$20	$50
Finback, 1988 Kenner	$20	$65
Groundbreaker, 1988 Kenner	$20	$65
Nightbeat, 1988 Kenner	$20	$60
Roadgrabber, 1988 Kenner	$20	$55
Skullgrin, clear insert, 1988 Kenner	$20	$50
Submarauder, clear insert, 1988 Kenner	$20	$50

Generation 1, Series 6, 1989

Bludgeon, 1989 Kenner	$10	$30
Crossblades, 1989 Kenner	$10	$40
Groundshaker, 1989 Kenner	$10	$30
Landmine,1989 Kenner	$20	$50
Skullgrin, 1989 Kenner	$10	$35
Skyhammer, 1989 Kenner	$20	$50
Thunderwing, 1989 Kenner	$10	$40

Generation 1, Series 7, 1990

Axer, 1990 Kenner	$8	$20
Gutcruncher, 1990 Kenner	$10	$45
Megatron, 1990 Kenner	$20	$60
Prowl, 1990, Kenner	$8	$20
Sprocket, 1990 Kenner	$10	$35

World's Greatest Super-Heroes (Mego, 1972-78)
12-1/2" Figures

Amazing Spider-Man, 1978, 1972-78, Mego	$40	$100

Transformers — Kickback, Generation 1, Series 2, Kenner, 1985, $25 MIP

	NM	MIP
Batman, 1978, 1972-78, Mego, magnetic	$100	$250
Batman, 1978, 1972-78, Mego	$60	$125
Captain America, 1978, 1972-78, Mego	$75	$200
Hulk, 1978, 1972-78, Mego	$30	$100
Robin, magnetic, 1978, 1972-78, Mego	$125	$250
Spider-Man, 1972-78, Mego, web shooting	$75	$150
Superman, 1972-78, Mego	$50	$125

8" Figures

	NM	MIP
Aquaman, 1972, Mego, carded	$50	$150
Aquaman,1972, Mego, Solid box, no window	$50	$800
Aquaman, 1972, Mego, boxed	$50	$150
Batgirl, 1973, Mego, boxed	$125	$300
Batgirl, 1973, Mego, carded	$125	$250
Batman, 1972, Mego, removable mask, Kresge card only	$200	$750
Batman, 1972, Mego, painted mask, boxed	$60	$150
Batman w/removable cowl, 1972, Mego, solid box, no window	$125	$1000
Batman, fist fighting, 1975, Mego, boxed	$150	$450
Batman, painted mask, 1972, Mego, carded	$60	$150
Batman, removable mask, 1972, Mego, boxed	$200	$600
Bruce Wayne, 1974, Mego, boxed, Montgomery Ward Exclusive	$1200	$2000
Captain America, 1972, Mego, carded	$60	$150
Captain America, 1972, Mego, boxed	$60	$200
Catwoman, 1973, Mego, boxed	$150	$350
Catwoman, 1973, Mego, carded	$150	$450
Clark Kent, 1974, Mego, boxed, Montgomery Ward Exclusive	$1200	$2000

World's Greatest Super-Heroes. Left to right: Robin with painted mask, boxed, 1972, $150 MIP; Robin with painted mask, carded, 1972, $90 MIP.

	NM	MIP
Conan, 1975, Mego, boxed	$150	$400
Conan, 1975, Mego, carded	$150	$500
Dick Grayson, 1974, Mego, boxed, Montgomery Ward Exclusive	$1200	$2000
Falcon, 1974, Mego, boxed	$60	$150
Falcon, 1974, Mego, carded	$60	$450
Green Arrow, 1973, Mego, boxed, with hat, belt and bow and arrow accessories	$150	$450
Green Arrow, 1973, Mego, carded	$150	$550
Green Goblin, 1974, Mego, boxed	$90	$275
Green Goblin, 1974, Mego, carded	$90	$1000
Human Torch, Fantastic Four, 1975, Mego, boxed	$25	$90
Human Torch, Fantastic Four, 1975, Mego, carded	$25	$50
Incredible Hulk, 1974, Mego, carded	$20	$50
Incredible Hulk, 1974, Mego, boxed	$20	$100
Invisible Girl, Fantastic Four, 1975, Mego, boxed	$30	$150
Invisible Girl, Fantastic Four, 1975, Mego, carded	$30	$60
Iron Man, 1974, Mego, boxed	$75	$125
Iron Man, 1974, Mego, carded	$75	$450
Isis, 1976, Mego, boxed	$75	$250
Isis, 1976, Mego, carded	$75	$125
Joker, 1973, Mego, boxed	$60	$200
Joker, 1973, Mego, carded	$60	$150
Joker, fist fighting, 1975, Mego, boxed	$150	$600
Lizard, 1974, Mego, carded	$75	$450
Lizard, 1974, Mego, boxed	$75	$200

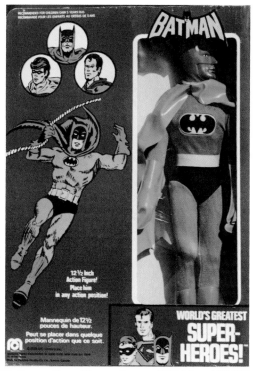

World's Greatest Super-Heroes—Batman, 1978, Mego, $125 MIP.

	NM	MIP
Mr. Fantastic, Fantastic Four, 1975, Mego, boxed	$30	$140
Mr. Fantastic, Fantastic Four, 1975, Mego, carded	$30	$60
Mr. Mxyzptlk, open mouth, 1973, Mego, boxed	$50	$75
Mr. Mxyzptlk, open mouth, 1973, Mego, carded	$50	$150
Mr. Mxyzptlk, smirk, 1973, Mego, boxed	$60	$150
Penguin, 1973, Mego, boxed	$60	$150
Penguin, 1973, Mego, carded	$60	$125
Peter Parker, 1974, Mego, boxed, Montgomery Ward Exclusive	$1200	$2000
Riddler, 1973, Mego, boxed	$100	$250
Riddler, 1973, Mego, carded	$100	$600
Riddler, 1975, Mego, fist fighting, boxed	$150	$600
Robin, 1972, Mego, painted mask, boxed	$60	$150
Robin, 1972, Mego, painted mask, carded	$60	$90
Robin, 1972, Mego, removable mask, boxed	$250	$750
Robin, 1972, removable mask, solid box	$250	$1500
Robin, 1975, Mego, fist fighting, boxed	$125	$450
Shazam, 1972, Mego, boxed	$75	$200
Shazam, 1972, Mego, carded	$75	$150
Spider-Man, 1972, Mego, carded	$20	$50
Spider-Man, 1972, Mego, boxed	$20	$100
Supergirl, 1973, Mego, boxed	$300	$450
Supergirl, 1973, Mego, carded	$300	$450
Superman, 1972, Mego, boxed	$50	$200

A selection of Hasbro's WWF series from 1994. Prices hover anywhere between $15 to $30 each, depending on the figure.

	NM	MIP
Superman, 1972, Mego, carded	$50	$125
Superman, 1972, Mego, solid box, no window	$50	$800
Tarzan, 1972, Mego, boxed	$50	$150
Tarzan, 1976, Mego, Kresge card only	$60	$225
Thing, Fantastic Four, 1975, Mego, boxed	$40	$150
Thing, Fantastic Four, 1975, Mego, carded	$40	$60
Thor, 1975, Mego, boxed	$150	$400
Thor, 1975, Mego, carded	$150	$450
Wonder Woman, 1972-78, Mego, boxed	$100	$350
Wonder Woman, 1972-78, Mego, Kresge card only	$100	$450
Wondergirl, 1972-78, Mego, carded	$125	$400

WWF World Wrestling Federation (Hasbro, 1990-94)

Figures

	NM	MIP
1-2-3- Kid, 1994, Hasbro	$15	$38
Adam Bomb, 1994, Hasbro	$10	$18
Akeem, 1990, Hasbro	$15	$38
Andre the Giant, 1990, Hasbro	$25	$75
Ax, 1990, Hasbro	$5	$15
Bam Bam Bigelow, 1994, Hasbro	$6	$15
Bart Gunn, 1994, Hasbro	$10	$18
Berzerker, 1993, Hasbro	$3	$8
Big Bossman with Jailhouse Jam, 1992, 1992, Hasbro	$4	$8
Big Bossman, 1990, 1990, Hasbro	$4	$8
Billy Gunn, 1994, Hasbro	$10	$18
Bret "Hitman" Hart with Hart Attack, 1992, 1992, Hasbro	$5	$13

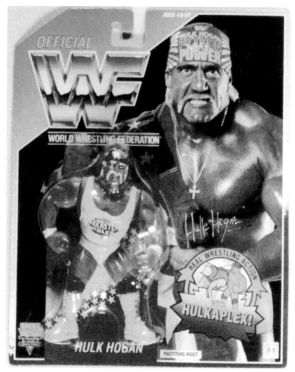

WWF World Wrestling Federation—Hulk Hogan with Hulkaplex,
Hasbro, 1992, $10 MIP.

	NM	MIP
Bret Hart, 1993 mail-in, 1993, Hasbro	$38	n/a
Bret Hart, 1994, 1994, Hasbro	$4	$8
British Bulldog with Bulldog Bash, 1992, 1992, Hasbro	$4	$8
Brutus "The Barber" Beefcake with Beefcake Flattop, 1992, 1992, Hasbro	$6	$13
Brutus the Barber, 1990, 1990, Hasbro	$6	$13
Bushwackers, two-pack, Hasbro	$5	$10
Butch Miller, 1994, Hasbro	$3	$8
Crush, 1993, 1993, Hasbro	$6	$13
Crush, 1994, 1994, Hasbro	$3	$8
Demolition, two-pack, Hasbro	$10	$23
Doink the Clown, 1994, Hasbro	$4	$8
Dusty Rhodes, 1991, Hasbro	$63	$150
Earthquake, 1991, Hasbro		$15
Earthquake with Aftershock, 1992, Hasbro	$4	$13
El Matador, 1993, Hasbro	$3	$8
Fatu, 1994, Hasbro	$3	$8
Giant Gonzales, 1994, Hasbro	$3	$8
Greg "the Hammer" Valentine with Hammer Slammer (1992), 1992, Hasbro	$5	$15
Hacksaw Jim Duggan, 1991, 1991, Hasbro	$3	$8
Hacksaw Jim Duggan, 1994, 1994, Hasbro	$3	$8
Honky Tonk Man, 1991, Hasbro	$13	$25
Hulk Hogan with Hulkaplex, 1992, 1992, Hasbro	$5	$10
Hulk Hogan, 1990, 1990, Hasbro	$6	$13
Hulk Hogan, 1991, 1991, Hasbro	$5	$10
Hulk Hogan, 1993, mail-in, 1993, Hasbro	$38	$50

WWF Best of 1998 (Series 1) —D.O.A. 8-Ball, Jakks Pacific, $8 MIP.

	NM	MIP
Hulk Hogan, 1993, no shirt, 1993, Hasbro	$5	$10
I.R.S., 1993, Hasbro	$4	$8
Jake the Snake Roberts, 1990, Hasbro	$5	$10
Jim Neidhart, 1993, Hasbro	$3	$8
Jimmy Superfly Snuka, 1991, Hasbro	$6	$13
Kamala, 1993, Hasbro	$5	$13
Koko B. Ware with Bird Man Bounce, 1992, 1992, Hasbro	$10	$30
Legion of Doom, two-pack, Hasbro	$10	$20
Lex Luger, 1994, Hasbro	$8	$15
Ludwig Borga, 1994, Hasbro	$20	$35
Luke Williams, 1994, Hasbro	$5	$15
Macho Man Randy Savage with Macho Masher, 1992, 1992, Hasbro	$15	$35
Macho Man, 1990, 1990, Hasbro	$12	$25
Macho Man, 1991, 1991, Hasbro	$15	$35
Macho Man, 1993, 1993, Hasbro	$7	$15
Marty Jannetty, 1994, Hasbro	$5	$15
Mountie, 1993, Hasbro	$6	$15
Mr. Perfect with Perfect Plex, 1992, 1992, Hasbro	$8	$20
Mr. Perfect with Texas Twister, 1992, 1992, Hasbro	$15	$35
Mr. Perfect, 1994, 1994, Hasbro	$12	$25
Nailz, 1993, Hasbro	$12	$25
Nasty Boys, two-pack, Hasbro	$15	$80
Owen Hart, 1993, Hasbro	$15	$45
Papa Shango, 1993, Hasbro	$7	$15
Razor Ramon, 1993, 1993, Hasbro	$15	$30

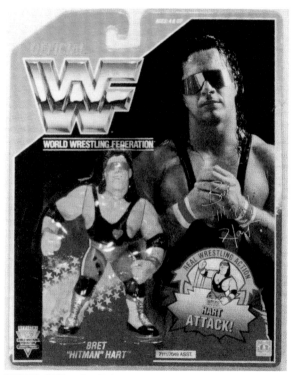

WWF World Wrestling Federation—Bret "Hitman" Hart with Hart Attack, Hasbro, 1994, $8 MIP.

	NM	MIP
Razor Ramon, 1994, 1994, Hasbro	$9	$18
Repo Man, 1993, Hasbro	$7	$15
Ric Flair, 1993, Hasbro	$7	$15
Rick Martel, 1993, Hasbro	$5	$15
Rick Rude, 1990, Hasbro	$15	$30
Rick Steiner, 1994, Hasbro	$9	$18
Ricky "The Dragon" Steamboat with Steamboat Springer, 1992, 1992, Hasbro	$7	$15
Rockers, two-pack, Hasbro	$10	$20
Rowdy Roddy Piper, 1991, Hasbro	$15	$30
Samu, 1994, Hasbro	$5	$15
Scott Steiner, 1994, Hasbro	$8	$18
Sgt. Slaughter with Sgt.'s Salute, 1992, 1992, Hasbro	$15	$30
Shawn Michaels, 1993, 1993, Hasbro	$10	$25
Shawn Michaels, 1994, 1994, Hasbro	$6	$15
Sid Justice, 1993, Hasbro	$6	$15
Skinner, 1993, Hasbro	$6	$15
Smash, 1990, Hasbro	$12	$25
Tatanka, 1993, 1993, Hasbro	$7	$15
Tatanka, 1994, 1994, Hasbro	$7	$15
Ted DiBiase, 1990, 1990, Hasbro	$10	$20
Ted DiBiase, 1991, 1991, Hasbro	$7	$15
Ted DiBiase, 1994, 1994, Hasbro	$7	$15
Texas Tornado with Texas Twister, 1992, 1992, Hasbro	$10	$50
Typhoon with Tidal Wave, 1992, 1992, Hasbro	$15	$30
Ultimate Warrior with Warrior Wham, 1992, 1992, Hasbro	$20	$40

	NM	MIP
Ultimate Warrior, 1990, 1990, Hasbro	$12	$25
Ultimate Warrior, 1991, 1991, Hasbro	$10	$20
Undertaker with Graveyard Smash, 1992, 1992, Hasbro	$9	$18
Undertaker, 1993, mail-in, 1993, Hasbro	$25	$50
Undertaker, 1994, 1994, Hasbro	$15	$25
Virgil, 1993, Hasbro	$7	$15
Warlord, 1993, Hasbro	$6	$15
Yokozuna, 1994, Hasbro	$15	$30

Barbie Doll

Little could Ruth Handler have realized her first foray into dollmaking would help create not only a fabulous doll, but also a touchstone of cultural politics and one of the most amazing success stories in the history of children's toys.

With Handler as the catalyst, Mattel's first Barbie doll named after Handler's daughter, Barbara debuted at the American Toy Fair in New York City in 1959. The 11-1/2-inch, fresh-faced doll with a ponytail and black-and-white striped swimsuit became an instant hit, selling more than 350,000 units its first year. Since then, more than 1 billion Barbie dolls have been sold in 150 countries.

First introduced as a teenage fashion model, Barbie has enjoyed more than 80 careers in the past five decades. She's been everything from an astronaut to a paleontologist to a presidential candidate.

Before her death in April 2002 at the age of 85, Handler fashioned not only a wonderful toy for little girls, but also one of the most popular and prized collectibles in the toy market. A Ponytail Barbie doll #1 has sold for as much as $10,000 in mint condition.

A 1962 Bubblecut Barbie doll set for a fraternity dance. $350 MIB.

The inspiration for Barbie came as Handler watched her daughter, Barbara, playing with paper dolls. Barbara and her friends liked to play teenage or adult make-believe with paper dolls, imagining the dolls in roles as college students, cheerleaders, and adults with careers. Handler recognized that experimenting with the future from a safe distance through play was an important part of growing up. She also noticed a marketing void and was determined to fill that niche with a three-dimensional fashion doll.

Along the way, Barbie doll has had a supporting cast that began with boyfriend Ken in 1961. (Ken was named after Ruth and Elliot Handler's son.) Barbie doll's best friend Midge was introduced in 1963. Barbie doll's little sister, Skipper, was introduced in 1964, while twins Tutti and Todd arrived in 1966. Sisters Stacy and Kelly were introduced in 1992 and 1995, respectively, and baby sister Krissy in 1999.

Barbie doll has come a long way from Ruth Handler's simple mission to create a toy for her daughter. Today, both children and adults collect her with passion and glee.

Welcome to the world of Barbie doll collecting, whether you've been interested for a while or are just discovering the wonders of the doll.

"Barbie in Switzerland" fashions and accessories, 1964, $130 mint to $250 MIB.

Barbie Doll

Prices listed are for dolls in Mint No Box (MNB) and Mint in Box (MIB) condition.

The "Barbie & Friends" section includes vintage and modern regular-issue and pink box dolls.

Barbie & Friends dolls

	MNB	MIB
All American Barbie, 1991, No. 9423	$4	$20
All American Christie, 1991, No. 9425	$4	$25
All American Ken, 1991, No. 9424	$4	$15
All American Kira, 1991, No. 9427	$4	$20
All American Teresa, 1991, No. 9426	$4	$30
All Star Ken, 1981, No. 3553	$7	$25
All Stars Barbie, 1989, No. 9099	$5	$25
All Stars Christie, 1989, No. 9352	$5	$20
All Stars Ken, 1989, No. 9361	$5	$20
All Stars Midge, 1989, No. 9360	$5	$30
All Stars Teresa, 1989, No. 9353	$5	$30
Allan, bendable leg, 1965, No. 1010	$150	$400
Allan, straight leg, 1964, No. 1000	$55	$125
American Beauties Mardi Gras Barbie,1988, No. 4930	$40	$100
American Beauties Army Barbie,1989, No. 3966	$20	$40
American Beauty Queen, 1991, No. 3137	$5	$45
American Beauty Queen, black, 1991, No. 3245	$5	$35

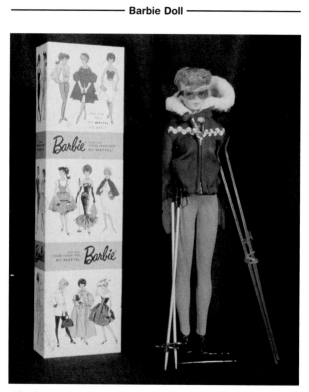

"Ski Queen" fashions and accessories (on a 1963 titian Ponytail Barbie doll), $75 mint to $180 MIB.

	MNB	MIB
American Girl (see Bendable Leg)		
Angel Face Barbie, 1982, No. 5640	$8	$40
Animal Lovin' Barbie, black, 1989, No. 4828	$5	$75
Animal Lovin' Barbie, white, 1989, No. 1350	$5	$40
Animal Lovin' Ken, 1989, No. 1351	$5	$20
Animal Lovin' Nikki, 1989, No. 1352	$7	$20
Astronaut Barbie, black, 1985, No. 1207	$30	$40
Astronaut Barbie, white, 1985, No. 2449	$25	$75
Babysitter Courtney, 1991, No. 9434	$4	$15
Babysitter Skipper, 1991, No. 9433	$4	$15
Babysitter Skipper, black, 1991, No. 1599	$4	$10
Baggie Casey, blond (sold in plastic bag), 1975, No. 9000	$75	$250
Ballerina Barbie on Tour, gold, 1st version, 1976, No. 9613	$45	$125
Ballerina Barbie, 1st version, 1976, No. 9093	$20	$65
Ballerina Cara, 1976, No. 9528	$25	$65
Barbie & Her Fashion Fireworks, 1976, No. 9805	$20	$60
Barbie & the Beat, 1990, No. 3751	$5	$30
Barbie & the Beat Christie, 1990, No. 2752	$5	$15
Barbie & the Beat Midge, 1990, No. 2754	$6	$20
Barbie Hair Happenings (department store exclusive, redhead), 1971, No. 1174	$400	$1,000
Barbie with Growin' Pretty Hair, 1971, No. 1144	$100	$300
Bathtime Fun Barbie, 1991, No. 9601	$3	$20

Ponytail #2. The model is identical to #1 except holes in feet are eliminated. $3,500-$7,000.

	MNB	MIB
Bathtime Fun Barbie, black, 1991, No. 9603	$3	$15
Beach Blast Barbie, 1989, No. 3237	$3	$20
Beach Blast Christie, 1989, No. 3253	$4	$15
Beach Blast Ken, 1989, No. 3238	$4	$15
Beach Blast Miko, 1989, No. 3244	$4	$15
Beach Blast Skipper, 1989, No. 3242	$4	$15
Beach Blast Steven, 1989, No. 3251	$4	$15
Beach Blast Teresa, 1989, No. 3249	$5	$15
Beautiful Bride Barbie, 1978, No. 9907	$60	$125
Beauty Secrets Barbie, 1st issue, 1980, No. 1290	$12	$65
Beauty Secrets Christie, 1980, No. 1295	$12	$65
Beauty, Barbie doll's dog, 1979, No. 1018	$12	$30

Bendable Leg "American Girl"

	MNB	MIB
Bendable Leg "American Girl" Barbie, short hair, 1965, No. 1070	$850	$1,900
Bendable Leg "American Girl" Barbie, Color Magic Face, 1966, No. 1070	$1,300	$2,900
Bendable Leg "American Girl" Barbie, long hair, 1965, No. 1070	$1,300	$2,800
Bendable Leg "American Girl" Barbie, side-part, long hair, 1966, No. 1070	$2,400	$4,000
Bendable Leg "American Girl" Barbie, Swirl Ponytail or Bubblecut hairstyle, 1965, No. 1070	$950	$3,000
Benetton Barbie, 1991, No. 9404	$6	$45
Benetton Christie, 1991, No. 9407	$6	$35
Benetton Marina, 1991, No. 9409	$6	$35

A mint-in-box, first-issue Bubblecut Barbie doll. Value: $1,400 MIB.

	MNB	MIB
Black Barbie, 1980, No. 1293	$30	$100
Brad, bendable leg, 1970, No. 1142	$75	$150
Brad, talking, 1970, No. 1114	$65	$150

Bubblecut Barbie dolls

	MNB	MIB
Bubblecut Barbie Sidepart, all hair colors, 1961, No. 850	$425	$900
Bubblecut Barbie, blond, brunette, titian, 1962, No. 850	$150	$350
Bubblecut Barbie, brunette, 1961, No. 850	$900	$1,400
Bubblecut Barbie, white ginger, 1962, No. 850	$450	$900
Busy Barbie, 1971, No. 3311	$100	$300
Busy Francie, 1971, No. 3313	$175	$425
Busy Ken, 1971, No. 3314	$60	$165
Busy Steffie, 1971, No. 3312	$125	$350
Butterfly Art Barbie, 1999	$5	$15
Calgary Olympic Skating Barbie, 1987, No. 4547	$25	$60
California Dream Barbie, 1988, No. 4439	$5	$20
California Dream Christie, 1988, No. 4443	$6	$15
California Dream Ken, 1988, No. 4441	$8	$15
California Dream Midge, 1988, No. 4442	$3	$15
California Dream Skipper, 1988, No. 4440	$13	$20
California Dream Teresa, 1988, No. 4403	$15	$20
Carla, European exclusive, 1976, No. 7377	$65	$140
Casey, Twist 'n Turn, 1967, No. 1180	$85	$275
Chris, titian, blond, brunette (Tutti's friend), 1967, No. 3570	$65	$250
Christie, talking, 1970, No. 1126	$65	$200

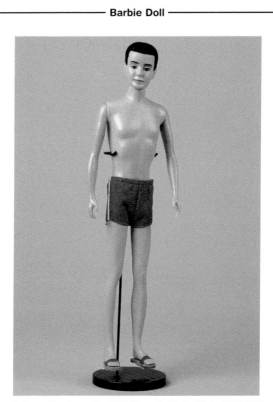

Ken doll was first issued in 1961. Note the flocked hair. $200 MIB.

	MNB	MIB
Christie, Twist 'n Turn, 1970, No. 1119	$125	$500
Coach Ken & Tommy, white or black, 2000	$7	$15
Color Magic Barbie, Golden Blond, 1966, No. 1150	$650	$2,400
Color Magic Barbie, Midnight Black, 1966, No. 1150	$1,200	$3,500
Cool City Blues: Barbie, Ken, Skipper, 1989, No. 4893	$20	$45
Cool Shavin' Ken, 1996, No. 15469	$10	$15
Cool Times Barbie, 1989, No. 3022	$5	$25
Cool Times Christie, 1989, No. 3217	$5	$20
Cool Times Ken, 1989, No. 3219	$5	$20
Cool Times Midge, 1989, No. 3216	$7	$20
Cool Times Teresa, 1989, No. 3218	$9	$20
Cool Tops Courtney, 1989, No. 7079	$7	$20
Cool Tops Kevin, 1989, No. 9351	$5	$20
Cool Tops Skipper, black, 1989, No. 5441	$5	$15
Cool Tops Skipper, white, 1989, No. 4989	$7	$15
Corduroy Cool Barbie, 2000, No. 24658	$5	$10
Costume Ball Barbie, black, 1991, No. 7134	$6	$15
Costume Ball Barbie, white, 1991, No. 7123	$6	$25
Costume Ball Ken, black, 1991, No. 7160	$6	$20
Costume Ball Ken, white, 1991, No. 7154	$6	$30
Crystal Barbie, black, 1984, No. 4859	$10	$25
Crystal Barbie, white, 1984, No. 4598	$10	$35
Crystal Ken, black, 1983, No. 9036	$15	$25
Crystal Ken, white, 1983, No. 4898	$8	$30

Fashion Queen Barbie doll, 1963. $145-$500.

	MNB	MIB
Dance Club Barbie, 1989, No. 3509	$5	$45
Dance Club Devon, 1989, No. 3513	$5	$40
Dance Club Kayla, 1989, No. 3512	$5	$85
Dance Club Ken, 1989, No. 3511	$5	$40
Dance Magic Barbie, 1990, No. 4836	$7	$25
Dance Magic Barbie, black,1990, No. 7080	$7	$25
Dance Magic Ken, 1990, No. 7081	$6	$20
Dance Magic Ken, black, 1990, No. 7082	$6	$20
Day-to-Night Barbie, black, 1985, No. 7945	$10	$35
Day-to-Night Barbie, Hispanic, 1985, No. 7944	$17	$40
Day-to-Night Barbie, white, 1985, No. 7929	$10	$40
Day-to-Night Ken, black, 1984, No. 9018	$8	$20
Day-to-Night Ken, white, 1984, No. 9019	$8	$25
Dentist Barbie, 1997, No. 17255	$15	$30
Doctor Barbie, 1988, No. 3850	$8	$45
Doctor Ken, 1988, No. 4118	$5	$40

Dolls of the World/International

	MNB	MIB
Arctic, 1997, No. 16495	$20	$30
Australian, two box variations, 1993, No. 3626	$10	$35
Austrian, 1999, No. 21553	$15	$25
Brazillian, 1990, No. 9094	$15	$60
Canadian, 1988, No. 4928	$15	$75
Chilean, 1998, No. 18559	$10	$20
Chinese, 1994, No. 11180	$10	$30
Czechoslovakian, 1991, No. 7330	$30	$110
Dutch, 1994, No. 11104	$10	$35
English, 1992, No. 4973	$12	$80

Swirl Ponytail Barbie originally came in a red one-piece swimsuit.
$1,200 MIB.

	MNB	MIB
Eskimo, 1982, No. 3898	$30	$100
Eskimo, 1991, No. 9844	$8	$60
French, 1997, No. 16499	$10	$25
German, 1987, No. 3188	$45	$100
German, 1995, No. 12598	$10	$25
Ghanaian, 1996, No. 15303	$15	$25
Gift Set (Chinese, Dutch, Kenyan), 1994, No. 12043	$30	$70
Gift Set (Irish, German, Polynesian), 1995, No. 13939	$30	$65
Native American #3, 1995, No. 12699	$10	$30
Nigerian, 1990, No. 7376	$15	$60
Norwegian, pink flowers, limited to .$3,000, 1996, No. 14450	$12	$65
NW Coast Native American Barbie, 2000, No. 24671	$12	$25
Oriental, 1981, No. 3262	$55	$130
Parisian, 1980, No. 1600	$65	$150
Parisian, 1991, No. 9843	$8	$60
Peruvian, 1986, No. 2995	$30	$80
Peruvian, 1999, No. 21506	$15	$25
Polish, 1998, No. 18560	$15	$25
Polynesian, 1995, No. 12700	$10	$30
Princess of India, 2000, No. 28374	$8	$20
Princess of the French Court, 2000, No. 28372	$8	$20
Princess of the Incas, 2000, No. 28373	$8	$20
Puerto Rican, 1997, No. 16754	$15	$25

Color Magic Barbie doll can change hair and clothes color. $2,400-$3,500 MIB.

	MNB	MIB
Royal, 1980, No. 1601	$65	$175
Russian, 1989, No. 1916	$20	$25
Russian, 1997, No. 16500	$20	$75
Scottish, 1981, No. 3263	$50	$130
Scottish, 1991, No. 9845	$8	$60
Spanish, 1983, No. 4031	$40	$110
Spanish, 1992, No. 4963	$12	$45
Spanish, 2000, No. 24670	$12	$25
Swedish, 1983, No. 4032	$35	$100
Swedish, 2000, No. 24672	$12	$25
Swiss, 1984, No. 7451	$35	$100
Thai, 1998, No. 18561	$10	$2
Dramatic New Living Barbie, 1970, No. 1116	$75	$275
Dramatic New Living Skipper, 1970, No. 1117	$50	$175
Dream Bride, 1992, No. 1623	$10	$40
Dream Date Barbie, 1983, No. 5868	$10	$25
Dream Date Ken, 1983, No. 4077	$10	$25
Dream Glow Barbie, black, 1986, No. 2242	$12	$25
Dream Glow Barbie, Hispanic, 1986, No. 1647	$25	$70
Dream Glow Barbie, white, 1986, No. 2248	$12	$45
Fashion Play Barbie, Hispanic, 1990, No. 5954	$2	$15
Fashion Queen Barbie, 1963, No. 870	$145	$500
Feelin'Fun Barbie, two versions, white, 1st issue, 1988, No. 1189	$5	$20
Flight Time Barbie, black, 1990, No. 9916	$5	$20
Flight Time Barbie, white, 1990, No. 9584	$5	$30
Flight Time Ken, 1990, No. 9600	$5	$20

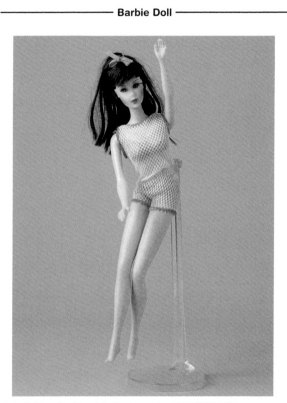

Twist 'n Turn Barbie with pivoting waist, 1967. $500 MIB.

	MNB	MIB
Fluff, 1971, No. 1143	$100	$210
Francie with Growin' Pretty Hair, 1971, No. 1129	$75	$225
Francie, bendable leg, blond, brunette, 1966, No. 1130	$150	$350
Francie, Hair Happenins, 1970, No. 1122	$150	$400
Francie, straight leg, brunette, blond, 1966, No. 1140	$150	$400
Francie, Twist N Turn, "Black Francie" 1st issue, red hair, 1967, No. 1100	$900	$1,600
Growing Up Ginger, 1977, No. 9222	$30	$140
Growing Up Skipper, 1977, No. 7259	$30	$150
Happy Birthday Barbie, 1981, No. 1922	$8	$45
Happy Birthday Barbie, 1984, No. 1922	$8	$35
Happy Birthday Barbie, 1991, No. 9561	$8	$20
Happy Birthday Barbie, black, 1991, No. 9561	$8	$30
Hawaiian Barbie, 1975, No. 7470	$25	$68
Hawaiian Barbie, 1977, No. 7470	$30	$80
Hawaiian Fun Barbie, 1991, No. 5040	$3	$20
Hawaiian Fun Christie, 1991, No. 5044	$3	$20
Hawaiian Fun Jazzie, 1991, No. 9294	$3	$20
Hawaiian Fun Ken, 1991, No. 5041	$3	$15
Hawaiian Fun Kira, 1991, No. 5043	$3	$15
Hawaiian Fun Skipper, 1991, No. 5042	$3	$15
Hawaiian Fun Steven, 1991, No. 5045	$3	$15
Hawaiian Ken, 1979, No. 2960	$13	$50
Hawaiian Ken, 1984, No. 7495	$7	$30

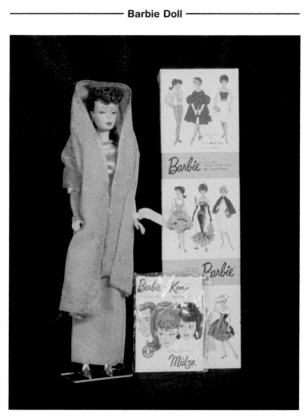

"Arabian Nights," 1962 Ponytail Barbie. $400 MIB.

	MNB	MIB
High School Chelsie, 1989, No. 3698	$5	$20
High School Dude, Jazzie's boyfriend, 1989, No. 3600	$5	$20
High School Jazzie, 1989, No. 3635	$5	$20
High School Stacie, 1989, No. 3636	$5	$20
Julia, Twist N Turn, one-piece nurse $dress, 2nd issue, 1969, No. 1127	$100	$250
Julia, Twist N Turn, two-piece nurse $outfit, 1st issue, 1969, No. 1127	$125	$300
Ken, bendable leg, brunette, 1965, No. 750	$155	$300
Ken, bendable leg, talking, 1970, No. 1124	$60	$125
Ken, flocked hair, brunette, blond, 1961, No. 750	$100	$200
Ken, painted hair, brunette, blond, 1962, No. 750	$50	$175
Kevin, 1991, No. 9325	$5	$10
Kissing Barbie, 1979, No. 2597	$8	$65
Kissing Christie, 1979, No. 2955	$10	$65
Lights & Lace Barbie, 1991, No. 9725	$4	$30
Lights & Lace Christie, 1991, No. 9728	$4	$30
Lights & Lace Teresa, 1991, No. 9727	$4	$25
Live Action Barbie, 1970, No. 1155	$60	$150
Live Action Barbie Onstage, 1970, No. 1152	$75	$250
Live Action Christie, 1970, No. 1175	$60	$250
Live Action Ken, 1970, No. 1159	$55	$150
Live Action Ken on Stage, 1970, No. 1172	$40	$150
Live Action P.J., 1970, No. 1156	$65	$250

The first Black Barbie doll released in 1980. Value: $100 MIB.

	MNB	MIB
Live Action P.J. on Stage, 1970, No. 1153	$75	$175
Lovin' You Barbie, 1983, No. 7072	$20	$100
Magic Curl Barbie, black, 1982, No. 3989	$8	$25
Magic Curl Barbie, white, 1982, No. 3856	$10	$35
Magic Moves Barbie, black, 1985, No. 3137	$15	$35
Magic Moves Barbie, white, 1985, No. 2126	$15	$35
Malibu Barbie, 1971, No. 1067	$15	$60
Malibu Barbie (Sunset), 1975, No. 1067	$15	$40
Malibu Christie, 1975, No. 7745	$10	$40
Malibu Francie, 1971, No. 1068	$15	$45
Malibu Ken, 1976, No. 1088	$8	$25
Malibu P.J., 1975, No. 1087	$5	$45
Malibu Skipper, 1977, No. 1069	$8	$45
Midge, bendable leg, blond, brunette, titian, 1965, No. 1080	$250	$425
Midge, straight leg, blond, brunette, titian, 1963, No. 860	$65	$175
Miss Barbie (sleep eyes), 1964, No. 1060	$400	$1,200
Mod Hair Ken, 1972, No. 4224	$45	$65
Music Lovin' Barbie, 1985, No. 9988	$15	$45
Music Lovin' Ken, 1985, No. 2388	$15	$45
Music Lovin' Skipper, 1985, No. 2854	$20	$75
My First Barbie, 1991, No. 9942	$3	$25
My First Barbie, aqua and yellow dress, 1981, No. 1875	$10	$30
My First Barbie, black, 1990, No. 9943	$5	$25
My First Barbie, Hispanic, 1991, No. 9944	$3	$20
My First Barbie, pink checkered dress, 1983, No. 1875	$5	$35

The first black Ken, Sunsational Malibu Ken, 1981. $35 MIB.

	MNB	MIB
My First Barbie, pink tutu, black, 1987, No. 1801	$5	$20
My First Barbie, pink tutu, white, 1987, No. 1788	$5	$20
My First Barbie, white, 1990, No. 9942	$4	$20
My First Barbie, white dress, black, 1984, No. 9858	$7	$25
My First Barbie, white dress, white, 1984, No. 1875	$5	$30
My First Barbie, white tutu, black, 1988, No. 1281	$6	$15
My First Barbie, white tutu, Hispanic, 1988, No. 1282	$6	$20
My First Barbie, white tutu, white, 1988, No. 1280	$5	$20
My First Ken, 1st issue, 1989, No. 1389	$4	$15
My First Ken, Prince, 1990, No. 9940	$4	$15
New Good Lookin' Ken, 1970, No. 1124	$75	$150
New Look Ken, 1976, No. 9342	$23	$65
Newport Barbie, two versions, 1974, No. 7807	$25	$140
Nurse Whitney, 1987, No. 4405	$20	$45
Ocean Friends Barbie, 1996, No. 15430	$5	$17
Ocean Friends Ken, 1996, No. 15430	$5	$17
Ocean Friends Kira, 1996, No. 15431	$5	$17
Olympic Gymnast, blond, 1996, No. 15123	$10	$25
P.J., talking, 1970, No. 1113	$65	$250
P.J., Twist N Turn, 1970, No. 1118	$125	$300
Party Treats Barbie, 1989, No. 4885	$8	$25
Peaches n' Cream Barbie, black, 1984, No. 9516	$8	$40

Barbie doll Ponytail #1, 1959. $9,000 MIB.

	MNB	MIB
Peaches n' Cream Barbie, white, 1984, No. 7926	$8	$45
Perfume Giving Ken, black, 1989, No. 4555	$6	$25
Perfume Giving Ken, white, 1989, No. 4554	$6	$25
Perfume Pretty Barbie, black, 1989, No. 4552	$8	$25
Perfume Pretty Barbie, white, 1989, No. 4551	$8	$25
Perfume Pretty Whitney, 1987, No. 4557	$8	$35
Pink n' Pretty Barbie, 1982, No. 3551	$12	$45
Pink n' Pretty Christie, 1982, No. 3554	$10	$40
Playtime Barbie, 1984, No. 5336	$15	$20

Ponytail Dolls

	MNB	MIB
Ponytail Barbie #1, blond, 1959, No. 850	$4,000	$7,500
Ponytail Barbie #1, brunette, 1959, No. 850	$5,000	$9,000
Ponytail Barbie #2, blond, 1959, No. 850	$3,500	$7,000
Ponytail Barbie #2, brunette, 1959, No. 850	$4,000	$7,000
Ponytail Barbie #3, blond, 1960, No. 850	$500	$1,300
Ponytail Barbie #3, brunette, 1960, No. 850	$750	$1,400
Ponytail Barbie #4, blond, 1960, No. 850	$250	$575
Ponytail Barbie #4, brunette, 1960, No. 850	$350	$400
Ponytail Barbie #5, blond, 1961, No. 850	$175	$400
Ponytail Barbie #5, brunette, 1961, No. 850	$250	$450
Ponytail Barbie #5, titian, 1961, No. 850	$250	$500
Ponytail Barbie #6, blond, brunette, titian 1962, No. 850	$150	$400
Ponytail Swirl Style Barbie, blond, brunette, titian, 1964, No. 850	$350	$625
Ponytail Swirl Style Barbie, platinum, 1964, No. 850	$500	$1,200

	MNB	MIB
Pose n' Play Skipper (packaged in baggie), 1973, No. 1117	$20	$55
Pretty Changes Barbie, 1978, No. 2598	$8	$45
Pretty Party Barbie, 1983, No. 7194	$12	$30
Quick Curl Barbie, 1972, No. 4220	$20	$80
Quick Curl Cara, 1974, No. 7291	$20	$60
Quick Curl Deluxe Barbie, 1976, No. 9217	$20	$95
Quick Curl Deluxe Cara, 1976, No. 9219	$20	$80
Quick Curl Deluxe P.J., 1976, No. 9218	$20	$50
Quick Curl Deluxe Skipper, 1976, No. 9428	$20	$50
Quick Curl Francie, 1972, No. 4222	$20	$55
Quick Curl Kelley, 1972, No. 4221	$20	$75
Quick Curl Miss America, blond, 1974, No. 8697	$35	$75
Quick Curl Miss America, brunette, 1973, No. 8697	$45	$175
Quick Curl Skipper, 1974, No. 4223	$20	$50
Ricky, 1965, No. 1090	$55	$160
Rocker Barbie, 1st issue, 1986, No. 1140	$7	$40
Rocker Barbie, 2nd issue, 1987, No. 3055	$7	$25
Rocker Dana, 1st issue, 1986, No. 1196	$7	$40
Rocker Dana, 2nd issue, 1987, No. 3158	$7	$20
Rocker Dee-Dee, 1st issue, 1986, No. 1141	$7	$30
Rocker Dee-Dee, 2nd issue, 1987, No. 3160	$7	$20
Rocker Derek, 1st issue, 1986, No. 2428	$7	$30
Rocker Derek, 2nd issue, 1987, No. 3173	$7	$20
Rocker Diva, 1st issue, 1986, No. 2427	$7	$30
Rocker Diva, 2nd issue, 1987, No. 3159	$7	$20

	MNB	MIB
Rocker Ken, 1st issue, 1986, No. 3131	$7	$30
Rollerskating Barbie, 1980, No. 1880	$8	$60
Rollerskating Ken, 1980, No. 1881	$8	$40
Safari Barbie, 1983, No. 4973	$8	$30
Scott, 1979, No. 1019	$15	$60
Sea Lovin' Barbie, 1984, No. 9109	$8	$35
Sea Lovin' Ken, 1984, No. 9110	$8	$30
Secret Messages Barbie, white or black, 2000, No. 26422	$7	$15
Sensations Barbie, 1987, No. 4931	$5	$12
Sensations Becky, 1987, No. 4977	$5	$12
Sensations Belinda, 1987, No. 4976	$5	$12
Sensations Bobsy, 1987, No. 4967	$5	$12
Sit 'n Style Barbie, 2000, No. 23421	$7	$15
Ski Fun Barbie, 1991, No. 7511	$6	$15
Ski Fun Ken, 1991, No. 7512	$6	$15
Ski Fun Midge, 1991, No. 7513	$6	$25
Skipper, bendable leg, brunette, blond, titian, 1965, No. 1030	$65	$250
Skipper, straight leg, brunette, blond, titian, 1964, No. 950	$50	$195
Skipper, straight leg, reissues, brunette, blond, titian, 1971, No. 950	$125	$400
Skipper, Twist N Turn, blond or brunette, curl pigtails, 1969, No. 1105	$95	$350
Skipper, Twist N Turn, blond, brunette, redhead, long straight hair, 1968, No. 1105	$95	$350

	MNB	MIB
Skooter, bendable leg, brunette, blond, titian, 1966, No. 1120	$100	$350
Skooter, straight leg, brunette, blond, titian, 1965, No. 1040	$55	$180
Snowboard Barbie, 1996, No. 15408	$10	$20
Sparkle Barbie, 1996, No. 15419	$10	$20
Sport n' Shave Ken, 1980, No. 1294	$8	$40
Stacey, talking, blond or redhead, side ponytail, 1968, No. 1125	$175	$475
Stacey, Twist and Turn, blond or redhead, long ponytail with spit curls, 1968, No. 1165	$150	$475
Stacey, Twist N Turn, blond or redhead, short rolled flip, 1969, No. 1165	$175	$475
Standard Barbie, blond, brunette, long straight hair with bangs, 1967, No. 1190	$250	$550
Standard Barbie, centered eyes, 1971, No. 1190	$350	$700
Standard Barbie, titian, long straight $hair with bangs, 1967, No. 1190	$300	$600

Stars 'n Stripes

	MNB	MIB
Air Force Barbie, 1990, No. 3360	$15	$50
Air Force Ken, white or black, 1994, No. 11554/11555	$15	$25
Air Force Thunderbirds Barbie, white or black, 1994, No. 11552/11553	$15	$25
Army Barbie, white or black, 1993, No. 1234/5618	$10	$40

	MNB	MIB
Army Ken, white or black, 1993, No. 1237/5619	$15	$30
Marine Corps Barbie, white or black, 1992, No. 7549/7594	$10	$35
Marine Corps Ken, black or white, 1992, No. 5352/7574	$20	$40
Navy Barbie, white or black, 1991, No. 9693/9694	$10	$35
Style Magic Barbie, 1989, No. 1283	$5	$20
Style Magic Christie, 1989, No. 1288	$5	$20
Style Magic Skipper, 1989, No. 1915	$10	$20
Style Magic Whitney, 1989, No. 1290	$5	$20
Summit Barbie, Asian, 1990, No. 7029	$10	$25
Summit Barbie, black, 1990, No. 7028	$12	$25
Summit Barbie, Hispanic, 1990, No. 7030	$10	$28
Summit Barbie, white, 1990, No. 7027	$8	$25
Sun Gold Malibu Barbie, black, 1983, No. 7745	$5	$15
Sun Gold Malibu Barbie, Hispanic, 1985, No. 4970	$3	$20
Sun Gold Malibu Barbie, white, 1983, No. 1067	$5	$15
Sun Gold Malibu Ken, black, 1983, No. 3849	$3	$15
Sun Gold Malibu Ken, Hispanic, 1985, No. 4971	$3	$20
Sun Gold Malibu Ken, white, 1983, No. 1088	$3	$15
Sun Gold Malibu P.J., 1983, No. 1187	$5	$15
Sun Gold Malibu Skipper, 1983, No. 1069	$5	$15
Sun Lovin'Malibu Barbie, 1978, No. 1067	$5	$20
Sun Lovin'Malibu Ken, 1978, No. 1088	$5	$20
Sun Lovin'Malibu P.J., 1978, No. 1187	$5	$20

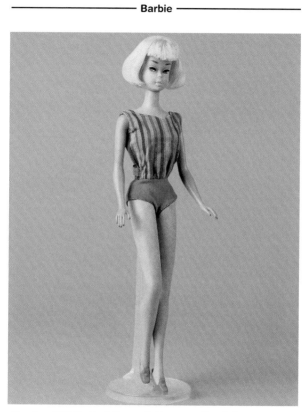

American Girl Barbie doll, so noted because of her hair.

	MNB	MIB
Sun Lovin'Malibu Skipper, 1978, No. 1069	$5	$20
Sun Valley Barbie, 1974, No. 7806	$20	$130
Sun Valley Ken, 1974, No. 7809	$20	$100
Sunsational Malibu Barbie, 1982, No. 1067	$6	$25
Sunsational Malibu Barbie, Hispanic, 1982, No. 4970	$8	$25
Sunsational Malibu Christie, 1982, No. 7745	$6	$20
Sunsational Malibu Ken, black, 1981, No. 3849	$15	$35
Sunsational Malibu P.J., 1982, No. 1187	$6	$30
Sunsational Malibu Skipper, 1982, No. 1069	$5	$35
Sunset Malibu Christie, 1973, No. 7745	$20	$65
Sunset Malibu Francie, 1971, No. 1068	$25	$65
Sunset Malibu Ken, 1972, No. 1088	$15	$50
Sunset Malibu P.J., 1971, No. 1187	$10	$50
Sunset Malibu Skipper, 1971, No. 1069	$20	$50
Super Hair Barbie, black, 1987, No. 3296	$8	$20
Super Hair Barbie, white, 1987, No. 3101	$8	$25
Super Sport Ken, 1982, No. 5839	$8	$20
Super Talk Barbie, 1994, No. 12290	$10	$20
Super Teen Skipper, 1978, No. 2756	$7	$20
Supersize Barbie, 1977, No. 9828	$75	$200
Supersize Bride Barbie, 1977, No. 9975	$150	$295
Supersize Christie, 1977, No. 9839	$75	$275
Supersize Super Hair Barbie, 1979, No. 2844	$85	$175
Superstar Ballerina Barbie, 1976, No. 4983	$20	$60
Superstar Barbie, 1977, No. 9720	$15	$70
Superstar Barbie, 1988, No. 1604	$45	$95
Superstar Barbie 30th Anniversary, black, 1989, No. 1605	$6	$35

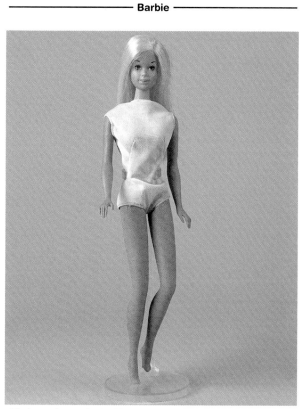

The instantly popular Malibu Barbie, 1971.

	MNB	MIB
Superstar Barbie 30th Anniversary, white, 1989, No. 1604	$8	$25
Superstar Christie, 1977, No. 9950	$20	$75
Superstar Ken, 1978, No. 2211	$17	$75
Superstar Ken, black, 1989, No. 1550	$5	$30
Superstar Ken, white, 1989, No. 1535	$7	$50
Superstar Malibu Barbie, 1977, No. 1067	$10	$35
Sweet 16 Barbie, 1974, No. 7796	$25	$125
Sweet Roses P.J., 1983, No. 7455	$15	$25
Swimming Champion Barbie, 2000, No. 24590	$7	$15
Talk With Me Barbie, 1997, No. 17350	$25	$50
Talking Barbie, chignon with nape curls, blond, brunette, titian, 1970, No. 1115	$200	$500
Talking Barbie, side ponytail with spit curls, blond or brunette, 1968, No. 1115	$150	$425
Talking Busy Barbie, 1972, No. 1195	$125	$300
Talking Busy Ken, 1972, No. 1196	$80	$160
Talking Busy Steffie, 1972, No. 1186	$175	$350
Talking Ken, 1969, No. 1111	$75	$175
Teacher Barbie, painted on panties, black, 1996, No. 13915	$15	$20
Teacher Barbie, painted on panties, white, 1996, No. 13914	$15	$25
Teacher Barbie, w/out panties, white, 1995, No. 13914	$25	$50
Teen Dance Jazzie, 1989, No. 3634	$7	$35
Teen Fun Skipper Cheerleader, 1987, No. 5893	$5	$15
Teen Fun Skipper Party Teen, 1987, No. 5899	$5	$15
Teen Fun Skipper Workout, 1987, No. 5889	$5	$15
Teen Jazzie (Teen Dance), 1989, No. 3634	$4	$35

	MNB	MIB
Teen Looks Jazzie Cheerleader, 1989, No. 3631	$4	$20
Teen Looks Jazzie Workout, 1989, No. 3633	$4	$20
Teen Scene Jazzie, two box versions, 1991, No. 5507	$5	$35
Teen Sweetheart Skipper, 1988, No. 4855	$5	$25
Teen Talk Barbie, 1992, No. 5745	$15	$45
Teen Talk Barbie, "Math is Tough" variation, 1992, No. 5745	$50	$275
Teen Time Courtney, 1988, No. 1950	$5	$10
Teen Time Skipper, 1988, No. 1951	$5	$10
Tennis Barbie, 1986, No. 1760	$5	$25
Tennis Ken, 1986, No. 1761	$5	$25
Todd, 1967, No. 3590	$95	$200
Tracy Bride, 1983, No. 4103	$8	$45
Tropical Barbie, black, 1986, No. 1022	$3	$15
Tropical Barbie, white, 1986, No. 1017	$3	$20
Tropical Ken, black, 1986, No. 1023	$3	$15
Tropical Ken, white, 1986, No. 4060	$3	$20
Tropical Miko, 1986, No. 2056	$3	$20
Tropical Skipper, 1986, No. 4064	$3	$20
Truly Scrumptious, standard, 1969, No. 1107	$225	$625
Truly Scrumptious, talking, 1969, No. 1108	$200	$600
Tutti, all hair colors, floral dress w/yellow ribbon, 1967, No. 3580	$45	$150
Tutti, all hair colors, pink, white gingham suit, hat, 1966, No. 3550	$50	$170
Tutti, Germany, 1978, No. 8128	$40	$125
Twiggy, 1967, No. 1185	$150	$350
Twirley Curls Barbie, black, 1983, No. 5723	$10	$35
Twirley Curls Barbie, Hispanic, 1982, No. 5724	$10	$40
Twirley Curls Barbie, white, 1982, No. 5579	$10	$40

Battery-Operated Toys

Armies of colorful, playful tin toys are frequently found at toy shows and flea markets. Among the most popular are battery-operated toys.

The heyday of battery-operated toys began in the 1940s, with Japanese companies leading the charge. Popular wind-up and friction toys were soon replaced with longer-lasting battery-operated versions.

Thousands of designs were made with toys featuring a variety of creative characters—from bubble-blowing monkeys to robots to cigar-smoking clowns. Disney creations and other cartoon characters like Popeye were also popular. The ingenuity of the Japanese created some truly unique novelty toys, valued today for their motion, design and humorous appeal.

Toys were often complex and could replicate several motions, such as walking, lifting or drumming. Tin lithography was usually quite interesting and detailed.

It is often difficult to identify the manufacturer of a battery-operated toy. Many companies used only initials to mark toys; some didn't mark them at all. Major manufacturers of battery-operated toys from the 1940s-1960s include Marx, Linemar (Marx's Japanese subsidiary), Alps, Marusan, Yonezawa, Bandai, Asahi Toy, and Modern Toy (MT).

Considering battery-operated toys were simply dime store staples, their values have risen remarkably. Nutty Mad Indian (left), 1960s, Marx, is worth $250.

Manufacture of tin toys dropped off in the 1960s in favor of cheaper methods and materials.

Determining Value

As in other collecting areas, toys with character ties generally command more money. Space-related battery-operated toys are also popular.

It's difficult to find most battery-operated toys in mint condition in original boxes. Battery-operated toys are highly susceptible to rust, corrosion, and yellowing of fabric or plush.

Having the original box greatly increases the toy's desirability. Instructions were often printed on the box, and the name of the toy on the box often didn't match the toy exactly.

The complexity of the toy also determines value. A toy with three or more actions will generally be worth more than a toy that performs only one action. Even though they may be nice display pieces, toys that don't work command much less.

This book lists toys in excellent, near mint, and mint in package conditions. To be graded in mint condition, a toy should be operational, clean, free of rust or corrosion, and have the original box. Lesser condition toys and those that are not operational are not graded here. Some collectors acquire them for parts.

Telephone Bear, 1950s, $450 in mint condition.

Battery-Operated Toys

	EX	NM	MIP
ABC Fairy Train, 1950s, MT, 14-1/2" long	$80	$95	$160
Accordion Player Bunny, 1950s, Alps, 12" tall, 9" long	$250	$350	$500
Aircraft Carrier, 1950s, Marx, 20" long, six actions	$325	$500	$750
American Airlines DC-7, 1960s, Linemar, 17-1/2" long, 19" wingspan	$200	$325	$450
Anti-Aircraft Unit No. 1, 1950s, Linemar, 12-1/2" long	$150	NM$225	$310
Barber bear, 1950s, Linemar, 9-1/2" tall	$300	$400	$500
Bengali—The Exciting New Growling, Prowling Tiger, 1961, Linemar, 18-1/2" tall	$150	$250	$300
Big John the Indian Chief, 1960s, TN, 12-1/2" tall	$150	$200	$250
Bimbo the Clown, 1950s, Alps, 9-1/4" tall	$190	$325	$400
Blushing Gunfighter, 1960s, Y Co., 11" tall	$75	$100	$125
Bobby the Drumming Bear, 1950s, Alps, 10" tall	$175	$275	$380
Brave Eagle, 1950s, TN, 11" tall	$100	$150	$200
Brewster the Rooster, 1950s, Marx, 9-1/2" tall	$200	$250	$300
Bubble Blowing Bear, 1950s, MT, 9-1/2" tall	$150	$225	$250

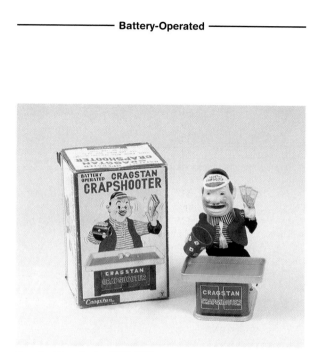

Cragstan Crapshooter, $225 MIP.

	EX	NM	MIP
Bubble Blowing Boy, 1950s, 7" tall	$150	$175	$250
Bubble Blowing Monkey, 1950s, Alps, 10" tall	$150	$175	$250
Bubble Blowing Popeye, 1950s, Linemar, 11-3/4" tall	$1000	$1500	$2500
Bunny the Magician, 1950s, Alps, 14-1/2" tall	$400	$500	$600
Burger Chef, 1950s, Y Co., 9" tall	$175	$250	$350
Busy Housekeeper, 1950s, Alps, 8-1/2" tall	$250	$350	$400
Cabin Cruiser with Outboard Motor, 1950s, Linemar, 12" long	$100	$135	$200
Camera Shooting Bear, 1950s, Linemar, 11" tall	$450	$600	$850
Cappy the Baggage Porter Dog, 1960s, Alps, 12" tall	$150	$200	$250
Caterpillar, 1950s, Alps, 16" long	$80	$125	$175
Charlie the Drumming Clown, 1950s, Alps, 9-1/2" tall	$150	$225	$300
Charlie Weaver, 1962, TN, 12"	$75	$100	$150
Charm the Cobra, 1960s, Alps, 6" tall	$90	$130	$175
Chee Chee Chihuahua, 1960s, Mego, 8" tall	$50	$75	$100

Indian Joe, 1960s, $175 mint value.

	EX	NM	MIP
Chippy the Chipmunk, 1950s, Alps, 12" long	$75	$120	$155
Circus Fire Engine, 1960s, MT, 11" long	$110	$175	$235
Climbing Donald Duck on Friction Fire Engine, 1950s, Linemar, 12" long	$400	$600	$900
Clown on Unicycle, 1960s, MT, 10-1/2" tall	$180	$280	$375
Coney Island Rocket Ride, 1950s, Alps, 13-1/2" tall	$300	$450	$600
Cragstan Crapshooter, 1950s, Y Co., 9-1/2" tall	$125	$175	$225
Cragstan Mother Goose, 1960s, Y Co., 8-1/4" tall	$100	$150	$200
Cragstan Playboy, 1960s, Cragstan, 13" tall	$75	$150	$200
Crawling Baby, 1940s, Linemar, 11" long	$50	$75	$100
Dandy, the Happy Drumming Pup, 1950s, Alps, 8-1/2" tall	$85	$150	$200
Dennis the Menace, 1950s, Rosko, 9" tall, with xylophone	$175	$225	$300
Disney Acrobats, 1950s, Linemar, 9" tall; Mickey, Donald, and Pluto	$300	$625	$800
Disney Fire Engine, 1950s, Linemar, 11" long	$600	$800	$1000
Disneyland Fire Engine, 1950s, Linemar, 18" long	$350	$550	$750

	EX	NM	MIP
Donald Duck, 1960s, Linemar, 8" tall	$200	$300	$400
Drinking Captain, 1960s, S & E, 12" tall	$100	$150	$200
Drumming Mickey Mouse, 1950s, Linemar, 10" tall	$1000	$1500	$2000
Drumming Polar Bear, 1960s, Alps, 12"	$100	$150	$200
Feeding Bird Watcher, 1950s, Linemar, 9" tall	$300	$350	$600
Fido the Xylophone Player, 1950s, Alps, 8-3/4" tall	$150	$350	$600
Flintstone Yacht, 1961, Remco, 17" long	$90	$145	$200
Frankenstein Monster, 1960s, TN, 14" tall	$150	$200	$250
Fred Flintstone Bedrock Band, 1962, Alps, 9-1/2" tall	$500	$650	$1000
Fred Flintstone Flivver, 1960s, Marx, 7" long	$400	$600	$900
Fred Flintstone on Dino, 1961, 22"	$600	$800	$1000
Godzilla Monster, 1970s, Marusan, 11-1/2" tall	$150	$200	$300
Great Garloo, 1960s, Marx, 23" tall green monster	$450	$550	$750
Green Caterpillar, 1950s, Daiya, 19-1/2" long	$150	$250	$350
Gypsy Fortune Teller, 1950s, Ichida, 12" tall, twenty cards	$1500	$2000	$2500

	EX	NM	MIP
Hobo Clown with Accordion, 1950s, Alps, 10-1/2" tall	$400	$500	$650
Hooty the Happy Owl, 1960s, Alps, 9" tall	$250	$100	$145
Hungry Cat, 1960s, Linemar, 9" tall	$250	$450	$700
Ice Cream Baby Bear, 1950s, MT, 9-1/2"	$200	$300	$400
Indian Joe, 1960s, Alps, 12" tall	$100	$150	$175
Jo-Jo the Flipping Monkey, 1970s, TN, 10" tall	$35	$55	$80
Jolly Bambino, 1950s, Alps, 9" tall	$250	$350	$500
Jolly Daddy, 1950s, Marusan, 8-3/4" tall	$165	$250	$350
Jolly Drummer Chimpy, 1950s, Alps, 9" tall	$125	NM $150	$175
Jolly Pianist, 1950s, Marusan, 8" tall	$100	$150	$200
Jolly Santa on Snow, 1950s, Alps, 12-1/2" tall	$150	$225	$300
Jumbo the Bubble Blowing Elephant, 1950s, Y Co., 7-1/4" tall	$75	$110	$150
Knitting Grandma, 1950s, T-N, 8-1/2" tall	$200	$300	$400
Lion, 1950s, Linemar, 9" long	$100	$150	$200
Mac the Turtle, 1960s, Y Co., 8" tall	$85	$135	$185

	EX	NM	MIP
Magic Snowman, 1950s, MT, 11-1/4" tall	$175	$225	$325
Main Street, 1950s, Linemar, 19-1/2" long	$1000	$1500	$2000
Marching Bear, 1960s, Alps, 10" tall	$150	$225	$300
Marshal Wild Bill, 1950s, Y Co., 10-1/2" tall	$225	$325	$425
Mickey the Magician, 1960s, Linemar, 10" tall	$1000	$1500	$2500
Mighty Kong, 1950s, Marx, 11" tall	$250	$1500	$500
Mischievous Monkey, 1950s, MT, 18" tall	$200	$300	$400
Motorcycle Cop, 1950s, 10-1/2" long, 8-1/4" tall	$500	$750	$1000
Mr. Traffic Policeman, 1950s, A-1, 14" tall	$175	$270	$365
Musical Bear, 1950s, Linemar, 10" tall	$200	$300	$400
Musical Jackal, 1950's, Linemar, 10" tall	$150	$225	$600
Nutty Mad Indian, 1960s, Marx, 12" tall	$150	$200	$250
Nutty Nibs, 1950s, Linemar, 11-1/2" tall	$700	$850	$1400
Panda Bear, 1970s, MT, 10" long	$30	$45	$65
Peppermint Twist Doll, 1950s, Haji, 12" tall	$150	$225	$300

	EX	NM	MIP
Peppy Puppy, 1950s, Y Co., 8" long	$75	$100	$125
Phantom Raider, 1963, Ideal, 33", freighter turned warship	$35	$100	$225
Picnic Bunny, 1950s, Alps, 10" tall	$150	$175	$225
Pierrot Monkey Cycle, 1950s, M-T, 8" tall	$325	$460	$650
Piggy Cook, 1950s, 9-1/2" tall	$150	$250	$350
Pipie the Whale, 1950s, Alps, 12" long	$250	$325	$500
Pistol Pete, 1950s, Marusan, 10-1/4" tall	$250	$325	$500
Popcorn Eating Bear, 1950s, MT, 9" tall	$150	$200	$250
Rambling Ladybug, 1960s, M-T, 8" long	$60	$90	$125
Rembrandt the Monkey Artist, 1950s, Alps, 8" tall	$170	$240	$365
Ricki the Begging Poodle, 1950s, Rock Valley, 9" long	$35	$45	$65
Rocking Chair Bear, 1950s, MT, 10" tall	$150	$200	$250
Sam the Shaving Man, 1960s, Plaything Toy, 11-1/2" tall	$150	$225	$300
Santa Claus on Handcar, 1960s, MT, 10" tall	$100	$140	$200
Santa Claus on Reindeer Sleigh, 1950s, M-T, 17" long	$400	$600	$825

	EX	NM	MIP
Santa Claus on Scooter, 1960s, MT, 10" tall	$110	$150	$200
Santa Copter, 1960s, MT, 8-1/2" high	$150	$200	$250
Serpent Charmer, 1950s, Linemar, 7" tall	$225	$350	$500
Shaggy the Friendly Pup, 1960s, Alps, 8" long	$35	$45	$65
Shutterbug Photographer, 1950s, T-N, 9" tall	$600	$800	$1000
Skating Circus Clown, 1950s, TPS, 6" tall	$450	$595	$800
Skiing Santa, 1960s, MT, 12" tall	$160	$230	$300
Slalom Game, 1960s, T-N, 15-1/4" long	$100	$160	$225
Sleeping Baby Bear, 1950s, Linemar, 9" long	$250	$350	$450
Smokey Bear, 1950s, SAN, 9" tall	$250	$300	$500
Snoopy Sniffer, 1960s, MT, 8" long	$50	$75	$100
Struttin' Sam, 1950s, Haji, 10-1/2" tall	$300	$400	$500
Super Susie, 1950s, Linemar, 9" tall	$500	$750	$1000
Switchboard Operator, 1950s, Linemar, 7-1/2" tall	$400	$500	$1000
Tarzan, 1966, Marusan, 13" tall	$500	$765	$1000
Teddy Bear Swing, 1950s, T-N, 17" tall	$300	$380	$600

	EX	NM	MIP
Telephone Bear, 1950s, Linemar, 7-1/2" tall	$250	$350	$450
Tom and Jerry Handcar, 1960s, M-T, 7-3/4" long	$175	$250	$350
Topo Gigio Playing the Xylophone, 1960s, TN	$265	$440	$525
Twirly Whirly, 1950s, Alps, 13-1/2" tall	$290	$450	$600
Walking Esso Tiger, 1950s, Marx, 11-1/2" tall	$300	$400	$500
Western Locomotive, 1950s, MT, 10-1/2" long	$45	$65	$80
Yeti the Abominable Snowman, 1960s, Marx, 12" tall	$250	$335	$500
Yo-Yo Clown, 1960s, Alps, 9" tall	$150	$200	$300
Yo-Yo Monkey, 1960s, YM, 12" tall	$100	$150	$200
Yo-Yo Monkey, 1960s, Alps, 9" tall	$150	$200	$300
Yummy Yum Kitty, 1950s, Alps, 9-1/2" tall	$170	$270	$325
Zero Fighter Plane, 1950s, Bandai, 15" wingspan	$150	$230	$300

Captain America hand puppet, Ideal, 1960s, $85 MIB.

Character Toys

By Tom Bartsch

From comic books to television shows to movies and more, characters have been a part of our lives for many years. And many times these same characters have appeared as toys.

The sheer volume of character toys outweighs any other collecting category by far, simply because you can find the likeness of characters almost anywhere. Because of these factors, character toys are among the most popular collectibles on the market, a major representation of which you will find in the following pages.

The beauty of character toys is that they are not limited to action figures or die-cast vehicles. Prices can range from under a dollar to several hundred thousand dollars for Superman's first appearance in a comic book (Action Comics #1, 1938).

The key to finding out which one is worth hundreds and which one is worth $50 is in the details. For starters, find out the name of the manufacturer. Then check out the details of the item. Sometimes the difference in valuable samples compared to average-priced ones is the color or an accessory. Do your research before taking the plunge.

Tom Bartsch is editor of Toy Shop *magazine and associate editor of* Toy Cars & Models, *both published by Krause Publications, Iola, Wis.*

Mad Hatter Marionette, Peter Puppet Playthings Inc., 1950s, $210 MIP.

Character Toys

Batman Toys

	EX	NM	MIP
Batman Cartoon Kit, 1966, Colorforms	$25	$55	$85
Batman Kite, 1982, Hiflyer	$8	$15	$30
Batman Trace-a-Graph, 1966, Emenee	$30	$75	$160
Batman Wind-Up, 1989, Billiken, tin litho	$25	$50	$100
Batscope Dart Launcher, 1966, Tarco	$25	$45	$90
Bat Troll Doll, 1966, Wish-Nik, vinyl, dressed in a blue felt Batman outfit w/cowl and cape	$100	$200	$350
Cave Tun-L, 1966, New York Toy, 26" x 26" x 2" tunnel	$600	$1500	$2350
Gotham City Stunt Set, 1989, Tonka	$15	$55	$85
Joker Wind-up, 1989, Billiken, tin litho	$40	$100	$185
Puppet Theater Stage, 1966, Ideal, marketed by Sears, 19" x 11" x 20" cardboard stage w/hand puppets	$125	$350	$600
Shooting Arcade, 1970s, AHI, graphics of Joker, Catwoman, and Penguin	$35	$100	$175

Captain Marvel Toys

	EX	NM	MIP
Captain Marvel Beanbags, 1940s, Captain Marvel, Mary Marvel, or Hoppy, each	$50	$175	$300

Indiana Jones vehicles by Micro Machines, 1996, plus an Indiana Jones figure. About $35 MIP.

	EX	NM	MIP

Captain Marvel Beanie, 1940s, cap shows image of Captain Marvel
flying toward word "Shazam," blue
.... $85................. $275...................... $450

Captain Marvel Beanie, 1940s, girl's cap shows image of Captain
Marvel flying toward word "Shazam," pink, rare
.... $300................. $750...................... $1000

Captain Marvel Buzz Bomb, 1950s, Fawcett, paper airplane in
envelope .... $25................. $85...................... $125

Captain Marvel Jr. Ski Jump, 1947, Reed and Associates, paper, in
envelope .... $10................. $20.......................... $60

Captain Marvel Jr. Statuette, 1940s, Fawcett, hand-painted
plastic .... $500................. $1500...................... $2500

Captain Marvel Lightning Race Cars, 1940s, Automatic Toy Co., set of
four cars w/wind-up keys, rare
.... $500................. $1750...................... $3000

Captain Marvel Lightning Wind-Up Race Car, 1947, Fawcett, 4" long
tin wind-up in green, yellow, orange, or blue, four cars and box
.... $1500................. $3000...................... $4000

Captain Marvel Statuette, 1940s, Fawcett, hand-painted plastic, shows
Captain Marvel standing w/arms crossed, on base w/name
engraved................... $1000................. $2500...................... $4000

Mary Marvel Statuette, 1940s, Fawcett, hand-painted
plastic .... $500................. $1750...................... $3000

Dick Tracy Toys

Auto Magic Picture Gun, 1950s, 6-1/2" x 9" metal picture gun and
filmstrip .... $30................. $100...................... $175

Automatic Police Station, 1950s, Marx, tin litho police station
and car........................ $250................. $800...................... $1500

B.O. Plenty Wind-Up, 1940s, Marx, 8-1/2" tall holding baby Sparkle,
litho tin, walks, hat tips up and down when key is wound
.... $120................. $300...................... $600

Monkees Deluxe Bass Guitar, Lapin, $250.

	EX	NM	MIP
Black Light Magic Kit, 1952, Stroward, ultra-violet bulb, cloth, invisible pen, brushes, and fluorescent dyes	$50	$100	$200
Bonny Braids Stroll Toy, 1951, Charmore, tin litho, Bonny doll in carriage	$35	$80	$160
Camera Dart Gun, 1971, Larami, 8mm camera-shaped toy w/dart-shooting viewer	$30	$60	$125
Crimestopper Club Kit, 1961, Chicago Tribune, premium kit containing badge, whistle, decoder, magnifying glass, fingerprinting kit, ID card, crimestopper textbook	$35	$60	$100
Crimestopper Play Set, 1970s, Hubley, Dick Tracy cap gun, holster, handcuffs, wallet, flashlight, badge, and magnifying glass	$35	$70	$50
Detective Kit, 1944, Dick Tracy Junior Detective Manual, Secret Decoder, ruler, Certificate of Membership, and badge	$175	$500	$800
Dick Tracy Candid Camera, 1950s, Seymour Sales, w/50mm lens, plastic carrying case, and 127 film	$45	$100	$175
Dick Tracy Crime Lab, 1980s, Ja-Ru, click pistol, fingerprint pad, badge, and magnifying glass, available in orange and bright yellow	$8	$15	$30
Dick Tracy Crime Stoppers Laboratory, 1955, Porter Chemical, 60 power microscope, fingerprint pack, glass slides, and magnifying glass and textbook	$100	$225	$400
Dick Tracy Detective Set, 1930s, Pressman, color graphics of Junior and Dick Tracy, ink roller, glass plate, and Dick Tracy fingerprint record paper	$85	$200	$350
Dick Tracy Figure, Lakeside, bendy	$15	$30	$50

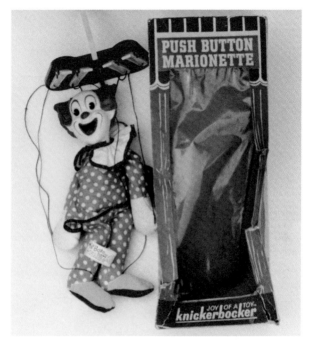

Bozo the Clown marionette, Knickerbocker, $85.

	EX	NM	MIP

Dick Tracy Jr. Bombsight, 1940s, Miller Bros. Hat,
cardboard...................... $40.................... $70........................ $175

Dick Tracy Puzzle, 1952, 11" x 14"
frame tray .... $25.................... $85........................ $150

Dick Tracy Target Game, 1940s, Marx, 17" circular cardboard target,
w/dart gun and box..... $100.................. $275........................ $500

Dick Tracy Target Set, 1969, Larami, red, green, or glue; shoots rubber
bands .... $15.................... $35......................... $75

Handcuffs, 1946, John Henry, metal toy handcuffs on display header
card................................ $25.................... $55........................ $110

Hemlock Holmes Hand Puppet, 1961, Ideal,
includes record .... $40.................... $90........................ $175

Junior Detective Kit, 1944, Sweets Company, certificate,
secret code dial, wall chart, file cards, and
tape measure................. $70.................. $250........................ $425

Mobile Commander, 1973, Larami, toy telephone
w/plastic connecting tube, plastic gun, and
badge .... $20.................... $40......................... $85

Playstone Funnies Kasting Kit, 1930s, Allied, molds
for casting figures of Tracy and other
characters .... $40.................... $80......................... $35

Secret Detector Kit, 1938, Quaker, Secret Formula Q-11 and negatives.
.... $100.................. $400........................ $600

Shoulder Holster Set, 1950s, J. Hapern, leather holster w/Dick Tracy's
profile .... $45.................... $90........................ $185

Looney Tunes Toys

Bugs Bunny Hand Puppet, 1940s, Zany,
rubber head .... $35.................. $100........................ $175

Elmer Fudd Hand Puppet, 1940s, Zany,
rubber head .... $30.................... $70........................ $150

Joan Palooka marionette, National Mask & Puppet, 1952, $110.

	EX	NM	MIP
Foghorn Leghorn Hand Puppet, 1940s, Zany, rubber head	$30	$75	$160
Pepe Le Pew Goofy Gram, 1971, Dakin	$25	$50	$100
Sylvester Hand Puppet, 1940s, Zany rubber head	$32	$80	$160
Sylvester Soaky, Colgate	$10	$30	$60
Tweety Hand Puppet, 1940s, Zany, rubber head	$30	$80	$160
Tweety Soaky, 1960s, Colgate, 8-1/2", plastic	$10	$30	$60

Peanuts Toys

	EX	NM	MIP
Lucy's psychiatrist booth and three action figures, Model No. 575	$90	$200	$275
Peanuts Skediddler Clubhouse Set, 1970, Mattel, three rubber skediddlers, Snoopy, Lucy, Charlie Brown, Model No. 3803	$125	$185	$250
Push 'N' Fly Snoopy, 1980, Romper Room/Hasbro, pull toy featuring Snoopy the Flying Ace, Model No. 824	$12	$20	$50
See 'N' Say Snoopy Says, 1969 Mattel, Model No. 4864	$40	$80	$100
Snoopy and Charlie Brown Copter, 1979, Aviva/Hasbro, plastic, Model No. 600	$15	$25	$50
Snoopy and his Flyin' Doghouse, 1974, Mattel, Model No. 8263	$60	$100	$175
Snoopy Deep Diver Submarine, 1980s, Knickerbocker, plastic, Model No. 0553	$35	$55	$70
Snoopy Jack-in-the-Box, 1980, Romper Room/Hasbro, plastic doghouse jack-in-the-box, Model No. 818	$8	$15	$35

Tom and Jerry puzzle, Whitman, $20 MIP.

	EX	NM	MIP

Snoopy Playhouse, 1977, Determined, plastic doghouse
    w/furniture, Snoopy, and Woodstock, Model
    No. 120 .... $40 .... $70 .... $100

Snoopy's Dog House, 1978, Romper Room/Hasbro, Snoopy walks on
    roof, Model No. 815 ..... $20 .... $45 .... $80

Talking Peanuts Bus, 1967, Chein, metal, characters seen in windows,
    Model No. 261 .... $150 .... $350 .... $725

Popeye Toys

Boxing Gloves, 1960s,
    Everlast .... $25 .... $60 .... $130

Brutus in Jeep, 1950s, tiny
    plastic car .... $15 .... $35 .... $70

Construction Trucks, 1981,
    Larami .... $6 .... $15 .... $30

Erase-O-Board and Magic Screen Set, 1957, Hassenfeld
    Bros. .... $30 .... $90 .... $160

Funny Color Foam, 1983, Creative
    Aerosol .... $5 .... $15 .... $60

Jack-in-the-Box, 1961,
    Mattel .... $60 .... $120 .... $210

Jeep Lucky Spinner, 1936,
    KFS .... $125 .... $250 .... $500

Magic Slate, 1959, Lowe ...... $20 .... $40 .... $85

Marble Set, 1935, Akro Agate,
    #116 .... $300 .... $850 .... $1500

Marble Shooter, 1940s, milk glass
    container .... $20 .... $40 .... $80

Olive Oyl Marionette, 1950s, Gund,
    11-?" tall .... $40 .... $120 .... $200

	EX	NM	MIP
Olive Oyl Squeak Toy, 1979, Cribmates, on a stick	$5	$13	$20
Olive Oyl Toboggan, 1979, KFS	$6	$15	$30
Popeye and Olive Oyl Sand Set, 1950s, Peer Products, bucket, shovel	$20	$50	$100
Popeye Bathtub Toy, 1960s, Stahlwood, floating boat	$20	$40	$85
Popeye Bingo, 1980, Nasta	$6	$10	$20
Popeye Blow Me Down Airport, 1935, Marx	$500	$1000	$1600
Popeye Coloring Set, 1960s, Hasbro, numbered, w/pencils	$12	$30	$60
Popeye Goes Swimming Colorforms, 1963, Colorforms	$15	$35	$65
Popeye Magic Play Around, 1950s, Amsco, characters w/magnetic bases that slide across play set	$35	$70	$140
Popeye Paint and Crayon Set, 1934, Milton Bradley	$50	$125	$200
Popeye Play Set, 1979, Cribmates, Popeye, Olive Oyl, and Swee' Pea squeak toys, mirror, rattle, and pillow	$15	$30	$45
Popeye Pull Toy, 1950s, Metal Masters, 10-1/2" x 11-1/2", xylophone, wood w/paper litho labels, metal wheels	$100	$225	$450
Popeye's Submarine, 1973, Larami	$10	$30	$50
Puzzle, 1932, Saalfield, Popeye in Four	$50	$100	$200

	EX	NM	MIP

Puzzle, 1959, England, 120 pieces, "What a Catch"
.... $25.................... $55........................ $80

Swee' Pea Hand Puppet, 1960s, Gund, bonnet on head, cloth body
decorated w/baby lambs
.... $15.................... $40........................ $80

Swee' Pea Squeak Toy, 1970s, frowning or smiling
.... $12.................... $25........................ $60

Whistling Wing Ding, 1950s, Mego
.... $20.................... $40........................ $75

Wimpy Tugboat, 1961, Ideal, inflatable
.... $20.................... $40........................ $60

Superman Toys

Cinematic Picture Pistol, 1940, Daisy, non-electric, film is viewed
through view in back of gun, metal gun w/one pre-loaded 28
scene Superman film, Model
No. 96......................... $300.................. $850...................... $1600

Dangle Dandies Mobile, 1955, Killogg's, set of eight cut outs
on boxes of Rice Krispies and Corn Flakes
.... $75.................. $100........................ $175

Flying Noise Balloon, 1966, Van Dam, oversized balloon
makes noise in flight, Superman illustration on balloon
and card......................... $12.................... $23........................ $40

Official Magic Kit, 1956, Bar-Zim, magic balls, disappearing cards,
multiplying corks, vanishing trick, shell game, balancing belt, and
directions in illustrated box
.... $350.................. $750...................... $1500

Paint-by-Numbers Watercolor Set, 1954, Transogram, 16 watercolors
and 44 action scenes..... $75.................. $200........................ $325

Super Heroes String Puppets, 1978, Madison, string controlled cloth
and vinyl marionette .... $25.................... $75........................ $110

	EX	NM	MIP

Superman and Supergirl Push Puppets, 1968, Kohner, set of two: 5-1/4" on bases in window box
.... $200................. $600..................... $1000

Superman Back-a-Wack, 1966, Dell, blue plastic paddle w/gold imprinted "S" logo and name, elastic string and red ball, on illustrated card. Model 1194
.... $50................. $100..................... $150

Superman Figure, Presents, 15" vinyl/cloth figure on base .... $25................. $40.......................... $60

Superman Golden Muscle Building Set, 1954, Peter Puppets Playthings, handles, springs, hand grippers, jump rope, wall hooks, measuring tape, progress chart, membership certificate and button, illustrated box............................... $700................. $1000..................... $1500

Superman Hand Puppet, 1966, Ideal, 11", cloth body, vinyl head..................... $50................. $75....................... $100

Superman Pogo Stick, 1977, 48" w/a vinyl bust on top .... $50................. $100....................... $200

Superman Push Puppet, 1966, Kohner, 5-1/4" on base, in window box................. $50................. $75....................... $100

Superman Roller Skates, 1975, Larami, plastic w/color bust of Superman shaped around front of each skate, in illustrated window box................. $20................. $50.................... $75

Superman Senior rubber Horseshoe Set, 1950s, in box .... $55................. $100....................... $175

Superman Sky Hero, 1977, Marx, rubber band glider w/color Superman image, on card, Model No. 9310...................... $25................... $40......................... $75

Superman Space Satellite Launcher Set, 1950s, Kellogg's, premium set of generic plastic gun w/firing "satellite wheel" and illustrated instruction sheet, in mailer box
.... $150................. $500..................... $1000

	EX	NM	MIP

Superman Tank, 1958, Linemar, large battery operated tin, 3-D Superman w/cloth cape, in illustrated box.............................. $350................ $1750...................... $3000

Superman Water Gun, 1967, Multiple Toymakers, 6" plastic, Model No. 484 .... $30................. $100........................ $185

Donald Duck Disney Dipsy Car, Marx, 1953, $770.

Disneyana

Walt Disney was involved in animation as early as 1920, but his first truly notable character was Oswald the Rabbit, introduced in 1927. Disney did not own the rights to Oswald, however, and he eventually fell into the hands of another animator, Walter Lantz.

Although Mickey Mouse first appeared in the 1928 short "Plane Crazy," the third Mickey cartoon, "Steamboat Willie," seems to have been the first released (on Nov. 18, 1928). Mickey was a success from then on. Minnie Mouse also appeared in "Steamboat Willie," and Pluto emerged in 1930 but was not known by that name until 1931. Goofy debuted in 1932 and Donald Duck came along in 1934.

Mickey Mouse toys were first produced in 1930, and since then the stream of Disneyana (apparently all of it deemed collectible) has been endless.

Source: O'Brien's Collecting Toys Identification & Value Guide, *tenth edition, edited by Elizabeth A. Stephan, 2001, Krause Publications, Iola, Wis.*

Donald Duck go-kart, Marx, 1960s, approximately $60-$75.

Disneyana

C6=Good condition; evident overall wear, well played with but acceptable to many collectors.
C8=very good condition; minor overall wear, very clean.
C10=mint, mint in box condition; like new.

Cinderella	C6	C8	C10

Cinderella and Prince Dancing Wind-up, plastic, Irwin Co., 1950s, 5"
  high ....$$65..................$100.........................$150
Hand Puppet, "1957" ....$22...................$33............................$60
Handcar, Jaq and Gus, 8" long$383................$575.........................$775
Soaky, w/movable arms, 1960s$15 ....$30............................$50
Umbrella Wind-up, spins and dances,
  Irwin, 4-3/4" high..........$62..................$95.........................$140

Donald Duck	C6	C8	C10

Acrobat, Linemar, 1950s,
  8-1/2" high ....$325..................$525.........................$750
Climbing Fireman Wind-up, Linemar,
  1950s, 13-1/2" ....$300..................$475.........................$650
Doll, composition and cloth, long-billed, in Russian costume,
  9" high........................$1000.................$1750........................$2500
Donald Duck and Pluto in Roadster, Sun Rubber, 1930s,
  6-1/2" long ....$80...................$120.........................$200
Donald Duck Figure, celluloid, long billed, Borgfeldt (Japan),
  1930s, 5" high ....$262..................$395.........................$550
Donald Duck on Tractor, plastic, friction, Marx, 1950s,
  3-1/2" long ....$120..................$200.........................$300
Donald Duck Wind-up, "984," Schuco (German),
  6" high........................$158..................$235.........................$375

*Sun Rubber Mickey Mouse and Donald Duck fire truck, original
condition, missing front wheel, $120.*

Goofy	**C6**	**C8**	**C10**
Figure, tin, 1930	$400	$600	$850
Goofy on a Unicycle Wind-up, tin, Linemar, 5-1/2" high	$500	$750	$1100
Goofy the Walking Gardener Wind-up, tin, Marx	$482	$625	$965
Goofy Tricycle Wind-up, Linemar, 1950s, 4" tall	$650	$975	$1300
Goofy with Whirling Tail Wind-up, plastic, Marx, 1950s, 8" high	$92	$140	$185
Goofy with Whirling Tail Wind-up, Linemar, 1950s, 5" tall	$300	$450	$600
Goofy's Disneyland Stock Car Wind-up, Linemar, 1950s, 6" long	$200	$300	$425
Goofy's Stock Car Wind-up, Linemar, 1950s, 6" long	$200	$300	$425
Soaky	$20	$30	$60

Jiminy Cricket	**C6**	**C8**	**C10**
Doll, latex head, hands and feet w/cloth body, 13" high	$60	$90	$150
Doll, felt and cloth, Crown Toy, 14" high	$150	$225	$325
Doll, felt and cloth, Crown Toy, 15-1/2" high	$150	$225	$325
Doll, cloth body w/rubber head and wooden feet, Gund, 12"	$22	$40	$65
Doll, jointed wood, Ideal, 1940, 9" high	$225	$375	$500
Doll, Knickerbocker, c. 1940, 10" high	$300	$450	$650

Disneykins set from Marx, $210.

Face Mask, Gillette, 1939 ......$25.................$38..................... $65
Hand Puppet, vinyl and cloth, Gund
....................................$32...................$48..................... $65
Jiminy Cricket Pushing Bass Fiddle Walkie, Marx
....................................$15...................$22......................... $45
Jiminy Cricket Tin Wind-up, in black tuxedo, top hat
　　has yellow band, Linemar, 1950s, 5-1/2" tall
....................................$300..................$450..................... $650
Soaky....................................$10...................$30..................... $50

Mickey Mouse	**C6**	**C8**	**C10**

Acrobat, clockwork trapeze w/celluloid Mickey, Japan, 1930s,
　　9" high.........................$243..................$365..................... $485
Bandleader Doll, black shako, red jacket, this doll was
　　produced in conjunction with Mickey's first color cartoon
　　"The Band Concert," Knickerbocker, 1935,
　　12" high.....................$650................$1200..................... $1850
Circus, two wood figures revolving on swinging mechanism,
　　6/3785, Geo. Borgfeldt, 1931, 11" long
....................................$500..................$850..................... $1300
Doll, felt, Character Co., c. 1939-40,
　　18" high.........................$70..................$105..................... $200
Doll, felt, Steiff, early 1930s,
　　12" high.....................$600..................$950..................... $1350
Figure, cast iron, Mickey Holding Flag,
　　1930s ....$140..................$210..................... $350
Figure, celluloid and wood, Mickey on Hobby Horse,
　　c. 1935, 4-1/2"...........$1050................$1800..................... $2500
Figure, lead, Allied Toys, 1933,
　　2-1/2" high ....$70..................$105..................... $160

Walt Disney's Snow White and the Seven Dwarfs Weaving Loom set from Hasbro, $85.

Figure, Fun-E-Flex, 1930s,
    3-1/2" high ....$150..................$225.........................$300
Mickey Mouse Express Tin Wind-up, train set, Marx, 1950s, 14" long,
    base 21" x 13" ....$700.................$1100......................$1700
Mickey Mouse Meteor Five-Car Train Tin Wind-up, Marx,
    43" long......................$800.................$1000......................$1500
Mickey Mouse Pirate Ship,
    Ideal............................$138.................$210.........................$275
Movie Fun Optical Toy, Mastercraft, 1950s,
    7" x 7" x 5"..................$150.................$225.........................$300
Newsreel, includes three records and five films, Mattel,
    9-1/2" high ....$110.................$165.........................$225
Push Puppet, Mickey Mouse Drummer, Kohner,
    1950s...........................$100.................$150.........................$200
Rocking Mickey Mouse on Pluto Wind-up,
    Linemar ....$800.................$1400......................$2000
Running Mickey on Pluto Wind-up, celluloid, M-T Co.,
    1940s, 5-1/2" long.....$2000.................$3750......................$6750
Scooter Jockey Wind-up, plastic, Mavco Co., 1950s,
    6" high........................$400.................$600.........................$800
Washing Machine, tin litho, shows two scenes
    w/Mickey, Minnie, Pluto, Ohio Art Co., 1932 or 1933,
    7" high........................$100.................$150.........................$220

Pinocchio	C6	C8	C10

Cleo the Goldfish Squeeze Toy,
    Sun Rubber..................$23.................$35.........................$60
Donkey Doll, stuffed,
    Knickerbocker...............$95.................$142.........................$225
Donkey Figure, rubber, Seiberling Rubber,
    1940, 4" ....$70.................$105.........................$160

Mickey Mouse Safety Patrol, Fisher-Price, $265-$575 (good-mint).

Figaro, tin friction toy, Linemar, 1950s,
    3" long............................$70..................$105....................$150
Gepetto Figure, wood, holding his chin, Multi Products,
    1940, 5-1/2" ....$70..................$105....................$140
Jiminy Cricket, 1940 ....$100..................$200....................$300
Pinocchio Doll, jointed wood and composition, Ideal,
    12" high.....................$300..................$450....................$625
Pinocchio Doll, jointed, c. 1940,
    19-3/4" high ....$400..................$600....................$830
Pinocchio Figure, molded wood fiber, Multi Products,
    1940, 5" high..............$100..................$150....................$200
Pinocchio the Acrobat Tin Wind-up, "Watch Him Go!",
    Marx, 1939 ....$385..................$575....................$770
Pinocchio Wind-up, wood and papier-mâché, George Borgfeldt,
    1940, 10-1/2" high ......$318..................$475....................$700

Pluto	C6	C8	C10

Drum Major Tin Wind-up, Linemar, 1950s,
    6-1/2" tall ....$250..................$400....................$600
Figure, lead, Allied Toys, 1933,
    2-1/2" high ....$60..................$90....................$150
Hand Puppet, Gund, 1950s.....$15..................$22....................$50
Musical Pluto, plastic, Marx, 1960s,
    8" x 8" base ....$400..................$600....................$850
Playful Pluto & Goofy Wind-up, two-piece set,
    Linemar, 1950s............$800..................$1300....................$2000
Pluto Pulling Cart, friction, Linemar, 1950s,
    8-1/2" long ....$392..................$588....................$785
Watch Me Roll Over Wind-up, Marx,
    1939.............................$130..................$195....................$300
Wise Pluto Wind-up, Marx, 1939,
    8" long........................$212..................$318....................$475

Linemar Rocking Mickey Mouse on Pluto Wind-up, $2,000. Photo courtesy Don Hultzman

Snow White and The Seven Dwarfs	C6	C8	C10
Bashful Doll, Ideal, 1938, 12" high	$80	$120	$200
Bashful Marionette, Madame Alexander, 1938, 9-1/2" tall	$100	$150	$250
Doc Doll, Ideal, 1938, 12" high	$82	$123	$190
Dopey and Doc Pull Toy, 14" long	$200	$300	$425
Dopey Doll, Ideal, 1938, 12" high	$150	$225	$350
Dopey Tin Wind-up, Marx, 1938	$263	$395	$575
Grumpy Doll, composition w/velvet clothes, Knickerbocker, 9" high	$100	$150	$250
Grumpy Doll, Ideal, 1938, 11" high	$80	$120	$185
Happy Doll, Ideal, 1938, 12" high	$110	$165	$250
Seven Dwarfs Puppet-Marionettes, price for the set, Pelham	$1500	$2250	$3500
Sleepy Doll, Ideal, 1938, 12" high	$120	$180	$300
Sneezy Marionette, Madame Alexander, 1938, 9-1/2" tall	$100	$150	$250
Snow White and the Seven Dwarfs Figures, lead, by Lincoln Logs, price for the set	$500	$850	$1200
Snow White Doll, Ideal, 1938, 15" high	$150	$225	$350
Wicked Witch, Madame Alexander, 1938, 9-1/2" tall	$100	$150	$250

Pluto puppets, 10 inches tall, marked "Walt Disney Prod." One puppet is made by Gund ($50) and has some paint off the nose. The other is unmarked.

Dolls

By Dawn Herlocher

There is probably no rational explanation for the feelings collectors have for their dolls. Perhaps it's because they awaken memories and dreams, stirring our feelings of nostalgia, or the simple pleasure gained in admiring the beauty of these present-day reminders of a long vanished era.

The attraction to dolls seems to be immediate and universal, made obvious by the thousands of new enthusiasts who have excitedly embraced the world of doll collecting in recent years.

No two dolls are exactly alike. A study of their various features indicates the factors that influence the value of a doll, including rarity, condition, quality of material, artistry, availability, originality, history of providence, and the ever-important visual appeal. All of these factors contribute to a doll's charisma.

Please take the time to thoroughly inspect a doll. An antique bisque doll head should be checked not only on the outside, but also from the inside, for at times a repair or hairline crack will be only visible from the inside. Remember not to confuse maintenance with repairs. Reset eyes, restrung bodies, and patched leather are examples of necessary maintenance and are not repairs to a doll.

Modern dolls should always be in perfect, complete condition. Inspect the markings of a doll. You may find them on the back of the head, the torso, the bottom of a foot, or even on the derriere. Of course, many fine dolls will have absolutely no markings. Learn from every doll you see or handle, for there is almost as much fun in learning about a doll as there is in owning it. Visit doll shows and museums.

I encourage you to read and study as much as you can about dolls. The two volumes of Dorothy S., Elizabeth A., and Evelyn J. Coleman's *The Collector's Encyclopedia of Dolls* (Crown Publishing 1972 and 1986) are accurate guidebooks to doll manufacturing prior to 1930. *Antique Trader's Doll Makers and Marks* (Krause Publications, 1999) is a concise directory for doll identification. If you don't own a copy, visit a library that does.

Talk to other collectors. Consider joining a doll club. Clubs that are members of the United Federation of Doll Clubs (U.F.D.C.) "represent the highest standards of excellence for collectors to create, stimulate and maintain interest in all matters pertaining to doll collecting." Write the U.F.D.C. at P.O. Box 14146, Parkville, MO 64152 to obtain the address of a club near you.

Our distinctive approach to pricing is a quick and easy way to determine the value of a particular doll.

The astute collector or interim care-giver can use this book for comparative purposes when assessing and evaluating their dolls, whether building a new collection or researching an existing one of a thousand dolls.

Dawn Herlocher is the author of 200 Years of Dolls Identification and Price Guide *published by Krause Publications, Iola, Wis.*

Twenty-one-inch Madame Alexander Coco Portrait dolls including Renoir; Scarlett; Lissy. Approximately $1,200 each. Courtesy of McMaster's Doll Auctions

Dolls

Prices in this section are based on dolls in good condition, appropriately dressed with no damage.

Alexander Doll Company

Individual Personalities

Dr. Dafoe: 14", Dionne Quintuplets doctor; cloth, chubby body; composition limbs; swivel composition head and shoulder plane; gray, mohair wig; painted blue eyes with upper lashes only; smiling mouth; chin dimple; typically unmarked; white jumpsuit and doctor's coat; tagged "DR. DAFOE/MmE. ALEXANDER"; gold octagon Dr. Dafoe wrist tag. **$1,800**

Minister: Dr. Dafoe body and face; identified by clothing and/or wrist tag. **$1,200**

Priest: Dr. Dafoe body and face; identified by clothing and/or wrist tag. **$1,300**

Baby Jane: 16", named for child star Juanita Quigley; all composition; jointed at neck, shoulder, and hip; chubby cheeks; brown, human-hair wig; brown sleep eyes; long, painted upper and lower lashes; open, smiling mouth with four teeth, felt tongue; typically marked "BABY JANE/ALEXANDER"; clothing tag "BABY JANE/ MmE. ALEXANDER."..**$1,200**

Hard Plastic

Shari Lewis: 21" hard plastic and vinyl body; jointed at shoulder, elbows, hip, and knees; high heel feet; heart-shaped face; synthetic, dark blond pony tail; feathered brows; blue, sleep eyes; real upper, painted lower lashes; very, very turned-up nose; pierced ears; closed, unsmiling full mouth; typically marked "MmE 19©58 ALEXANDER." **$1,000**

Sleeping Beauty: 21" hard plastic and vinyl body; jointed at shoulder, elbows, hip, and knees; high heel feet; beautiful round-shaped face, synthetic, very blond wig; lightly feathered and shaped brows; blue, sleep eyes; real upper, painted lower lashes; original satin gown trimmed in gold; gold tiara with rhinestone stars; gold brocade net floor-length cape; rhinestone necklace and ring. Typically marked "ALEXANDER"; clothing tag "MADAME ALEXANDER PRESENTS WALT DISNEY'S AUTHENTIC SLEEPING BEAUTY." **$1,500**

Cabbage Patch Dolls

1978 Helen Blue, signed birthmark, 1,000 issued **$2,000**

1980 Christmas Set, Nicholas, Noel, signed birthmark, 2,500 issued **$500**

1980 Grand Edition, signed birthmark, 1,000 issued **$700**

1981 New Ears Edition, stamped birthmark, 15,000 issued...........**$200**

1982 Christmas Set, Christy, Nicole, Baby Rudy, Cabbage Patch Kids Editions, stamped birthmark, 1,000 issued **$600**

1982 Cabbage Patch Kids 10 Character Kids Set, stamped birthmark, 2,500 issued.. **$400 each; set $4,000**

1983 Oriental, stamped birthmark, 1,000 issued **$600**

1983 Indian, stamped birthmark, 1,000 issued **$500**

1983 Hispanic, stamped birthmark, 1,000 issued **$400**

1983 Bald Babies, stamped birthmark, mass produced....................**$75**

1983 Baby with pacifier, stamped birthmark, mass produced **$100**

1983 White with freckles, stamped birthmark, mass produced.........**$75**

1983 Black with freckles, stamped birthmark, mass produced **$100**

1983 Red fuzzy haired boy, stamped birthmark, mass produced.....**$100**

1984 Single tooth, stamped birthmark, mass produced...................**$200**

1984 Popcorn hairdo, stamped birthmark, mass produced..............**$200**

1985 Christmas, Sandy, Claude, stamped birthmark, 2,500 issued . **$100**

1985 Four Seasons, Crystal, Morton, Sunny, Autumn, stamped birthmark, 2,000 issued... **$100**

1986 Christmas, Hillary, Nigel, monogram birthmark, 2,000 issued **$100**

1986 Georgia, monogram birthmark, 4,000 issued......................... **$100**

1987 Iddy Buds, monogram birthmark, 750 issued........................ **$500**

1987 Sleeping Beauty, Prince Charming, monogram birthmark, 1,250 issued... **$250**

1988 Nursery Edition, Baby Marilyn, Suzann, Baby Tyler Bo, Baby Dorothy Jane, Baby Sybil Sadie, monogram birthmark, 2,000 issued... **$75**

1989 Christmas Joy, monogram birthmark, 500 issued **$300**

Effanbee Doll Company

Composition

Doll House Doll: 6"; composition head and hands; cloth-covered wire armature body; molded and painted shoes; molded and painted hair; painted blue eyes; closed mouth; original, detailed costume; typically marked "EFFanBEE".. **$100**

Button Nose: 8"; all composition; jointed at neck, shoulder, and hip; molded and painted hair; painted, round, side-glancing eyes; closed, slightly-smiling mouth; original detailed costume; typically marked "Effanbee" **$400**

Oriental facial features **$600**

Little Sister and Big Brother: 12" and 16"; composition socket head; shoulder plate and hands; cloth body and limbs; floss hair; painted eyes; small closed mouth; original Little Sister's pink and white and Big Brother's blue and white outfits; typically marked "Effanbee."

Little Sister: 12".. **$300**

Big Brother: 16" **$350**

All original composition dolls, including: 16-inch Effanbee Baby Brother, $350; 16-inch Madame Alexander McGuffey Ana, $650; 12-inch Effanbee Baby Sister, $300; 14-inch Madame Alexander Alice, $750. Courtesy of David Cobb's Doll Auctions

Candy Kid: 13"; all composition, jointed at neck, shoulder, and hip; chubby child figure; molded and painted hair; painted eyes; pointed eyebrows; closed mouth; original gingham outfit; holding small stuffed monkey; typically marked "EFFANBEE" **$500**

Hard Plastic/Vinyl

Happy Boy: 10"; all vinyl; jointed at neck and shoulder; character face; molded and painted hair; molded and painted closed eyes; open/closed mouth; molded upper tooth; freckles; appropriately dressed; typically marked "1960/Effanbee" or "Effanbee" ... **$100**

Mickey The All American Boy: 11"; all vinyl; jointed at neck, shoulder, and hip; molded hat and hair; painted eyes; closed smiling mouth; freckles; appropriately dressed; typically marked "Mickey/Effanbee" **$175**

Patsy Ann: 15"; all vinyl; jointed at neck, shoulder, and hip; rooted hair; sleep eyes; closed smiling mouth; appropriately dressed; typically marked "Effanbee Patsy Ann/1959" **$250**

Miss Chips: 18"; all vinyl; jointed at neck, shoulder, and hip; rooted hair, full bangs; very large, side-glancing sleep eyes; closed mouth; appropriately dressed; typically marked "Effanbee 19©65/1700" **$125**

Rootie Kazootie: 19", vinyl hands and character flange neck; cloth body; molded and painted hair, long curl coming down forehead; round, painted eyes; open/closed laughing mouth; appropriately dressed; typically marked "Rootie/Kazootie/Effanbee" **$350**

Honey Walker: 20"; vinyl head; hard plastic walker body; jointed at shoulder and hip, just above the knees, and at ankles; feet molded for high heel shoes; rooted hair; sleep eyes; pierced ears; closed mouth; appropriately dressed; typically marked "EFFanBEE" **$450**

My Fair Baby: 21"; all vinyl; jointed at neck, shoulder, and hip; rooted hair; sleep eyes; open nurser mouth; body has crier; appropriately dressed; typically marked "EFFanBEE/1960" **$125**

American Composition, including: 19-inch Arranbee Debuteen with box, $1,200+; 19-inch Effanbee Patsy Ann with box, $1,400+; 20-inch Effanbee Ann Shirley with box, $1,000; 13-inch Ideal Shirley Temple in original tagged NRA dress, $1,200; 11-inch Effanbee Patsy Jr. with box, $1,100; 12-inch Cameo Scootles with box, $1,100; 8-inch Effanbee Toddler Tinyette, $450; and 9-inch Patsyette on skates, $500. Courtesy of David Cobb's Doll Auctions

Mary Jane: 30"; vinyl socket head; plastic body; jointed at shoulder and hip; rooted hair; sleep/flirty eyes; closed, slightly-unsmiling mouth; freckles over nose; appropriately dressed, typically marked "Effanbee/Mary Jane".. **$450**

Ideal® Novelty and Toy Company
Hard Plastic & Vinyl

Little Lost Baby: 22"; three-faced, vinyl head; foam stuffed suit encased body; one face smiling awake, one sleeping, and one crying, all with molded and painted features; lever at base of neck turns head; marked with tag "Little Lost Baby/1968 Ideal Toy Corp".. **$175**

Cuddly Kissy: 17"; vinyl head; cloth body; rooted hair; sleep eyes; open/closed mouth; appropriately dressed; press stomach, and hands come together, head tilts forward, lips pucker, and doll makes a kissing sound; marked "Ideal Toy Corp/KB-17-E".. **$175**

Bonnie Braids: 13"; vinyl head; hard plastic body; jointed at shoulder and hip; molded and painted hair with saran braids coming through holes on each side of head; blue, sleep eyes with real lashes; open mouth with three painted teeth; original dress; typically marked "1951/Chicago Tribune/Ideal Doll" **$350**

Dorothy Hamil: 11-1/2"; vinyl head and arms; plastic body; bendable legs; rooted hair; painted eyes; open/closed mouth with painted teeth; appropriately dressed; typically marked "1977 DH/Ideal" within oval, "H-282/Hong Kong" on head, "1975/Ideal" in oval on hip, and "U.S. Pat. No. 3903640/Hollis NY 11423/Hong Kong P" **$75**

Tammy: 12"; vinyl head and arms; plastic body; jointed at neck, shoulder, and hip; rooted hair; painted, side-glancing eyes; closed mouth; appropriately dressed; typically marked "Ideal Toy Corp./B-5 12," "Ideal Toy Corp/B-5 12-1/2" **$150**

Twenty-inch Effanbee composition painted-eye American child, $2,500; 27-inch Ideal composition Shirley Temple with original box, $4,200; 21-inch Dollcraft Novelty composition Tonto, $1,500, and Lone Ranger, $1,800; 17-inch Effanbee composition Ann Shirley, $475; 13-inch Ideal composition Howdy Doody with wood-segmented body, $750; 13-inch Madame Alexander Snow White, $550; 11-inch Ideal composition Shirley Temple, $1,300. Courtesy of David Cobb's Doll Auctions

Tammy's family:

Big Brother Ted: 12-1/2"; typically marked "B-12 1/2 M-2" **$175**

Mother: 12-1/2"; typically marked "W-1 3 L" or "W-13" **$225**

Father: 13"; typically marked "M13-2" or "B-12 1/2" **$175**

Little Sister Pepper: 9"; typically marked "6-9 W/2," "G9W," or "P-9DD-9-6" **$100**

Little Brother Freckled-Face Pete: 8"; typically marked, "P-8" .. **$250**

Pepper's Friend Patti: 9"; typically marked "P-9" or "G-9-W" ... **$300**

Pepper's Friend Dodi: 9"; typically marked "DO-9-E" **$100**

Pepper's Freckled-Face Friend Salty: 8"; original baseball cap, glove, bat, ball, and catcher's mask; typically marked "P-8" **$350**

Tammy's Boyfriend Bud: 12-1/2"; typically marked "B-12 1/2 M-2" **$300**

007 James Bond: 12-1/2"; vinyl head and arms; plastic body; molded and painted hair and facial features; appropriately dressed; typically marked "Ideal Toy Corp/B-12-1/2-2" **$150**

Tiffany Taylor: 14"; vinyl head; shapely plastic body; jointed at neck, shoulder, and hip; swivel cap wig (spins to change hair color from blond to brunette); painted eyes; closed mouth; appropriately dressed; typically marked "1974/Ideal" in an oval, "Hollis, NY 11423/2M 5854 01/2" "1973/CG-19-H-230" **$100**

Bye-Bye Baby: 25"; vinyl head; plastic body; nicely molded, lifelike hands and feet; softly molded and painted hair; sleep eyes; open nurser mouth; appropriately dressed; typically marked "Ideal Toy Corp./HB-25" **$500**

Kissy: 22"; vinyl head; plastic body; rooted hair; sleep eyes; open/ closed mouth; appropriately dressed; typically marked "®IDEAL/ IDEAL CORP./K-21-L//IDEAL TOY CORP. K-22 PAT. PEND." Note: Kissy dolls made a kissing sound, advertised as "Go get Kissy if you want a little kiss, do her arms like this (squeeze arms together) she'll give a little kiss." **$250**

Kissin Cousins: 11-1/2" **$100**

Tiny Kissy Baby: 16" **$150**

Rare and irresistible bisque Kewpies, with drum, $1,750; in egg shell, $3,500; and soldier, $1,600. Courtesy Frasher's Auctions

Kewpies

Kewpie Value Comparisons

2" all bisque, painted eyes*..$200
2" celluloid shoulder joints, painted eyes $75
3" all bisque, painted eyes*..$225
3" celluloid shoulder joints, painted eyes $100
4" all bisque, painted eyes*..$250
4" celluloid shoulder joints, painted eyes $125
5" all bisque, painted eyes*..$300
5" celluloid shoulder joints, painted eyes $150
6" all bisque, painted eyes*..$450
6" celluloid shoulder joints, painted eyes $175
7" all bisque, painted eyes*..$550
8" all bisque, painted eyes*..$700
8" celluloid shoulder joints, painted eyes $275
8" composition head and body, painted eyes $350
9" all bisque, painted eyes*..$850
10" all bisque, painted eyes*..$1,100
10" bisque head, composition body, glass eyes.......................$6,000
10" celluloid shoulder joints, painted eyes $400
12" all bisque, painted eyes*..$1,700
12" bisque head, composition body, glass eyes.......................$6,800
12" bisque head, cloth body, painted eyes...............................$2,600
12" bisque head, cloth body, glass eyes $3,500
12" celluloid shoulder joints, painted eyes $450
12" composition head and body, painted eyes $600
12" composition head, cloth body...$350
14" bisque head, composition body, glass eyes.......................$7,500
15" celluloid shoulder joints, painted eyes $600
20" bisque head, composition body, glass eyes.......................$16,000
20" celluloid shoulder joints, painted eyes $750

    * Add an additional $400-500 for jointed hips or molded and painted shoes and socks.

Fifteen-inch Ideal hard plastic Toni complete with original box and play wave set, $950. Courtesy of McMaster's Doll Auctions

Knickerbocker Dolls & Toy Company

Vinyl

Prices listed are for dolls in near-mint, original condition. If damaged, redressed, or undressed, expect the value to be less than one half to one fourth the amounts listed.

Annie: 7"; vinyl character head; (Aileen Quinn); plastic body; rigid vinyl limbs; rooted hair; painted eyes; smiling mouth; original, red cotton dress with white collar, white socks, and black shoes; marked "1982 CPI Inc. 1982 CTNYNS, Inc/1982 Knickerbocker Toy Co. Inc. H-15" **$85**

Daddy Warbucks: 7"; (Albert Finney); vinyl character head; plastic body; rigid vinyl limbs; solid dome; painted eyes; closed mouth; original, black suit and tie; white shirt and red cummerbund; marked "1982 CPI Inc. 1982 CTNYNS Inc./1982 Knickerbocker Toy Co. Inc H-22" **$65**

Miss Hannigan: 7" (Carol Burnett); vinyl character head; plastic body; rigid vinyl limbs; rooted hair; painted eyes; closed mouth; original, purple dotted dress with ruffle and purple shoes; marked "1982 CPI Inc. 1982 CTNYNS Inc./1982 Knickerbocker Toy Co. Inc H-22" **$85**

Punjab: 7" (Geoffrey Holder); dark vinyl character head; dark plastic body; rigid vinyl limbs; molded and painted hair and facial features; closed mouth; original all-white suit with gold trim; marked "1982 CPI Inc. 1982 CTNYNS Inc./1982 Knickerbocker Toy Co. Inc H-22" **$85**

Molly: 5-3/4" (Toni Ann Gisondi); vinyl character head; plastic body; rigid vinyl limbs; rooted dark hair; painted eyes; open/closed, wide, smiling mouth; original, turquoise dress with calico sleeves and collar; marked "1982 CPI Inc. 1982 CTNYNS Inc./1982 Knickerbocker Toy Co. Inc H-17" **$45**

Fifteen and one-half-inch Gene Marshall in Somewhere Summer ensemble designed birthmark by Mel Odom for Ashton Drake Galleries, $275. Photo courtesy Ashton Drake

Little House on the Prairie Child: vinyl head, hands, and legs; cloth body; rooted hair; painted eyes; smiling mouth; original cotton dress with name printed on front pocket; marked "1978 ED FRIENDLY PRODUCTIONS INC/LIC JLM/Made in Taiwan T-2" on back of head; dress tagged "Little House on the Prairie Made by Knickerbocker Toy Co." **$65**

Soupy Sales: vinyl head; cloth body; molded and painted hair; character face; painted eyes; heavy brows; closed, smiling mouth; non-removable clothes with polka-dot bow tie. Marked "1965 Knickerbocker" on back of head, tagged "Soupy Sales/1966 Soupy Sales W.M.C." **$250**

Holly Hobbie: 10-1/2"; all vinyl; jointed at neck, shoulder, and hip; rooted, long hair; round, freckled character face; painted features; closed mouth; original calico dress and sun bonnet; marked "KTD/GAC/1974" **$75**

Mattel® Inc.

Tiny Cheerful Tearful: 6-1/2"; all vinyl; rooted hair; painted eyes; open mouth; press tummy to change expression from glad to sad; marked "1966 Mattel Inc. Hong Kong" **$75**

Kretor and Zark the Shark: 7" Kretor and 12" Zark; Kretor's a vinyl frogman; Zark's a plastic shark that swims in the water and carries Kretor with him; pull-string activated; marked "6389-0150/2" on Kretor's left foot; "1970 Mattel Inc./Hong Kong/U.S. U For/ Patented/Patented in Canada 1970" on Kretor's right foot; "1970 Mattel Inc./Hong Kong/U.S. Patent Pending" on Zark's underside; the set **$250**

The Sunshine Family (9-1/2" Steve, 9" Stephie, and 3" Sweets): vinyl heads and arms; plastic bodies; jointed knees; rooted hair; insert eyes; marked "1973 Mattel Inc." on heads; "1973/Mattel Inc./Taiwan"on back; wrist tag "The Sunshine Family"; the set **$165**

Eighteen-inch vintage Steiff felt child, $2,800. Courtesy of Sotheby's Auctions

Buffie: 10", vinyl head; plastic body; vinyl limbs; rooted hair; painted eyes; open/closed mouth with two upper teeth; freckles across nose; holding 3-1/2" Mrs. Beasley doll; marked "1967/Mattel Inc./U.S. & For/Pats. Pend Mexico" **$300**

Baby Small Talk: 11"; all black vinyl; rooted, black hair; painted, brown eyes; open/closed mouth with two upper and two lower teeth; pull-string talker; marked "1967 Mattel/Japan" on head **$75**

Gold Medal Big Jack: 12"; all rigid black vinyl; jointed at neck, shoulder, wrists, waist, hip, knees, and ankles; boxer; press back to make right arm move; marked "1971 Mattel, Inc./Hong Kong U.S. & Foreign Patented" **$250**

Guardian Goddesses: 12"; adult figure; test market dolls only; Moonmystic and Sunspell; arms go up and down; when limbs are pulled, gowns fly off and reveal "Super Girl" outfit, 1979-1980 .... **$500**

Cheerful Tearful: 13"; vinyl head; plastic body; vinyl limbs; rooted hair; painted eyes; open mouth; moving left arm makes face change from sad to glad expression; marked "1965 Mattel Inc./ Hawthorne Calif., U.S. Patents Pending/3036-014-1" **$65**

Saucy: 16"; vinyl head; plastic body; vinyl limbs; rooted hair; sleep eyes; rotating left arm causes eyes and mouth to form eight different expressions; marked "1972 Mattel Inc. Mexico" on head; "1972 Mattel Inc. Mexico/US Patent Pend." on back **$125**

Talking Miss Beasley: 16"; vinyl head; blue and white polka-dot cloth body with apron; rooted, blond hair; painted features; black plastic glasses; pull-string talker; cloth tag "Mattel Miss Beasley" sewn into seam.. **$400**

Chatty Cathy: 20"; vinyl head; plastic body; vinyl limbs; rooted hair; sleep eyes with lashes; open/closed mouth with molded and painted teeth; marked "Chatty Cathy 1960/Chatty Baby 1961 By Mattel Inc./U.S. Pat. 301718/Other U.S. and Foreign Pats. Pend./ Pat'd in Canada 1962"; dress tag reads "Chatty Cathy Mattel"**$350**

Chatty Cathy black version **$1,000**
Scooby-Doo: 21"; vinyl head; cloth body; rooted hair; blue, sleep eyes
    with liner and eye shadow; closed mouth; pull-string on left hip;
    marked "Mattel/Scooby Doo 1964" on tag sewn into seam... **$250**
Charmin Chatty: 25"; vinyl head and arms; plastic body; plastic legs;
    rooted hair; side-glancing, sleep eyes with lashes; closed, smiling
    mouth; record fits into slot on side of doll; pull-string operates
    talker; marked "Charmin Chatty 1961 Mattel, Inc." **$200**
Chatty Baby, 18" **$150**
Tiny Chatty Baby, 15" **$85**
Tiny Chatty Baby Brother, 15" **$100**
Singing Chatty **$200**

Modern Collectible Dolls

Hard Plastic/Vinyl

Annette Himstedt Children: 19"-31"; vinyl head and arms; cloth
    body; good wig; set eyes; closed or open/closed mouth; well-made
    appropriate costume; typically marked "Annette Himstedt/Puppen
    Kind," signature on neck, wrist tag with character name and
    clothing tag (designed birthmark by Annette Himstedt for Mattel)

    Timi, Toni, Panchita, Pancho, or **Melvin** **$600**

    Baby, Leischen, Tara, Annachen, Lona, or **Kima** **$800**

    Fiene Kai, Janka, Liliane, Adriene, or **Ayoka** **$1,200**

    Neblina, Taki, Freeke, Bibbi, or **Makimura** **$1,300**

    Michiko, Malin, Frederike, or **Tinka** **$1,500**

    Kasimir **$1,800**

Beatles: 5"; oversized vinyl heads; miniature plastic body; rooted hair;
    painted features; black suits; plastic guitars with "John," "Paul,"
    "George," or "Ringo" written across the front; marked "Remco
    Ind.Inc.1964 (Seltael, Inc, NEMS) .... **$600 set**

Captain Kangaroo: 11"-21"; vinyl character modelled head and hands; cloth body; molded cap; hair and moustache; painted or insert eyes; open/closed smiling mouth; dressed in oversized pocket suit; marked "1961 ROBT. KEESHAN/ASSOC. INC." or "B B" (by Baby Barry Toy Co.)

    11" **$250**

    15" **300**

    21" **500**

Dawn Model Agency (Dawn, Angie, Glori, Dale [black version], April, Dinah, Melanie, Daphne): 6"; jointed at neck, shoulder, and hip; rooted hair; painted eyes; closed mouth; original "mod" outfit; marked production year (1969-1972) "Topper Corp/Hong Kong" and "H11A," "11C," "A11A," "K10," "H-7/110," "11-7," "878/K11A," "2/H-11," "A8-10," "H-17," "4/H 72," "543/H11a," "92/H-17," "154/S11," "51/D10," "4/H86," "K10/A," "AK11/H-7," and possibly others (by Deluxe Reading) **$125**

FayZah Spanos Babies and Children: 25"; quality vinyl head and limbs; cloth body; good wig; acrylic-topped eyes; open/closed mouth; nicely dressed; marked "FAYZAH SPANOS" **$250**

Gene®: 16"; jointed at neck, shoulder, and hip; rooted hair; beautifully-sculptured and dramatically-painted facial features; original, designer costume; marked "1995 Mel Odom/Ashton Drake" (designed birthmark by award winning artist Mel Odom for Ashton Drake)

    Early premier issue **$750**

    Later retired issue (depending upon costume) **$200-400**

Julie Good-Krueger Children: 20"; all vinyl or vinyl head and limbs and cloth body; good wig; set eyes; closed or open/closed mouth; nicely dressed; marked "Julie Good-Krueger© (production date)"

    .... **$300**

Twenty-four-inch Jolie & Jacques, 1996 limited edition porcelain dolls by Fayzah Spanos, $400 each. Photo courtesy of the artist.

Lee Middleton Babies or Toddlers: 11"-22"; realistically-modelled vinyl head and limbs; cloth body; rooted or molded hair; sleeping or set eyes; closed or open/closed mouth; nicely dressed with tiny Bible tied to wrist; marked character name and production number "Lee Middleton (date) (fish or Christian symbol) The Middleton Doll Co" and signature

11" **$100**
20" **$200**
22" **$250**

Lilli: 11 1/2"; all quality vinyl; curvaceous body, jointed at neck, shoulder, and hip; rooted, long hair worn in a pony tail; heavily lined black and white painted eyes; closed mouth; fashionably dressed; marked "Germany" (by Bild Lilli) (very similar in appearance, in fact many believe Lilli was the impetus for Barbie®)

In original plastic tube with metal rod stand **$8,000**
Without tube **$5,000**

Contemporary Porcelain

Ashton Drake Fairy-Tale: 14"; porcelain head, arms, and legs; cloth body; good wig; glass eyes; closed mouth; appropriate costume and accessories; marked "Dianna Effner/production number."

Red Riding Hood (first in the series) **$175**
Cinderella (at the ball) **$125**
Cinderella (poor-girl) **$150**
Goldilocks **$100**
Rapunzel **$100**
Snow White **$150**

Franklin Mint Ladies: 20"-22"; porcelain head and limbs; cloth body; nice wig; painted or glass eyes; closed mouth; beautifully costumed; marked "Franklin Mint"/date and/or production number ...... **$300 and up**, for dolls made before 1990, depending upon character and costume

Noelle the Christmas Angel: 15"; porcelain in a pirouette pose; wig with blond curls; glass eyes; closed mouth; dressed in layers of diaphanous materials; marked "Noelle/Ann Timmerman" production number "1995" (designed by Ann Timmerman for the Little Bit of Heaven Collection from Georgetown Collection)**$165**

Royal Doulton: 8"-12"; porcelain heads and hands; cloth bodies with wire armatures; good wigs; painted eyes; closed mouth; wonderfully-detailed costumes; marked with the "Royal Doulton" stamp (designed by Eric Griffiths and costume by Peggy Nisbet)

8" **$150**

12" **$250**

Raggedy Ann & Andy®

Raggedy Ann & Andy Value Comparisons

Gruelle Family, 16"; Ann only .... **$8,500** plain nose

....**$8,500** black-outlined nose

Volland, 16"; Ann or Andy .... **$3,400** plain nose,

....**$4,600** black-outlined nose

14"; Beloved Belindy, ...**$3,800** black-outlined nose

14"-18"; Character..**$3,000** plain nose

Exposition Doll... **$9,000** plain nose

....**$9,000** black-outlined nose

Molly-'es, 17"-22"; Ann or Andy ....**$2,500** black-outlined nose

14"; Baby **$3,500**

Georgene, 13"; Ann; Awake/Asleep .... **$1,000** plain nose

....**$1,600** black-outlined nose

While Georgene manufactured Raggedys, the company rights were renewed in Johnny Gruelle's name, except in 1946. Tagged part "...1946 by Myrtle Gruelle Silsby..." This tag adds an additional $200 to any doll.

14"-18"; Beloved Belindy.................. **$2,600** black-outlined nose

15"; Ann or Andy ....**$600** plain nose

.... **$1,800** black-outlined nose

19"; Ann or Andy, ... **$500** plain nose
.... **$2,400** black-outlined nose
24"; Ann or Andy, ... **$700** plain nose
.... **$2,900** black-outlined nose
31"; Ann or Andy, ... **$1,300** plain nose
.... **$3,600** black-outlined nose
36"; Ann or Andy .... **$1,400** plain nose
45"; Ann or Andy .... **$1,600** plain nose
50"; Ann or Andy, ... **$2,000** plain nose
.... **$4,900** black-outlined nose

Knickerbocker Toy Co.

3"; Ann or Andy Huggers .... **$200** plain nose
6"; Ann or Andy .... **$75** plain nose
12"; Ann or Andy .... **$150** plain nose
15"; Ann or Andy .... **$200** plain nose
19"; Ann or Andy .... **$275** plain nose
24"; Ann or Andy .... **$400** plain nose
30"; Ann or Andy .... **$700** plain nose
36"; Ann or Andy .... **$1,000** plain nose
40"; Ann or Andy .... **$1,400** plain nose
45"; Ann or Andy .... **$1,700** plain nose
78"; Ann or Andy .... **$2,500** plain nose
15"; Beloved Belindy, ... **$1,500** plain nose
.... **$1,500** black-outlined nose
Camel with Wrinkled Knees .... **$500** plain nose
Raggedy Arthur .... **$400** plain nose
.... **$400** black-outlined nose
Applause 15"; Ann or Andy .... **$65** plain nose

Shirley Temple

Shirley Temple Doll Value Comparisons

8" 1982 vinyl	**$100**
11" Ideal all composition*	**$1,300**
12" 1957 vinyl	**$300**
1982 vinyl	**$125**
13" Ideal all composition*	**$1,200**
14" porcelain, Danbury Mint	**$250**
15" Ideal all composition*	**$1,200**
1957 vinyl	**$400**
1972 vinyl	**$300**
16" Ideal all composition*	**$1,200**
Baby Shirley	**$1,600**
1973 vinyl	**$200**
17" Ideal all composition*	**$1,400**
1957 vinyl	**$475**
18" Ideal all composition*	**$1,400**
Baby Shirley	**$1,700**
Brown Shirley	**$1,300**
19" 1957 vinyl	**$550**
20" Baby Shirley	**$1,800**
21" Baby Shirley	**$1,900**
22" Ideal all composition*	**$1,600**
23" Baby Shirley	**$2,000**
25" Ideal all composition*	**$1,700**
Baby Shirley	**$2,100**
27" Ideal all composition*	**$2,600**
36" 1984 vinyl	**$500**

* Add an additional **$300-$800** for Texas Ranger or Curly Top costumed doll.

Terri Lee Company
Terri Lee Family Value Comparisons

10" Tiny Terri Lee	**$500**
Tiny Jerrie Lee,	**$450**
16" Composition Terri Lee	**$700**
Hard plastic/vinyl Terri Lee	**$800**
Gene Autry	**$3,700**
Jerri Lee, lamb's-wool wig	**$900**
Patti Jo	**$1,600**
Benji, Bonnie Lu, or other friends	**$1,000**
Nanook Eskimo	**$2,000**
9 1/2" vinyl So-Sleepy	**$300**
10" vinyl Baby Linda Lee	**$300**
17" Mary Jane Sleep Eyes Copy	**$350**
19" Connie Lynn Baby	**$800**

Vogue Dolls, Inc.
Ginny Value Comparisons (all 8")

#1 Ginny painted eyes	**$500**
#2 Ginny sleep eyes, painted lashes, straight-leg non-walker	**$700**
#2 Ginny Poodle Cut	**$800**
#2 Ginny Fluffy Bunny	**$1,600**
#2 Ginny Crib Crowder Baby	**$1,200**
#3 Ginny sleep eyes, painted lashes, straight-leg walker	**$500**
#3 Ginny Black	**$2,200**
#3 Ginny Queen	**$1,200**
#4 Ginny sleep eyes, molded lashes, straight-leg walker	**$400**
#5 Ginny sleep eyes, molded lashes, jointed-knee walker	**$300**
#6 Ginny vinyl head, rooted hair	**$200**
Modern Ginny, all vinyl	**$100**
Sassoon Ginny painted eyes	**$75**
Sassoon Ginny sleep eyes	**$65**
Contemporary Ginny	**$30**

A 1957 Farmall 450 with silver stack in 1:16-scale by Ertl. Even well-played with examples of this model are commanding high prices. $1,144 MIP.

Farm Toys

By Elizabeth A. Stephan

Modern farm toy collecting was born in 1945 when Fred Ertl, Sr. made his first toy tractor — a sandcast Allis-Chalmers WC.

Ertl began his modest toymaking business in Dubuque, Iowa. By 1947, Ertl had to move his business to a larger facility, and he chose a small town twenty miles west of Dubuque — Dyersville. Today Dyersville is synonymous with farm toys.

Other farm toy companies popped up in the 1940s. Joseph Carter started the Carter Machine Company in the first half of the decade. Carter's line of toys consisted of John Deer and International tractors and implements. Trucks were added to the lineup in the 1950s. In 1971, Carter sold the line to Ertl.

Andy Reul started Reuhl Toys (the "h" was added to help with pronunciation) in the mid-'40s. Original models were made of wood, Bakelite, fiberglass, and plastic. Sold mainly through retail outlets, Reuhl went out of business in 1958 when the company lost two of its biggest clients — Caterpillar and Massey-Harris.

Many other farm toy manufacturers have originated in the same region — Eska, SpecCast, and Scale Models, just to name a few.

Before Ertl

Companies like Arcade, Hubley, and Vindex made the earliest cast-iron toy tractors and implements in the 1920s and '30s. Some other more localized toymakers like Kansas Toy and Novelty and Ralstoy made slush-mold models, but they lacked the detail that the earlier cast-iron models had. Farm toys would occasionally show up in the Sears catalog, too.

Most of these companies faded away by the 1950s. Ertl toys sold well and flourished because of their realistic detail, durable construction, and wide distribution.

By the late 1970s, the farm toy collecting hobby was in full swing. Why do people collect farm toys? I'm sure there are many reasons, but it seems to boil down to one word — nostalgia.

Listings are grouped together alphabetically under each tractor company name. The three main pricing grades used are excellent (EX), near mint (NM), and mint in pack (MIP).

Elizabeth A. Stephan is the co-editor of the Standard Catalog of Farm Toys *published by Krause Publications, Iola, Wis.*

Farm Toys

Abbreviations

n/a: not applicable. This is used when there isn't a value given for that toy in a certain condition grade.

npf: no price found. In some cases, a price cannot be found. Sometimes there aren't enough records on the sales of a particular model to make an honest evaluation of price. This doesn't always mean the toy is extremely valuable or not valuable at all, though.

ROPS: Rollover Protection System

PTO: Power Take Off

FWA: Front Wheel Assist

MFD: Mechanical Front Drive

Allis-Chalmers

	EX	NM	MIP
Allis-Chalmers Crawler, Product Miniature,1:16-scale, orange, 1950s	$126	$317	$523
Allis-Chalmers Crawler, Lionel 1:60-scale, orange, 1950s	$58	$127	$228
Allis-Chalmers 190, Ertl, 1:16-scale, orange, black A over C decal in grille, bar grille, 1960s, No. 192	$67	$112	$367
Allis-Chalmers 190 XT, Ertl, 1:16-scale, orange, 1960s, No. 192	$58	$98	$237
Allis-Chalmers 200, Ertl, 1:16-scale, orange, w/air cleaner, 1970s, No. 152	$73	$134	$248
Allis-Chalmers 7045, Ertl, 1:64-scale, orange and black, rectangular decal, 1980s, No. 1623	$98	$174	$222

A 1:16 scale Farmall 560 from 1964. This casting was used for years by Ertl, with many variations. This model features plastic front wheels and no fast hitch. $650 MIP.

	EX	NM	MIP
Allis-Chalmers B-110, Ertl, 1:16-scale, yellow, 1960s	$88	$207	$398
Allis-Chalmers C, American Precision, 1:12-scale, orange, 1950s	$98	$183	$367
Allis Chalmers D-14, Strombecker, 1:25-scale, orange, 1960s	$27	$79	$154
Allis-Chalmers D-17 Series III, Ertl, 1:16-scale, orange, no headlights, 1960s	$176	$352	$819
Allis-Chalmers Tractor/Belly Dump, Arcade, orange, 1930s	$148	$279	$748
Allis-Chalmers U w/Bottom Dump Trailer, Arcade, 1:24-scale, orange, red or green, 1930s	$148	$279	$748
Allis-Chalmers WC, Ertl, 1:16-scale, red, aluminum wheels, 1940s	$348	$798	npf
Allis-Chalmers WC, Dent, 1:24-scale, orange, rubber wheels, painted river casted separately, 1930s	$146	$373	$1183
Allis-Chalmers WD, Product Miniature, 1:16-scale, cream, 1950s	$87	$179	$382

Case

	EX	NM	MIP
Case 750 Dozer, Hong Kong, 1:16-scale, yellow and black, 1960s	$293	$722	$1026
Case Disc, Ertl, 1:16-scale, orange, 1970s	$18	$42	$79
Case Plow, Vindex, 1:16-scale, red w/pale green or yellow wheels, early 1930s	$712	$1193	npf
Case Spreader, Vindex, red w/pale green or yellow wheels, early 1930s	$1498	$2318	npf

A popular toy in sandboxes everywhere, the Ertl 1:16-scale John Deere 40 crawler debuted in 1954. The casting was used for years— the numbers on the side were simply updated to reflect any changes in the actual tractor line. $745 MIP.

	EX	NM	MIP

Case 1030, Ertl, 1:16-scale, beige and orange, late 1960s,
    No. 2004 .... $118................ $186...................... $472

Case 800, Monarch, 1:16-scale, orange and beige, 1960s
    .... $122............... $289...................... $547

Case 930, Ertl, 1:16-scale, beige and orange, plastic
front rims w/die-cast rear rims, mid 1960s,
    No. 200 .... $102................ $227...................... $687

Case CC, Kruse (Custom), 1:16-scale, gray, did not come in box,
    1970s .... $37.............. $56.......................... n/a

Case L, Vindex, 1:16-scale, gray w/red rims, nickel-plated driver,
    early 1930s .... $446.............. $1047..........................npf

Case SC, Monarch, 1:16-scale, orange, w/o fenders,
    1950s .... $114............... $273...................... $438

Farmall

Farmall 200, Classic Farm Toys, 1:16-scale, red,
    1980s .... $22................ $36........................ $52

Farmall 200, Lakone, 1:16-scale, red,
    1950s .... $148................ $382.................... $1343

Farmall 230, Lakone, 1:16-scale, red,
    1950s .... $148................ $382.................... $1343

Farmall 340, Ertl, 1:16-scale, red, smooth or ribbed front tires,
    one has word McCormick above International,
    one doesn't, 1960s ..... $262................ $483.................... $1188

Farmall 350, Freiheit (Custom), 1:16-scale, red, did not come
    in box, 1980s .... $167................ $242.......................... n/a

Farmall 400, Ertl, 1:16-scale, red,
    1950s .... $236................ $483.................... $1432

Farmall 450, Ertl, 1:16-scale, red,
    1950s .... $236................ $672.................... $1973

John Deere Model A tractor, 1:16-scale by Arcade, 1940. Finding one of these with a complete driver can be a real challenge. $3,082 MIP.

	EX	NM	MIP

Farmall 560, Ertl, 1:16-scale, red, no two-point or belt pulley,
plastic red front rims, 1960s, No. 408
.... $67................ $198.................... $632

Farmall 656, Ertl, 1:32-scale, red, 1970s, No. 40
.... $4................ $22.................... $48

Farmall 806, Ertl, 1:16-scale, red, one w/die-cast rear
rims, one w/plastic rear rims, 1960s,
No. 435 .... $98................ $257.................... $772

Farmall C, Jouef, 1:16-scale, red,
1970s........................ $97................ $268..........................npf

Farmall Cub, Design Fabricators, 1:16-scale, red, Farmall was decalled,
1950s........................ $89................ $221.................... $378

Farmall Cultivision A, Arcade, 1:16-scale, red,
1940s........................ $293................ $778.................... $2692

Farmall H, Scale Models, 1:16-scale, various colors,
1980s........................ $22................ $38..........................$53

Farmall M, Arcade, 1:16-scale, red,
1940s........................ $97................ $227.................... $658

Farmall Regular, Arcade, 1:16-scale, one all red, one w/gray body and
red wheels, 1930s ...... $388................ $792.................... $2689

Farmall Super C, Lakone, 1:16-scale,
red, 1950s.................. $116................ $278.................... $683

Ford

Ford 1961 Powermaster, Hubley, 1:12-scale, gray and red,
1960s........................ $116................ $203..........................$436

Ford 3600, Milton, 1:20-scale, blue,
1980s........................ $13................ $28..........................$34

Massey-Harris 44 tractor, 1:20-scale by Reuhl, 1954. All die-cast rims. $864 MIP.

	EX	NM	MIP

Ford 4000, Hubley, 1:12-scale, gray and red, 1960s,
No. 1506 .... $63 .... $134 .... $248

Ford 4600, Ertl, 1:12-scale, blue, three-point hitch, 1970s,
No. 805 .... $18 .... $39 .... $59

Ford 600, Product Miniature, 1:12-scale, gray and red,
1950s .... $148 .... $333 .... $659

Ford 7710, Ertl, 1:16-scale, blue, 1963 National Farm Toy Show
Tractor, No. 1522 ...... $197 .... $237 .... $358

Ford 8000, Ertl, 1:12-scale, blue,
1970s .... $38 .... $76 .... $132

Ford 8N, AMT/MPC, 1:12-scale, gray and red, also w/windup clock
work, 1950s .... $116 .... $228 .... $358

Ford 900, Product Miniature, 1:12-scale, gray and red,
1950s .... $224 .... $443 .... $759

Ford Commander 6000, Hubley, 1:12-scale, gray and blue,
1970s .... $49 .... $86 .... $143

Ford Select-O-Speed, Hubley, 1:12-scale, gray and red,
1960s .... $112 .... $198 .... $372

International

International Diesel Crawler TD 18, Arcade, 1:16-scale, orange,
1940s .... $437 .... $1057 .... $3114

International Disc, Ertl, 1:16-scale, red,
1960s .... $22 .... $57 .... $92

International 1456, Ertl, 1:16-scale, red,
1960s, No. 420 .... $98 .... $257 .... $772

International 240, Ertl, 1:16-scale, red, smooth or ribbed front tires,
one with McCormick above International, one without,
1960s .... $262 .... $483 .... $1492

Minneapolis-Moline R, 1:16-scale by Auburn. These rubber tractors were produced in black and white tire variations. The models shown here were produced in 1950. Auburn's toys have been generating greater interest among collectors in recent years. $74 MIP.

	EX	NM	MIP

International 340, Ertl, 1:16-scale, red, 404-style rear rims,
  1960s .... $262 .... $483 .... $1188

International 544, Ertl, 1:16-scale, red, 1960s,
  No. 414 .... $72 .... $159 .... $284

International 606, Deyen (Custom), 1:16-scale, red, did not come
  in box, 1980s .... $98 .... $158 .... n/a

John Deere

John Deere 24T Baler, Ertl, 1:16-scale, green 1960s,
  No. 545 .... $36 .... $78 .... $143

John Deere 40 Crawler w/Blade, Ertl, 1:16-scale, green,
  1950s .... $156 .... $276 .... $578

John Deere 44 Manure Spreader, Ertl, 1:16-scale, green, C-type hitch,
  1960s, No. 534 .... $36 .... $48 .... $106

John Deere 495 Planter, Ertl, 1:16-scale, green, two-legged decal,
  plastic wheels, clank hitch, static marker disc, 1960s,
  No. 539 .... $78 .... $103 .... $228

John Deere Bale Wagon, Ertl, 1:16-scale, green, 1980s,
  No. 522 .... $6 .... $11 .... $18

John Deere Combine, Vindex, 1:16-scale, silver,
  1930s .... $2856 .... $6836 .... npf

John Deere Combine, Eska, 1:16-scale, green, lift lever
  made like the ones on the two bottom plows,
  1950s .... $96 .... $183 .... $343

John Deere Corn Picker, Eska, 1:16-scale, green, square
  letter decal, fits 60-, 620- and 730-style tractors,
  1950s .... $157 .... $238 .... $418

John Deere Disc, Ertl, 1:16-scale, green and yellow, 1970s,
  No. 583 .... $43 .... $86 .... $133

John Deere Elevator, Eska, 1:16-scale, green, 1950s
  .... $77 .... $183 .... $372

	EX	NM	MIP

John Deere Flail Chopper, Nygren (Custom), 1:16-scale, green, did not come in box, 1980s..... $18................. $36.........................n/a

John Deere Flare Box Wagon, Arcade/Strombecker, 1:16-scale, green, cast-iron running gear, wood box, 1940s .... $192................. $394..................... $769

John Deere Gas Engine, Vindex, 1:12-scale, green w/silver trim on pulley and flywheel, 1930s .... $321................. $927.........................npf

John Deere Grain Wagon, Vindex, 1:16-scale, green box w/red running gear, short tongue, cast iron, 1930s .... $927.............. $1732.........................npf

John Deere Manure Spreader, Eska, 1:16-scale, green, long levers, 1950s .... $61................. $109..................... $238

John Deere 2020, Wader (Custom), 1:16-scale, green, 1960s......................... $636................. $1382.........................npf

John Deere 3020, Ertl, 1:16-scale, green, two long fuel filters, wide front end, 1960s.......... $42................. $128..................... $243

John Deere 430, Ertl, 1:16-scale, yellow, w/o three-point hitch, 1950s .... $267................. $473..................... $1059

John Deere 440, Ertl, 1:16-scale, yellow, w/three-point hitch, 1950s .... $267................. $452..................... $983

John Deere 4440, Ertl, 1:16-scale, green, International Harvester front spindles, 1970s, No. 512 .... $29................. $54.....................$76

John Deere 620, Ertl, 1:16-scale, green, three-point hitch, no light on seat, 1950s................. $183................. $367..................... $1092

John Deere 730, Ertl, 1:16-scale, green, w/o three-point hitch, w/o ribbed front tires, w/o ribbed hole for muffler, w/o power steering decal, 1950s.............. $223................. $736..................... $893

John Deere A, Arcade, 1:16-scale, green w/nickel plated driver, solid rubber tires, 1940s..... $257................. $762..................... $3082

	EX	NM	MIP

John Deere D, Vindex, 1:16-scale, green w/yellow wheels, nickel-plated
drive, 1930s .... $582.............. $1757..........................npf

John Deere M, Auburn Rubber, 1:32-scale, orange, blue, red, pink, light
green, dark green and orange w/plastic wheels,
1950s .... $16................. $38........................$56

Massey-Ferguson

Massey-Ferguson Loader, Corgi, 1:43-scale, red,
1970s .... npf................. npf..........................npf

Massey-Ferguson Loader, Corgi, 1:43-scale,
silver, 1960s................ npf................. npf..........................npf

Massey-Ferguson Farm Set, Mercury, 1:43-scale, red,
1960s .... $543................... n/a..........................n/a

Massey-Ferguson 175, Ertl, 1:16-scale, red,
1960s .... $63................ $102...................... $143

Massey-Ferguson 44, Dinky, 1:43-scale, red,
1970s .... $28................. $73...................... $109

Massey-Harris

Massey-Harris Disc Harrow, Reuhl, 1:20-scale,
red, 1950 .... $153................ $307...................... $482

Massey-Harris Mower, Lincoln, 1:16-scale,
red, 1950s.................. $38................. $71...................... $143

Massey-Harris No. 11 Spreader, King, 1:16-scale,
red, 1950s.................. $42................. $98...................... $207

Massey-Harris, Lincoln, 1:16-scale, red,
1950s.................. $78................ $206...................... $382

Massey-Harris 44, Reuhl, 1:20-scale, red, all die-cast rims,
1950s .... $287................ $472...................... $864

	EX	NM	MIP

Massey-Harris 745 D, Matchbox, 1:16-scale, red,
1950s .... $238 .... $312 .... $647

Minneapolis-Moline

Minneapolis-Moline Disc, Carter, 1:16-scale, red,
1950s .... $168 .... $298 .... $568

Minneapolis-Moline Plow, Carter, 1:16-scale, red w/yellow
wheel rims, 1950s .... $98 .... $212 .... $333

Minneapolis-Moline Wood Wagon, Werner, 1:12-scale,
prairie gold, did not come in box,
1940s .... $33 .... $47 .... n/a

Minneapolis-Moline 4 Star, Slik, 1:24-scale, brown belly w/yellow
wheel centers, 1950s ... $33 .... $78 .... $172

Minneapolis-Moline 445, Slik, 1:24-scale, prairie gold w/red wheel
centers, also w/brown belly, w/new style Moline decal,
1950s .... $72 .... $163 .... $296

Minneapolis-Moline 5 Star, Mohr (Custom), 1:16-scale, yellow, custom,
available in Row Crop, wide front end and LP gas,
1980s .... $98 .... $152 .... $183

Minneapolis-Moline G LP, Cottonwood Acres, 1:16-scale, yellow,
1980s .... $98 .... $152 .... $183

Minneapolis-Moline G-1000, Ertl, 1:16-scale, yellow w/yellow rims,
1960s, No. 17 .... $122 .... $216 .... $393

Minneapolis-Moline G-1335, Ertl, 1:16-scale, yellow w/white rims,
1970s, No. 19 .... $122 .... $178 .... $282

Minneapolis-Moline Jr., Ertl, 1:25-scale, yellow, 1960s,
No. 15 .... $68 .... $138 .... $288

Minneapolis-Moline M-602, Mohr (Custom), 1:16-scale, yellow and
brown, wide front end, 1980s
.... $123 .... $168 .... $208

	EX	NM	MIP
Minneapolis-Moline R, Auburn Rubber, 1:16-scale, red, 1950s	$22	$52	$74
Minneapolis-Moline UB, Slik, 1:16-scale, yellow, 1950s	$122	$253	$487
Minneapolis-Moline UTS, Spec-Cast, 1:16-scale, yellow, rubber tires, 1980s	$22	$33	$43
Minneapolis-Moline Z, Auburn Rubber, 1:32-scale, prairie gold w/ white, red tires, 1940s	$38	$66	$138

Oliver

	EX	NM	MIP
Oliver Combine, Slik, 1:16-scale, green, 1950s	$88	$168	$356
Oliver Corn Picker, Slik, 1:16-scale, green, 1950s	$88	$146	$238
Oliver Harrow, Slik, 1:25-scale, red or green, 1940s	$6	$18	$38
Oliver Mower, Slik, 1:16-scale, green, 1950s	$122	$289	$448
Oliver Plow, Arcade, 1:16-scale, red, 1940s	$78	$168	$523
Oliver Wagon, Ertl, 1:16-scale, green, die-cast rims, 1960s, No. 23	$38	$83	$206
Oliver, Slik, 1:32-scale, green, 1960s	$12	$28	$89
Oliver 1800 A, Ertl, 1:16-scale, green, die-cast rims, long checkerboard decal, 1960s, No. 604	$122	$278	$762
Oliver 1850, Ertl, 1:16-scale, green, plastic rims, 1960s, No. 604	$42	$113	$243

	EX	NM	MIP

Oliver 1855, Ertl, 1:16-scale, green, wide front, 1970s,
No. 609 .... $98................ $189...................... $382

Oliver 70 Orchard, Hubley, 1:25-scale,
various, 1930s............ $78................ $192...................... $483

Oliver 77, Slik, 1:16-scale, green w/red wheel centers, non-steerable,
1950s......................... $98................ $189...................... $462

Oliver 880, Slik, 1:16-scale, green w/white wheel centers,
1950s......................... $78................ $162...................... $383

Oliver OC-6, Slik, 1:16-scale, yellow,
1960s......................... $198................ $482...................... $782

Oliver Super 44, SpecCast, 1:16-scale, green, Toy Tractor Times,
1980s......................... $33................. $48........................ $57

Oliver Super 55, Slik, 1:12-scale, green w/green rims,
1950s .... $268................ $582...................... $892

Oliver Super 77, Slik, 1:16-scale, green w/green rims,
1950s .... $243................ $447...................... $856

Fisher-Price

By Bruce R. Fox and John J. Murray

The history of Fisher-Price is filled with extreme dedication and commitment, beginning with the courageous ambitions of three founders determined to succeed in a business during one of the most traumatic times in American history, the Great Depression.

On Oct. 1, 1930, Fisher-Price Toys was founded by Herman G. Fisher and Irving Price and located in East Aurora, New York. Fisher was previously president and general manager of All-Fair Toys and Games of Churchville, New York. Price had retired early after a successful career with F. W. Wollworth Company. Fisher brought along with him many workers and designers from All-Fair, as well as business associate Helen Schelle. Schelle was instrumental in the success of Fisher-Price. For that reason, she is considered a company co-founder.

Their perseverance, belief in each other's abilities, and faith in their product made their little company grow, not by mountainous leaps, but steadily, year after year. Even before the company made any money, the founders decided that if and when there was a profit, it would be shared by all employees. This philosophy became

Left to right: #104 Lookee Monk (rear left), $600-$2,000; #103 Barky Puppy (rear left center), $600-$2,000; #102 Drummer Bear (rear right center), $600-$2,000; #105 Bunny Scoot (rear right), $1,500-$3,500; #350 Go 'n' Back Mule (middle left), $400-$1,200; #101 Granny Doodle (middle center), $600-$1,500; #100 Doctor Doodle (middle right), $600-$1,500; #355 Go 'n' Back Bruno (front left), $800-$2,500; and #360 Go 'n' Back Jumbo (front right), $400-$1,200.

reality after 1936 and continued through the Quaker Oats acquisition until the company was spun off as a separate entity in 1990.

The world's largest preschool toy company for 70-plus years continues to grow under the umbrella of Mattel. The number one toy brand will continue to mesmerize children, many of whom will want their childhood memories on a shelf in their grownup world.

Bruce R. Fox and John J. Murray are the co-authors of Fisher-Price, Historical, Rarity, and Value Guide, 1931-Present, *third edition, published by Krause Publications, Iola, Wis.*

Clockwise from left: # 717 Ducky Flip-Flap (rear left), $350-$750; #245 Riding Horse (rear center), $500-$1,100; #722 Racing Bunny Cart (rear right), $275-$475; # 799 Duckie Transport (front right), $400-$875; # 465 Teddy Choo-Choo (front center), $475-$825; # 766 Prancing Horses (front left), $800-$1,800; and #462 Busy Bunny (middle center), $400-$900.

Fisher-Price

Top 10 Lists

As experts on collecting Fisher-Price toys, we are often asked which toys we feel are the most valuable. We have compiled our Top 10 lists for various toy categories as a quick reference to the cream of the toy crop.

−Bruce R. Fox and John J. Murray

Toy Category	Toy Number	Remarks	Value (G-M)	Year Intro.
Adventure People				
TV Action Team	309	With all parts	$75-$140	1977
Alpha Probe	325	With all parts	$65-$135	1980
Sky Surfer	375	With all parts	$60-$125	1977
Adventure Series Safari	304	With all parts	$55-$115	1975
North Woods Trailblazer	312	With all parts	$65-$110	1977
Wilderness Patrol	307	With all parts	$50-$105	1976
Daredevil Sport Van	318	With all parts	$55-$100	1978
Alpha Star	326	With all parts	$45-$95	1983
Aero-Marine Search team	323	With all parts	$45-$80	1979
Dune Buster	322	With all parts	$40-$75	1979
Bears				
Go 'n' Back Bruno	355		$800-$2,500	1931
Road Roller	152		$800-$2,200	1934
Drummer Bear	102	With hat	$600-$2,000	1931
Teddy Bear Parade	195		$800-$1,700	1938

Clockwise from left: #185 Donald Duck Xylophone (rear left), $475-$925; # 195 Teddy Bear Parade (rear center), $800-$1,700; # 795 Mickey Mouse Drummer (rear right), $600-$1,200; #180 Snoopy Sniffer (middle right), $125-$475; #770 Doc & Dopey Dwarfs (front right), $975-$2,600; #425 Donald Duck Pop-Up (front center), $450-$1,100; #432 Mickey Mouse Choo-Choo (front left), $425-$1,275; and #550 Donald Duck Cart (middle left), $425-$900.

Toy Category	Toy Number	Remarks	Value (G-M)	Year Intro.
Bruno Bak-Up	375		$600-$1,700	1932
Drummer Bear	102	With hat	$600-$1,700	1932
Pushy Bruno	777	With stick	$600-$1,600	1933
Teddy Drummer	775		$700-$1,400	1936
Blackie Drummer	785		$550-$1,225	1939
Teddy Choo-Choo	465		$475-$825	1937

Circus-Themed

Woodsy-Wee Circus	201	With box	$750-$2,500	1931
Tumbling Tim	166	With stick	$900-$2,100	1939
Big Performing Circus	250	With all parts	$550-$1,800	1932
Teddy Bear Parade	195		$800-$1,700	1938
Johnny Jumbo	712		$600-$1,600	1933
Woodsy Circus Wagon	202	With all parts	$450-$1,500	1933
Blackie Drummer	785		$550-$1,225	1939
Circus Wagon	156		$525-$1,100	1942
The Band Wagon	198		$475-$985	1940
Fisher-Price Circus	900	With all parts	$325-$685	1962

Comic Character/Advertiser

Raggedy Ann and Andy	711		$1,400-$3,875	1941
American Airlines Flaghip	170	With props/tail	$975-$3,300	1941
Popeye	700		$800-$2,500	1935
Popeye Cowboy	705		$700-$2,300	1937
Popeye the Sailor	703		$700-$2,100	1936
Boom-Boom Popeye	491		$600-$1,600	1937

Left to right: #407 Chick Cart (rear left), $40-$90; #406 Bunny Cart (rear left center), $40-$90; #52 Rabbit Cart (rear right center), $60-$125; #51 Ducky Cart (rear right), $60-$125; #28 Bunny Egg Cart (front left), $100-$225; and #325 Buzzy Bee (front right), $35-$70.

Toy Category	Toy Number	Remarks	Value (G-M)	Year Intro.
Popeye Spinach Eater	488		$600-$1,600	1939
Elsie's Dairy Truck	745	With bottles	$475-$925	1948
Huckleberry Hound Zilo	711		$385-$800	1961
Flintstone Zilo	712		$395-$800	1962

Disney Toys

Donald Duck Bak-Up	358	With wings	$1,800-$6,500	1936
Donald and Donna Duck	160	With wings	$1,200-$3200	1937
Walt Disney Carnival	483	With box	$1,300-$3,000	1936
Trotting Donald Duck	741	With wings	$1,400-$2,800	1937
WD Easter Parade	475	With box	$1,200-$2,800	1936
Mickey Mouse Band	530	With stick	$1,000-$2,800	1935
Doc & Dopey Dwarfs	770		$975-$2,600	1938
Dogcart Donald	149		$800-$2,500	1936
Dough-Boy Donald	744		$900-$2,375	1942
Dumbo Circus Racer	738	With arms	$975-$2,350	1941

Dogs

Barky Buddy	150	With hat	$800-$2,000	1934
Barky Puppy	103		$600-$2,000	1931
Woodsy-Wee Dog Show	209	With box	$600-$2,000	1932
Scotty Dog	710		$700-$1,500	1933
Musical Mutt	725		$500-$1,200	1935
Puppy Bak-up	365	With ears/tail	$400-$1,200	1932
Ice Cream Wagon	778		$485-$1,150	1940
Hot Dog Wagon	750		$425-$975	1938
Hot Dog Wagon	764		$375-$875	1939
Kiltie Dog	450		$300-$800	1936

Clockwise from left: #630 Fire Truck (front left), $60-$110; #926 Concrete-Mixer Truck (middle left), $245-$485; #983 Safety School Bus (rear), $295-$675; #809 Pop 'n Ring (rear right), $45-$135; #148 Jack 'n Jill TV-Radio (front right), $55-$110; and #642 Dinkey Engine (center), $50-$90.

Toy Category	Toy Number	Remarks	Value (G-M)	Year Intro.

Dolls

Musical Baby Ann	204		$125-$225	1975
My Friend Karen	8121		$125-$200	1990
Special Birthday Mandy	4009		$75-$140	1985
Baby/Black Baby Soft Sounds	213/214		$60-$125	1980
Suzie Soft Sounds	201		$50-$95	1982
My Friend Christie	8120		$50-$95	1990
My Friend Mandy	210		$45-$95	1977
My Friend Nicky	206		$35-$60	1984
Fisher-Price Dolls	200-206		$30-$60	1974/ 1975
My Baby Beth	209		$30-$50	1978
My Friend Mandy	211		$30-$50	1979
My Friend Jenny	212		$30-$50	1979
My Friend Mikey	205		$30-$50	1982
My Friend Mandy	215		$30-$50	1982
My Friend Jenny	217		$30-$50	1982
My Friend Becky	218		$30-$50	1982
My New My Friend Jenny	209		$30-$50	1984
My New My Friend Mandy	216		$30-$50	1984

Easter Carts

Bouncing Bunny Cart	723		$600-$1,100	1936
Busy Bunny Cart	719		$500-$1,000	1936
Howdy Bunny	757	With ears	$425-$975	1939

Clockwise from left: #747 Talk-Back Telephone (front left), $75-$225; #145 Husky Dump Truck (rear left), $70-$140; #984 Safety School Bus (rear center), $285-$475; #169 Snorky Fire Engine (rear right), $175-$400; #191 Golden Gulch Express (front right), $110-$225; and #159 "Ten Little Indians" TV-Radio (front center), $25-$60.

Toy Category	Toy Number	Remarks	Value (G-M)	Year Intro.
Busy Bunny	462		$400-$900	1937
Bouncing Bunny Cart	727		$350-$900	1938
Duckie Transport	799	With wings	$400-$875	1937
Rock-A-Bye Bunny	788		$425-$775	1940
Ducky Flip Flap	717	With wings	$350-$750	1937
Cottontail Cart	525		$385-$675	1940
Rooster Cart	469		$325-$675	1938

Elephants

Dumbo Circus Racer	738	With arms	$975-$2,350	1941
Pushy Elephant	525	With stick	$600-$1,800	1934
Chubby Chief	110	With hat	$600-$1,700	1932
Johnny Jumbo	712		$600-$1,600	1933
Go 'n' Back Jumbo	360	With ears/tail	$400-$1,200	1931
Tiny Ding Dong	767		$425-$1,050	1940
Jumbo Xylo	780		$375-$725	1937
Musical Elephant	145	With ears/tail	$350-$695	1948
Juggling Jumbo	735		$235-$390	1958
Jumbo Rolo	755		$235-$360	1951

Horses

Dandy Dobbin

Stick Horse	6001	With stick	$900-$2,100	1936
Prancing Horses	766		$800-$1,800	1937
Horse & Wagon	605/610		$600-$1,800	1933/ 1934

Left to right: #904 Beginners Circus (rear left), $95-$155; #979 Dump Truckers (rear center), $60-$110; #728 Pound & Saw Bench (rear right), $20-$35; #138 Pony Chime (middle left), $55-$115; #131 Milk Wagon (middle left center rear), $35-$65; #724 Jolly Jalopy (middle left center front), $30-$60; #136 Lacing Shoe—with Play Family (middle right center), $60-$120; #154 "Pop Goes the Weasel" TV-Radio (middle right), $30-$55; #192 School Bus (front left), $75-$175; #476 Cookie Pig (front center), $30-$65; and #195 "Mary Had A Little Lamb" TV Music Box (front right), $30-$65.

Toy Category	Toy Number	Remarks	Value (G-M)	Year Intro.
Wheel Horse	200	With reins/tail	$600-$1,800	1934
Wheel Horse	225	With reins/tail	$600-$1,700	1935
Riding Horse	237	With reins/tail	$500-$1,600	1936
Racing Pony	705		$600-$1,500	1933
Kicking Donkey	175	With ears	$600-$1,300	1937
Racing Ponies	760		$500-$1,300	1936
Riding Horse	245	With reins/tail	$500-$1,100	1937

Musical Toys

"Farmer-in-the-Dell"
    Music Box .... 763 ...... With strap .... $75-$150 1962
"Farmer-in-the-Dell"
    Music Box Barn .... 764 ...... With strap .... $65-$135 1964
"Humpty Dumpty"
    Pocket Radio .... 765 .... $55-$125 1976
Music Box Lacing Shoe . 991 ...... With all parts $60-$110 1964
Musical Ferris Wheel ..... 969 ...... With all parts ..... $55-$110 1966
"Jack 'n Jill" TV-Radio148/155 .... $55-$110 .... 1959/
                                                             1968
"Old Woman in the Shoe"
    TV-Radio .... 161 .... $55-$110 1968
"Little Boy Blue" TV-Radio
                     . 158 .... $30-$95 1967
Musical Tick-Tock Clock997 .... $55-$90 1962
"Winnie the Pooh" Two Tune
    Music Box TV ...... 175 .... $45-$90 1971

Left to right: #915 Play Family Farm (rear), $35-$75; #686 Play Family Car & Camper (front left), $30-$50; #685 Play Family Car & Boat (front center), $30-$55; and #732 Happy Hauler (front right), $25-$45.

Toy Category	Toy Number	Remarks	Value (G-M)	Year Intro.

One Year Only Generic F-P

Skipper Sam	155	With oars	$1,500-$3,800	1934
Bunny Scoot	105	With ears	$1,500-$3,500	1931
Penelope Penguin	345		$1,200-$3,500	1935
Go 'n' Back Bruno	355		$800-$2,500	1931
Granny Doodle & Family	101	With bonnet	$600-$2,000	1933
Lookee Monk	104	With hat	$600-$2,000	1931
Drummer Bear	102	With hat	$600-$2,000	1931
Pushy Drummer	520		$600-$2,000	1934
Hot Mammy	810		$600-$1,800	1934
Hot Diggety	800		$600-$1,800	1934

Play Family and Little People Playsets

Safety School Bus	983	With all parts	$295-$675	1959
Nifty Station Wagon	234	With all parts	$295-$675	1960
Amusement Park	932	With all parts	$285-$585	1963
Safety School Bus	984	With all parts	$285-$475	1961
Snorky Fire Engine	168	With all parts	$185-$425	1960
Snorky Fire Engine	169	With all parts	$175-$400	1961
Safety School Bus	990	With all parts	$175-$295	1962
Play Family Sesame Street/ Clubhouse	938/937	With all parts	$75-$195	1975/ 1977
Play Family Castle	973	With all parts	$80-$190	1974
School Bus	192	With all parts	$75-$175	1965

Pop-Up Kritters

Donald Duck Pop-Up	425	With wings	$450-$1,100	1938
Tailspin Tabby (Banjo), $ 400			$400-$1,000	1931

Clockwise from left: #768 "Happy Birthday" Pocket Radio (front left), $15-$35; #995 Change-A-Record Music Box (middle left), $25-$50; #107 Music Box Clock Radio (rear left), $15-$35; #118 Tumble Tower (rear center), $15-$25; #104 Animal Scramble Game (rear right), $15-$30; #175 "Winnie the Pooh" Two Tune TV (front right), $45-$90; #156 Jiffy Dump Truck (front center), $15-$30 ; and #448 Mini-Copter (center), $15-$35.

Toy Category	Toy Number	Remarks	Value (G-M)	Year Intro.
Dizzy Dino	407		$300-$800	1931
Stoopy Storky (Banjo)	410		$300-$800	1931
Lofty Lizzy	405		$300-$800	1931
Pop-Up Rooster	476	With wings	$375-$700	1936
Goofy Gerty	440		$200-$700	1935
Lop-Ear Looie	415		$150-$400	1934
Jumbo Jitterbug	422	With ears	$165-$375	1940
Dizzy Donkey	433		$85-$175	1939

Pre-War Push-Toys

Mickey Mouse Band	530	With stick	$1,000-$2,800	1935
Pushy Piggy	500	With stick	$800-$2,300	1932
Tumbling Tim	166	With stick	$900-$2,100	1939
Pushy Doodle	507	With stick	$600-$2,000	1933
Pushy Drummer	520	With stick	$600-$2,000	1934
Pushy Elephant	525	With stick	$600-$1,800	1934
Choo-Choo Local	517	With stick	$600-$1,800	1936
Tricky Tommy	470	With stick	$700-$1,600	1936
Pushy Bruno	777	With stick	$600-$1,600	1933
Pushy Pat	515	With stick	$600-$1,500	1933

Post-War Push-Toys

Musical Sweeper	100	With stick	$135-$235	1950
Looky Push Car	875	With stick	$120-$190	1962
Corn Popper	785	With stick	$65-$175	1957
Musical Sweeper	225	With stick	$70-$160	1953

Toy Category	Toy Number	Remarks	Value (G-M)	Year Intro.
Roller-Chime	123	With stick	$70-$135	1953
Pop 'n Ring	808/809	With stick	$45-$135	1956/ 1959
Musical Sweeper	230	With stick	$60-$125	1956
Musical Push Chime	722	With stick	$50-$125	1950
Music Box Sweeper	131	With stick	$60-$120	1961
Ducky Flip-Flap	715	With stick	$40-$85	1964

Trains

Toy Category	Toy Number	Remarks	Value (G-M)	Year Intro.
Streamline Express	215		$800-$2,300	1935
Choo-Choo Local	517	With stick	$600-$1,800	1936
Pushy Pat	515	With stick	$600-$1,500	1933
Tabby Ding Dong	730		$625-$1,450	1939
Mickey Mouse Choo-Choo	432		$425-$1,275	1938
Tiny Ding Dong	767		$425-$1,050	1940
Teddy Choo-Choo	465		$475-$825	1937
Donald Duck Choo-Choo	450		$325-$675	1940
Peter Bunny Engine	715		$200-$475	1941
Looky Chug-Chug	161	With coal car	$250-$400	1949

Trucks

Toy Category	Toy Number	Remarks	Value (G-M)	Year Intro.
Scoop Loader	300		$25-$75	1975
Shovel Digger	301		$25-$75	1975
Dump Truck	302		$25-$75	1975

Toy Category	Toy Number	Remarks	Value (Good-Mint), $	Year Introduced
Bull Dozer	311		$25-$75	1975
Roller Grader	313		$25-$75	1976
Boom Crane	314		$25-$75	1978
Cement Mixer	315		$25-$75	1978
Tow Truck	316		$25-$75	1978
Rescue Rig	337		$35-$65	1981
Police Patrol Squad	332		$35-$65	1981
Power Tow	338		$35-$65	1982
Fire Pumper	336		$35-$65	1983
Power & Light Service Rig	339		$35-$65	1983
Farm Set	331		$30-$55	1981
Hook & Ladder	319		$20-$50	1979
Race Car Rig	320		$20-$50	1979
Fire Fighters	321		$20-$50	1979
Highway Dump Truck	328		$20-$50	1980
Dozer Loader	329		$20-$50	1980
Rodeo Rig	330		$20-$50	1980
Load Master Dump	327		$20-$45	1984

Vehicles

Transport Trucks	900		$700-$1400	1934
Elsie's Dairy Truck	745		$475-$925	1948
Campbell Kid's Farm Truck	845		$325-$750	1954
Mickey Mouse Safety Patrol	733		$265-$575	1956

Toy Category	Toy Number	Remarks	Value (G-M)	Year Intro.
Egg Truck	749		$245-$575	1947
Doggy Racer	7		$285-$525	1942
Concrete-Mixer Truck	926		$245-$485	1959
Teddy Station Wagon	480		$285-$475	1942
Bunny Racer	474		$250-$475	1942
Teddy Trucker	711		$245-$395	1949

Xylophones

Toy Category	Toy Number	Remarks	Value (G-M)	Year Intro.
Donald & Donna Duck	160		$1,200-$3,200	1937
Mickey Mouse Xylophone	798		$575-$1,250	1939
Donald Duck Xylophone	185		$475-$925	1938
Mickey Mouse Xylophone	798		$450-$925	1942
Fred Flintstone Zilo	712		$395-$800	1962
Huckleberry Hound Xylophone	711		$385-$800	1961
Jumbo Xylophone	780		$375-$725	1937
Donald Duck Xylophone	177		$350-$675	1946
Mickey Mouse Xylophone	714		$300-$675	1963
Teddy Xylophone	752		$250-$425	1946

Games

Board games and tabletop games as we think of them really got their steam in the Victorian age. McLoughlin Bros. produced some of the best stuff of the era, with gorgeously lithographed packages and games. McLoughlin was purchased by the (now) much better-known Milton Bradley in 1920. Milton Bradley's re-issues of McLoughlin games don't command the same prices as the originals, as you would expect. Parker Brothers, too, is a venerable and recognized force in the world of games, producing them from 1883 until the present day.

Most collectors of games break the hobby into two segments: pre-war and post-war. Of course, most post-war games have a common denominator—television. Games based on TV shows are probably one of the hottest segments in the field. Their box graphics are bright and recognizable, and the shows they represent conjure up pure nostalgia. The market has fallen off a bit on these items in the past three years or so, but that just makes them easier for the collector to pick up.

These pop-culture games, along with early electronic games, are likely to be best bets for collectors. Avoid word games like Scrabble—they just don't appreciate much.

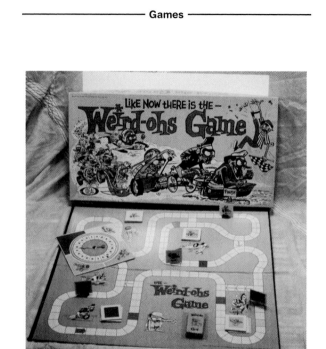

Weird-Ohs board game, Ideal, 1964, $230 MIP.

Games

Postwar Games
Board Games

	EX	NM	MIP
20,000 Leagues Under the Sea, 1950s, Gardner			
	$25	$55	$100
Addams Family, 1965, Ideal			
	$50	$75	$175
Alfred Hitchcock presents Mystery Game "Why," 1958,			
Milton Bradley	$20	$35	$55
All Star Baseball, 1960s, Cadaco-Ellis			
	$20	$50	$75
Annie Oakley (larger), 1955 Milton Bradley			
	$20	$50	$75
Apollo: A Voyage to the Moon, 1969, Tracianne			
	$12	$30	$40
Atom Ant Game, 1966, Transogram			
	$25	$60	$90
Babes in Toyland, 1961, Whitman			
	$15	$35	$50
Barbie, Queen of the Prom, 1960,			
Mattel	$30	$60	$85
Barbie's Little Sister Skipper Game,			
1964, Mattel	$15	$40	$60
Bart Starr Quarterback Game, 1960s			
	$175	$295	$450
Batman Game, 1966,			
Milton Bradley	$25	$60	$90

Bewitched Stymie Card Game, Milton Bradley, 1960s, $50 MIP.

Canadian version of "Battlestar Galactic" game, $25 MIP.

	EX	NM	MIP
Battlestar Galactica, 1978, Parker Brothers	$10	$15	$25
Beatles Flip Your Wig Game, 1964, Milton Bradley	$85	$150	$250
Beverly Hillbillies Game, 1963, Standard Toykraft, "If you like the T.V. show...you'll love the game..."	$25	$55	$80
Bewitched, 1965	$50	$80	$120
Bible Baseball, 1950's, Standard	$50	$75	$150
Bonanza Michigan Rummy Game, 1964, Parker Brothers	$20	$35	$70
Branded, 1966, Milton Bradley	$20	$50	$90
Calling All Cars, 1930s-40s, Parker Brothers	$40	$50	$100
Can You Catch It Charlie Brown?, 1976, Ideal	$10	$25	$35
Candyland, 1949, Milton Bradley	$25	$50	$75
Captain America, 1966, Milton Bradley	$40	$65	$105
Captain Kangaroo, 1956, Milton Bradley	$20	$45	$100
Challenge the Yankees, 1960s, Hasbro	$200	$400	$600
Charlie Brown's All Star Baseball Game, 1965, Parker Brothers	$18	$45	$65

The "Bonanza" game "as played by the Cartwrights at their Ponderosa ranch..." from 1964 is valued at $70 MIP.

"Benji" game from the 1970s, $22 MIP.

	EX	NM	MIP
Charlie's Angels (Farrah Fawcett box), 1977,			
Milton Bradley	$10	$20	$45
Charlotte's Web Game, 1974,			
Hasbro	$10	$25	$35
Chutes & Ladders, 1956,			
Milton Bradley	$10	MN$15	$25
Clue, 1949,			
Parker Brothers	$25	$40	$65
Columbo, 1973,			
Milton Bradley	$6	$10	$15
Coney Island, The Game of, 1956, Selchow &			
Righter	$20	$50	$100
Dallas, 1985,			
Maruca Industries	$17	$35	$55
Dennis The Menace Baseball Game,			
1960	$22	$50	$70
Dick Tracy Crime Stopper, 1963,			
Ideal	$20	$50	$75
Dick Van Dyke Board Game, 1964, Standard			
Toykraft	$65	$100	$175
Doctor Who, 1980s,			
Denys Fisher	$35	$75	$100
Dogfight, 1962,			
Milton Bradley	$35	$65	$100
Donald Duck Pins & Bowling Game, 1955s,			
Pressman	$35	$60	$90
Dr. Kildare, 1962,			
Ideal	$20	$35	$50

"Charlie's Angels" board game with Farrah Fawcett box, $45 MIP.

Beatles Flip Your Wig game, Milton Bradley, 1960s, $250 MIP.

	EX	NM	MIP
Dracula Mystery Game, 1960s, Hasbro	$80	$160	$225
Dungeons & Dragons, Electronic, 1980, Mattel	$12	$30	$40
Eliot Ness and the Untouchables, 1961, Transogram	$30	$70	$100
F.B.I., 1958, Transogram	$35	$55	$90
Family Affair, 1967, Whitman	$25	$40	$65
Flagship Airfreight: The Airplane Cargo Game, 1946, Milton Bradley	$40	$70	$115
Flash Gordon, 1977, Waddington/House Of Games	$10	$25	$35
Flintstones, 1971, Milton Bradley	$6	$15	$25
Flying Nun Game, The, 1968, Milton Bradley	$15	$25	$40
G.I. Joe Card Game, 1965, Whitman	$10	$15	$25
Gene Autry's Dude Ranch Game, 1950s, Warren/Built-Rite	$25	$50	$75
George of the Jungle Game, 1968, Parker Brothers	$40	$90	$125
Gilligan's Island, 1965, Game Gems	$125	$250	$600
Godzilla, 1960s, Ideal	$100	$250	$400
Gomer Pyle Game, 1960s, Transogram	$15	$30	$45
Gong Show Game, 1975, Milton Bradley	$15	$25	$40

"The Flintstones" game from 1971 is popular with character toy collectors, too, $25 MIP.

Knockout Electronic Boxing Game, Northwestern Products, $240 MIP.

	EX	NM	MIP
Good Ol' Charlie Brown Game, 1971,			
Milton Bradley	$8	$20	$30
Goodbye Mr. Chips Game, 1969,			
Parker Brothers	$8	$20	$30
Groucho's TV Quiz Game, 1954,			
Pressman	$30	$50	$75
Groucho's You Bet Your Life, 1955,			
Lowell	$25	$50	$75
Gunsmoke Game, 1950s,			
Lowell	$40	$65	$100
Hank Aaron Baseball Game, 1970s,			
Ideal	$50	$80	$125
Happy Days, 1976,			
Parker Brothers	$8	$20	$30
Hardy Boys Mystery Game, Secret of Thunder Mountain, 1978,			
Parker Brothers	$7	$15	$25
Hardy Boys Mystery Game, The, 1968,			
Milton Bradley	$6	$15	$25
Hobbit Game, The, 1978,			
Milton Bradley	$25	$60	$85
Hogan's Heroes Game, 1966,			
Transogram	$45	$85	$120
Honeymooners Game, The, 1986,			
TSR	$7	$12	$20
Hopalong Cassidy Chinese Checkers Game,			
1950s	$20	$50	$75
Hot Wheels Wipe-Out Game, 1968,			
Mattel	$15	$35	$50

From the Milton Bradley "Gamemaster" series, "Axis & Allies," a great World War II board game with miniature planes, troops, tanks, and ships, $45 MIP.

I Dream of Jeannie Game, Milton Bradley, 1965, $100 MIP.

	EX	NM	MIP
Howdy Doody Quiz Show, 1950s, Multiple Products	$20	$40	$75
Howdy Doody's Three Ring Circus, 1950, Harett-Gilmar	$35	$60	$100
Howdy Doody's TV Game, 1950s, Milton Bradley	$35	$50	$100
I Dream of Jeannie Game, 1965, Milton Bradley	$30	$75	$100
I Spy, 1965, Ideal	$35	$75	$100
Indiana Jones: Raiders of The Lost Ark, 1981, Kenner	$20	$35	$55
Jack and The Beanstalk, 1946, National Games	$25	$45	$65
Jackie Gleason's and AW-A-A-A-Y We Go!, 1956, Transogram	$60	$100	$150
James Bond 007 Goldfinger Game, 1966, Milton Bradley	$35	$60	$85
James Bond Message From M Game, 1966, Ideal	$100	$250	$350
Jerry Kramer's Instant Replay, 1970, EMD Enterprises	$15	$25	$40
Jonny Quest Game, 1964, Transogram	$200	$500	$700
Land of The Giants, 1968, Ideal	$60	$125	$175
Lassie Game, 1965, Game Gems	$10	$35	$75
Laugh-In's Squeeze Your Bippy Game, 1968 Hasbro	$35	$75	$100

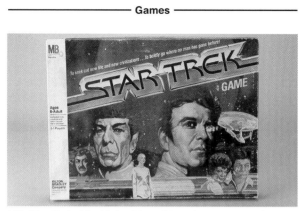

This "Star Trek—The Motion Picture" board game valued at $50 in mint condition.

"The Six Million Dollar Man" game from 1975 is an affordable $15 MIP item.

	EX	NM	MIP
Let's Make a Deal, 1964,			
Milton Bradley	$12	$30	$40
Life, The Game of, 1960,			
Milton Bradley	$8	$20	$30
Lord of the Rings, The, 1979,			
Milton Bradley	$40	$85	$110
Lost in Space Game, 1965,			
Milton Bradley	$35	$75	$100
M Squad, 1958,			
Bell Toys	$35	$75	$125
Masquerade Party, 1955,			
Bettye-B	$45	$75	$100
Matchbox Traffic Game, 1960s,			
Bronner	$25	$45	$70
McHale's Navy Game, 1962,			
Transogram	$30	$40	$65
Mickey Mantle's Big League Baseball,			
1958, Gardner	$125	$250	$325
Mickey Mouse, 1950,			
Jacmar	$35	$55	$90
Mighty Mouse Rescue Game, 1960s,			
Harett-Gilmar	$20	$50	$75
Mission: Impossible, 1967,			
Ideal	$40	$100	$135
Mr. Ed Game, 1962,			
Parker Brothers	$20	$50	$75
Monkees Game, 1968,			
Transogram	$45	$100	$150

Walt Disney Snap-Out Target game, T. Cohn, 1960s, $65.

	EX	NM	MIP
Munsters Drag Race Game, 1965, Hasbro	$250	$600	$1000
Muppet Show, 1977, Parker Brothers	$6	$15	$25
My Favorite Martian, 1963, Transogram	$50	$90	$125
Mystery Date, 1965, Milton Bradley	$60	$125	$225
Name That Tune, 1959, Milton Bradley	$12	$20	$30
Nancy Drew Mystery Game, 1957, Parker Brothers	$35	$100	$175
Newlywed Game (2nd Ed.), 1967, Hasbro	$11	$22	$35
Peanuts: The Game of Charlie Brown And His Pals, 1959, Selchow & Righter	$20	$30	$50
Planet of the Apes, 1974, Milton Bradley	$18	$45	$65
Playoff Football, 1970s, Crestline	$20	$35	$50
Pony Express, Game of, 1947, Polygon	$12	$40	$60
Rawhide, 1959, Lowell	$100	$250	$400
Red Barber's Big League Baseball Game, 1950s, G & R Anthony	$350	$800	$1000
Red Herring, 1945, Cadaco-Ellis	$12	$40	$60
Rifleman Game, 1959, Milton Bradley	$20	$50	$75

1954 Uncle Wiggily Game from Milton Bradley and 1977 Uncle Wiggily Game ($30 MIP) from Parker Brothers/General Mills.

	EX	NM	MIP
Rin Tin Tin Game, 1950s,			
Transogram	$20	$50	$65
Risk, 1959,			
Parker Brothers	$25	$50	$75
Road Runner Game, 1968,			
Milton Bradley	$10	$25	$35
S.O.S., 1947, Durable Toy &			
Novelty	$40	$70	$110
Scooby-Doo, Where are You?, 1973,			
Milton Bradley	$18	$40	$50
Sherlock Holmes, 1950s,			
National Games	$30	$60	$75
Sinking of The Titanic, The, 1976,			
Ideal	$25	$40	$60
Six Million Dollar Man, 1975,			
Parker Brothers	$5	$10	$15
Snagglepuss Fun at the Picnic Game, 1961,			
Transogram	$40	$50	$75
Snoopy & The Red Baron, 1970,			
Milton Bradley	$15	$35	$50
Snoopy Game, 1960, Selchow &			
Righter	$25	$45	$70
Sports Illustrated All Time All Star Baseball, 1973,			
Sports Illustrated	$75	$175	$250
Star Trek, 1979,			
Milton Bradley	$18	$40	$50
Television, 1953,			
National Novelty	$35	$75	$100

	EX	NM	MIP
Tell It To The Judge, 1959, Parker Brothers	$12	$35	$50
Three Musketeers, 1958, Milton Bradley	$35	$55	$90
Three Stooges Fun House Game, 1950s, Lowell	$100	$275	$400
Tom & Jerry Adventure in Blunderland, 1965, Transogram	$25	$45	$70
Trapped (Ellery Queen's), 1956, Bettye-B	$30	$70	$100
Treasure Island, 1954, Harett-Gilmar	$20	$40	$60
Twilight Zone Game, 1960s, Ideal	$75	$100	$200
Twister, 1966, Milton Bradley	$5	$15	$20
Wanted Dead or Alive, 1959, Lowell	$50	$75	$125
Wendy, The Good Little Witch, 1966, Milton Bradley	$60	$135	$175
What's My Line Game, 1950s, Lowell	$15	$35	$50
Who Framed Roger Rabbit?, 1987, Milton Bradley	$20	$35	$55
Wild, Wild West, The, 1966, Transogram	$150	$350	$500
Winnie The Pooh Game, 1959, Parker Brothers	$30	$50	$80

	EX	NM	MIP
Yogi Bear Break A Plate Game, 1960s, Transogram	$50	$80	$100
Zorro Game, Walt Disney's, 1966, Parker Brothers	$18	$40	$65

Card Games

	EX	NM	MIP
Archie Bunker's Card Game, 1972, Milton Bradley	$6	$15	$20
Baseball Card Game, Official, 1965, Milton Bradley	$20	$50	$60
Batman Card Game, 1966, Ideal	$20	$65	$85
Bewitched Stymie Game, 1960s, Milton Bradley	$15	$40	$50
Bullwinkle Card Game, 1962, Ed-U-Cards	$10	$30	$40
Daniel Boone Wilderness Trail, 1964, Transogram	$10	$40	$65
Dick Tracy Playing Card Game, 1934, Whitman	$25	$60	$75
Flintstones Cut-Ups Game, 1963, Whitman	$15	$45	$60
Howdy Doody Card Game, 1954, Russell	$20	$30	$50
Know Your States, 1955, Garrard Press	$10	$25	$45
Li'l Abner's Spoof Game, 1950, Milton Bradley	$65	$95	$135

	EX	NM	MIP
Man from U.N.C.L.E. Illya Kuryakin Card Game, 1966,			
Milton Bradley	$10	$25	$30
Monster Old Maid, 1964,			
Milton Bradley	$10	$40	$55
Munsters Card Game, 1966,			
Milton Bradley	$20	$45	$65
Nuclear War, 1965,			
Douglas Malewicki	$25	$40	$75
Superheroes Card Game, 1978,			
Milton Bradley	$15	$30	$55

Skill Games

	EX	NM	MIP
Chutes Away!, 1978,			
Gabriel	$15	$60	$85
Don't Break the Ice, 1960s,			
Schaper	$5	$16	$25
Hoc-Key, 1958,			
Cadaco-Ellis	$10	$35	$50
On Target, 1973,			
Milton Bradley	$12	$40	$60
Sharpshooter, 1962,			
Cadaco-Ellis	$12	$30	$40

Skill/Action Games

	EX	NM	MIP
Airways, 1950s, Lindstrom Tool &			
Toy	$30	$50	$75
Batman Batarang Toss, 1966,			
Pressman	$150	$250	$400

	EX	NM	MIP
Batman Pin Ball, 1966, Marx	$55	$95	$150
Bats in the Belfry, 1964, Mattel	$20	$55	$80
Bowl-A-Matic, 1963, Eldon	$100	$250	$350
Candid Camera Target Shot, 1950s, Lindstrom Tool & Toy	$35	$60	$70
Deputy Dawg Hoss Toss, 1973	$15	$25	$40
Fireball XL-5 Magnetic Dart Game, 1963, Magic Wand	$75	$125	$200
Hands Down, 1965, Ideal	$10	$15	$25
Hopalong Cassidy Bean Bag Toss Game, 1950s	$20	$40	$60
Howdy Doody Dominoes Game, 1950s, Ed-U-Cards	$60	$100	$150
Johnny Apollo Moon Landing Bagatelle, 1969, Marx	$20	$35	$55
Mechanical Shooting Gallery, 1950s, Wyandotte	$70	$135	$195
Mickey Mouse Haunted House Bagatelle, 1950s	$210	$350	$550
Mouse Trap, 1963, Ideal	$25	$45	$70
Pro Bowl Live Action Football, 1960s, Marx	$35	$65	$95
Rat Patrol Spin Game, 1967, Pressman	$30	$65	$85
Superman Spin Game, 1967, Pressman	$40	$65	$105

G.I. Joe

By Karen O'Brien

"G.I. Joe, G.I. Joe. Fighting man from head to toe. On the land, on the sea, in the air . . ."

To children in the 1960s, this familiar phrase signaled the arrival of a G.I. Joe television commercial. It is one of the few advertising slogans to stand the test of time, and still brings smiles to the grown-ups who remember dashing to the television to see the latest G.I. Joe figures.

G.I. Joe revolutionized the toy industry in the 1960s. A twelve-inch action figure made especially for boys had never been attempted and Hasbro's secret project had to overcome several challenges. Would the public embrace G.I. Joe as a military action figure? Or would it be perceived as a doll for boys? Hasbro decided that G.I. Joe was worth the gamble and launched an extensive advertising campaign portraying G.I. Joe as "America's Movable Fighting Man."

Today, G.I. Joe is acknowledged as the first action figure and its articulated design set the standard for all action toys following in its boot tracks. Hasbro shattered the potential stigma of "boys playing with dolls" by offering boys a fully articulated, movable man of action, not a doll. G.I. Joe accomplished for boys in 1964 what Barbie accomplished five years earlier for girls—it allowed boys to role-play any situation their imaginations could dream up.

Karen O'Brien is the editor of numerous books on toy collecting, including Toys & Prices, 11th edition *and* O'Brien's Collecting Toys Identification & Value Guide, *both published by Krause Publications, Iola, Wis.*

Covert Commando Team. 1997, $50 MIP.

Arctic Mission Team. 1997, $35 MIP.

G.I. Joe

Original Series and Adventure Team (1964-78)
Action Marine Series
Figure Sets

	EX	NM	MIP

Action Marine, 1964, Hasbro, fatigues, green cap, boots, dog tags, insignias and manual, Model No. 7700
.... $125............... $145...................... $375

Marine Medic Series, 1967, Hasbro, Red Cross helmet, flag and arm bands, crutch, bandages, splints, first aid pouch, stethoscope, plasma bottle, stretcher, medic bag, belt with ammo pouches. Model No. 90711 ..... $325............... $425.................... $3250

Talking Action Marine, 1967, Hasbro, Model No. 7790 .... $175............... $200...................... $850

Uniform/Equipment Sets

Beachhead Assault Field Pack Set, 1964, Hasbro, M-1 rifle, bayonet, entrenching shovel and cover, canteen with cover, belt, mess kit with cover, field pack, flamethrower, first aid pouch, tent, pegs and poles, tent camo and camo, Model No. 7713 .... $100............... $175...................... $325

Beachhead Flamethrower Set, 1964, Hasbro Model No. 7718 .... $15............... $30...................... $125

Beachhead Mess Kit Set, 1964, Hasbro, Model No. 7716 .... $25............... $40...................... $275

Beachhead Rifle Set, 1964, Hasbro, bayonet, cartridge belt, hand grenades and M-1 rifle, Model No. 7717 .... $30............... $50...................... $150

Communications Post and Poncho Set, 1964, Hasbro, field radio and telephone, wire roll, carbine, binoculars, map, case, manual, poncho, Model No. 7701 $125........... $175...................... $475

Cobra Viper Team, figure with flight pod, $50 MIP.

One of the many styles of G.I. Joe Footlocker, $175 MIP.

	EX	NM	MIP

Jungle Fighter Set, 1967, Hasbro, bush hat, jacket with emblems, pants, flamethrower, field telephone, knife and sheath, pistol belt, pistol, holster, canteen with cover, and knuckle knife,

    Model No. 7732 .... $450 .... $700 .... $3500

Marine Basics Set, 1966, Hasbro,

    Model No. 7722 .... $55 .... $85 .... $275

Paratrooper Camouflage Set, 1964, Hasbro, netting and foliage,

    Model No. 7708 .... $20 .... $35 .... $65

Paratrooper Parachute Pack, 1964, Hasbro,

    Model No. 7709 .... $30 .... $80 .... $125

Tank Commander Set, 1967, Hasbro, includes faux leather jacket, helmet and visor, insignia, radio with tripod, machine gun, ammo box, Model No. 7731 $325 .... $500 .... $1750

Action Pilot Series

Figure Sets

Action Pilot, 1964, Hasbro, orange jumpsuit, blue cap, black boots, dog tags, insignias, manual, catalog, and club application.

    Model No. 7800 .... $130 .... $165 .... $600

Uniform/Equipment Sets

Air Academy Cadet Set, 1967, Hasbro, deluxe set with figure, dress jacket, shoes, and pants, garrison cap, saber and scabbard, white M-1 rifle, chest sash, and belt sash,

    Model No. 7822 .... $225 .... $450 .... $1250

Air Force Basics Set, 1966, Hasbro,

    Model No. 7814 .... $30 .... $55 .... $200

Air Force Police Set, 1965, Hasbro,

    Model No. 7813 .... $70 .... $150 .... $250

G.I. Joe Action Soldier, blond, from 1965, $350 MIP.

	EX	NM	MIP

Air Force Security Set, 1967, Hasbro, Air Security radio and helmet, cartridge belt, pistol and holster,
Model No. 7815 .... $275.............. $350.................... $590

Air/Sea Rescue Set, 1967, Hasbro, includes black air tanks, rescue ring, buoy, depth gauge, face mask, fins, orange scuba outfit, Model No. 7825 .... $325.............. $550.................... $2500

Astronaut Set, 1967, Hasbro, helmet with visor, foil space suit, booties, gloves, space camera, propellant gun, tether cord, oxygen chest pack, silver boots, white jumpsuit, and cloth cap,
Model No. 7824 .... $100.............. $200.................... $3000

Fighter Pilot Set, 1967, Hasbro, working parachute and pack, gold helmet, Mae West vest, green pants, flash light, orange jump suit, black boots,
Model No. 7823 .... $400.............. $650.................... $2500

Scramble Communication Set, 1965, Hasbro, poncho, field telephone and radio, map with case, binoculars, and wire roll,
Model No. 7812 .... $35................ $75.................... $175

Scramble Parachute Set, 1964, Hasbro, Model No. 7811
.... $20................ $40.................... $150

Scramble Set, 1964, Hasbro, deluxe set, gray flight suit, orange air vest, white crash helmet, pistol belt with .45 pistol, holster, clipboard, flare gun, and parachute with insert,
Model No. 7807 .... $125.............. $225.................... $950

Survival Life Raft Set, 1964, Hasbro, raft with oar, flare gun, knife, air vest, first aid kit, sea anchor, and manual,
Model No. 7801 .... $75.............. $125.................... $550

Vehicle Sets

Crash Crew Fire Truck Set, 1967, Hasbro, Includes blue truck and fireproof silver suit, truck has working fire hose,
Model No. 8040 .... $950.............. $1700.................... $3500

Flocked hair G.I. Joe, part of the new look for the "Adventure Team" starting in 1970, $80 MIP.

	EX	NM	MIP

Official Space Capsule Set, 1966, Hasbro, space capsule, record, space
suit, cloth space boots, space gloves, helmet with visor,
Model No. 8020 .... $175............... $225...................... $350

Action Sailor Series
Figure Sets
Action Sailor, 1964, Hasbro, white cap, denim shirt and pants, boots,
dog tags, navy manual, and insignias,
Model No. 7600 .... $125............... $225...................... $350

Uniform/Equipment Sets

Deep Sea Diver Set, 1965, Hasbro underwater uniform, helmet, upper
and lower plate, sledge hammer, buoy with rope, gloves, compass,
hoses, lead boots, and weight belt,
Model No 7620 .... $325............... $425.................... $2000

Frogman Underwater Demolition Set, 1964, Hasbro, headpiece, face
mask, swim fins, rubber suit, scuba tank, depth gauge, knife,
dynamite, and manual,
Model No. 7602 .... $175............... $250.................... $1500

Landing Signal Officer, 1966, Hasbro, jumpsuit, signal paddles,
goggles, cloth head gear, headphones, clipboard (complete),
binoculars, and flare gun,
Model No. 7621 .... $225............... $350...................... $575

Navy Attack Helmet Set, 1964, shirt and pants, boots, yellow life vest,
blue helmet, flare gun, binoculars, signal flags,
Model No. 7610 .... $35................. $75...................... $150

Navy Basics Set, 1966, Hasbro,
Model No. 7628 .... $25................. $55...................... $125

Navy L.S.O. Equipment Set, 1966, Hasbro, helmet,
headphones, signal paddles, flare gun,
Model No. 7626 .... $40................. $80...................... $150

U.S. Army Infantry Soldier, limited collectors' edition, 1996, $30 MIP.

	EX	NM	MIP

Navy Machine Gun Set, 1965, Hasbro, MG and ammo box,
Model No. 7618 .... $40................. $80..................... $175
Sea Rescue Set, 1964, Hasbro, life raft, oar, anchor, flare gun, first-aid
kit, knife, scabbard, manual,
Model No. 7601 .... $95............... $135....................... $500
Shore Patrol Dress Jumper Set, 1964, Hasbro,
Model No. 7613 .... $75............... $125..................... $225

Vehicle Sets
Official Sea Sled and Frogman Set, 1966, Hasbro, without cave,
Model No. 8050 .... $150............... $300................. $550

Action Soldier Series
Figure Sets
Action Soldier, 1964, Hasbro, fatigue cap, shirt, pants, boots, dog tags,
army manual and insignias, helmet, belt with pouches, M-1 rifle,
Model No. 7500 .... $100............... $175..................... $350
Canadian Mountie Set, 1967, Hasbro, Sears Exclusive,
Model No. 5904 .... $850.............. $1500.................... $4000

Uniform/Equipment Sets
Adventure Pack with sixteen items, 1968, Hasbro, Adventure Pack
Footlocker, Model No. 8007.83
.... $75............... $125...................... $600
Adventure Pack, Army Bivouac Series, 1968, Hasbro,
Model No. 7549-83 .. $225............... $450.................... $3500
Combat Camouflaged Netting Set, 1964, Hasbro, foliage, and posts,
Model No. 7511 .... $25................. $40........................ $85
Combat Construction Set, 1967, Hasbro, orange
safety helmet, work gloves, jack hammer,
Model No. 7572 .... $325................. $400..................... $575

British S.A.S. limited collectors' edition, 1996, $30 MIP.

	EX	NM	MIP

Combat Demolition Set, 1967, Hasbro,
Model No. 7573 .... $65.............. $100...................... $525

Combat Engineer Set, 1967, Hasbro, pick, shovel, detonator, dynamite,
tripod, and transit with grease gun,
Model No. 7571 .... $125.............. $175...................... $625

Combat Field Pack Deluxe Set, 1964, Hasbro, field jacket, pack,
entrenching shovel with cover, mess kit, first-aid pouch, canteen
with cover, Model No. 7502
.... $75.............. $125...................... $325

Command Post Field Radio and Telephone Set, 1964,
Hasbro, field radio, telephone with wire roll, and map,
Model No. 7520 .... $35.............. $70...................... $135

Dress Parade Adventure Pack, 1968, Hasbro, Adventure
Pack with thirty-seven pieces,
Model No. 8009.83... $750.............. $1250...................... $3500

Heavy Weapons Set, 1967, Hasbro mortar launcher and shells,
M-60 machine gun, grenades, flak jacket, shirt and pants,
Model No. 7538 .... $175.............. $325...................... $1750

Mountain Troops Set, 1964, Hasbro, snow shoes, ice axe, ropes,
grenades, camouflage pack, web belt, manual,
Model No. 7530 .... $90.............. $175...................... $350

Sabotage Set, 1967, Hasbro, dingy and oar, blinker light, detonator with
strap, TNT, wool stocking cap, gas mask, binoculars,
green radio, and .45 pistol and holster,
Model No. 7516 .... $125.............. $250...................... $2000

Vehicle Sets

Official Combat Jeep Set, 1965, trailer, steering wheel, spare tire,
windshield, cannon, search light, shell, flag, guard rails, tripod,
tailgate, and hood, without Moto-Rev Sound,
Model No. 7000 .... $200.............. $375...................... $550

A-10 Thunder Bolt, $50 MIP.

Slugger Tank with figure, $35 MIP.

Action Soldiers of the World

Figure Sets	EX	NM	MIP

Australian Jungle Fighter, 1966, Hasbro, action figure with jacket, shorts, socks, boots, bush hat, belt, "Victoria Cross" medal, knuckle knife, flamethrower, entrenching tool, bush knife and sheath, Model No. 8105 $250 .... $400.................... $2500

British Commando, 1966, Hasbro, deluxe set with action figure, helmet, night raid green jacket, pants, boots, canteen and cover, gas mask and cover, belt, Sten sub machine gun, gun clip, and "Victoria Cross" medal, Model No. 8104 .... $300............... $425.................... $2500

Foreign Soldiers of the World, 1968, Hasbro, Talking Adventure Pack, Model No. 8111-83 .. $750............... $825.................... $5000

French Resistance Fighter, 1966, Hasbro, deluxe set with figure, beret, short black boots, black sweater, denim pants, "Croix de Guerre" medal, knife, shoulder holster, pistol, radio sub machine gun, and grenades, Model No. 8103 .... $200............... $250.................... $2250

German Storm Trooper, 1966, Hasbro, deluxe set with figure, helmet, jacket, pants, boots, Luger pistol, holster, cartridge belt, cartridges, "Iron Cross" medal, stick grenades, 9MM Schmeisser, field pack, Model No. 8100 $275 .... $425.................... $2500

Japanese Imperial Soldier, 1966, Hasbro, deluxe set with figure, Arisaka rifle, belt, cartridges, field pack, Nambu pistol, holster, bayonet, "Order of the Kite" medal, helmet, jacket, pants, short brown boots, Model No. 8101 $425............. $675.................... $2700

Russian Infantry Man, 1966, Hasbro, deluxe set with action figure, fur cap, tunic, pants, boots, ammo box, ammo rounds, anti-tank grenades, belt, bipod, DP light machine gun, "Order of Lenin" medal, field glasses and case, Model No. 8102 .... $275............... $400.................... $2250

G.I. Joe 3-3/4-inch Navy Seal Team, $30 MIP.

The Cobra Range, $20 MIP.

	EX	NM	MIP

Uniform/Equipment Sets

British Commando Set, 1966, Hasbro, Sten submachine gun,
 gas mask and carrier, canteen and cover, cartridge belt, rifle,
 "Victoria Cross" medal, manual,
 Model No. 8304 .... $125 .... $200 .... $325

French Resistance Fighter Set, 1966, Hasbro shoulder holster,
 Lebel pistol, knife, grenades, radio, 7.65 submachine gun,
 "Croix de Guerra" medal, counter-intelligence manual,
 Model No. 8303 .... $25 .... $50 .... $275

Adventure Team

Figure Sets

Air Adventurer, 1970, Hasbro, includes figure with Kung Fu grip,
 orange flight suit, boots, insignia, dog tags, rifle, boots, warranty,
 club insert, Model No. 7403
 .... $120 .... $375 .... $400

Black Adventurer, 1970, Hasbro, includes figure, shirt with insignia,
 pants, boots, dog tags, shoulder holster with pistol,
 Model No. 7404 .... $125 .... $150 .... $375

Land Adventurer, 1970, Hasbro, includes figure,
 camo shirt and pants, boots, insignia, shoulder holster
 and pistol, dog tags, and team inserts,
 Model No. 7401 .... $45 .... $75 .... $200

Talking Adventure Team Commander, 1970, Hasbro, includes figure,
 two-pocket green shirt, pants, boots, insignia, instructions, dog
 tag, shoulder holster and pistol. With life-like hair and beard.
 Model No. 7400 .... $65 .... $125 .... $400

Uniform/Equipment Sets

Adventure Team Headquarters Set, 1972, Hasbro, Adventure Team
 playset, Model No. 7490
 .... $50 .... $125 .... $200

	EX	NM	MIP

Adventure Team Training Center Set, 1973, Hasbro, rifle rack, logs, barrel, barber wire, rope ladder, three tires, two targets, escape slide, tent and poles, first aid kit, respirator and mask, snake, instructions. Model No. 7495
.... $75................ $125...................... $225

Danger Ray Detection, 1975, Hasbro, magnetic ray detector, solar communicator with headphones, two-piece uniform, instructions and comic, Model No. 7338-1
.... $45................ $90...................... $225

Demolition Set, 1971, Hasbro, armored suit, face shield, bomb, bomb disposal box, extension grips,
Model No. 7370 .... $20................ $45...................... $125

Dive to Danger, 1975, Hasbro, Mike Powers set, orange scuba suit, fins, mask, spear gun, shark, buoy, knife and scabbard, mini sled, air tanks, comic,
Model No. 8031 .... $150................ $250...................... $450

Emergency Rescue Set, 1971, Hasbro, shirt, pants, rope ladder and hook, walkie talkie, safety belt, flashlight, oxygen tank, axe, first-aid kit, Model No. 7374 $45 .... $75...................... $150

Flying Space Adventure Set, 1970, Hasbro,
Model No. 7425 .... $400................ $600...................... $1000

High Voltage Escape Set, 1971, Hasbro, net, jumpsuit, hat, wrist meter, wire cutters, wire, warning sign,
Model No. 7342 .... $40................ $75...................... $150

Jaws of Death, 1975, Hasbro, super deluxe set,
Model No. 7421 .... $325................ $500...................... $650

Jettison to Safety, 1975, Hasbro, infrared terrain scanner, mobile rocket pack, two-piece flight suit, instructions and comic.
Model No. 7339-2 ...... $85................ $200...................... $275

	EX	NM	MIP

Peril of the Raging Inferno, 1975, Hasbro, fireproof suit,
hood and boots, breathing apparatus, camera,
fire extinguisher, detection meter, gaskets,
Model No. 7416 .... $85 .... $150 .... $275

Search for the Abominable Snowman Set, 1973, Hasbro, Sears,
white suit, belt, goggles, gloves, rifle, skis and poles,
snow shoes, sled, rope, net, supply chest, binoculars,
Abominable Snowman, comic book,
Model No. 7439.16... $110 .... $175 .... $350

Secret Mission to Spy Island Set, 1970, Hasbro, comic,
inflatable raft with oar, binoculars, signal light, flare gun, TNT and
detonator, wire roll, boots, pants, sweater, black cap, camera,
radio with earphones, .45 submachine gun,
Model No. 7411 .... $75 .... $125 .... $250

Three-in-One Super Adventure Set, 1971, Hasbro,
Danger of the Depths, Secret Mission to Spy Island, and Flying
Space Adventure Packs,
Model No. 7480 .... $550 .... $975 .... $1250

Vehicle Sets

Secret of the Mummy's Tomb Set, 1970, Hasbro, with Land Adventurer
figure, shirt, pants, boots, insignia, pith helmet, pick, shovel,
Mummy's tomb, net, gems, vehicle with winch, comic,
Model No. 7441 .... $175 .... $300 .... $600

Sharks Surprise Set with Sea Adventurer, 1970, Hasbro,
Model No. 7442 .... $175 .... $325 .... $550

Adventures of G.I. Joe
Figure Sets

Aquanaut, 1969, Hasbro,
Model No. 7910 .... $175 .... $550 .... $3000

	EX	NM	MIP

Negro Adventurer, 1969, Hasbro, Sears Exclusive,
includes painted hair figure, blue jeans, pullover sweater, shoulder
holster and pistol, plus product letter from Sears,
Model No. 7905 .... $450............... $750.................... $2750

Sharks Surprise Set with Frogman, 1969, Hasbro, with figure, orange
scuba suit, blue sea sled, air tanks, harpoon, face mask,
treasure chest, shark, instructions, and comic,
Model No. 7980 .... $125............... $300.................... $750

Talking Astronaut, 1969, Hasbro, hard-hand figure with
white coveralls with insignias, white boots, dog tags,
Model No. 7615 .... $85............... $275.................... $1000

Uniform/Equipment Sets

Danger of the Depths Underwater Diver Set, 1969, Hasbro, Model No.
7920 .... $140............... $275..................... $500

Eight Ropes of Danger Set, 1969, Hasbro, diving suit,
treasure chest, octopus,
Model No. 7950 .... $110............... $225..................... $525

Fantastic Freefall Set, 1969, Hasbro, includes figure with parachute and
pack, blinker light, air vest, flash light, crash helmet with visor
and oxygen mask, dog tags, orange jump suit, black boots,
Model No. 7951 .... $150............... $325..................... $675

Flight for Survival Set with Polar Explorer, 1969, Hasbro, reissue,
Model No. 7982.83... $150............... $300.................... $500

PEZ®

By Shawn Peterson

The PEZ® dispenser has been around for 50 years. PEZ candy got its start even earlier, introduced in 1927 in Vienna, Austria as the world's first-ever breath mint. Edward Haas, an avid non-smoker, wanted to invent a product to rival cigarettes. His product, a small compressed sugar tablet with peppermint oil added, was sold in small pocket size tins and marketed as an alternative to smoking.

The name "PEZ" was derived from the German word for peppermint, "pfefferminz." Using the first, middle, and last letter of the word, Haas came up with the name "Pez."

Twenty years after the candy was invented, Oscar Uxa invented and patented a little mechanical box for dispensing the candy.

Haas reinvented the product by adding fruit flavors to the candy — and a three-dimensional cartoon head to the top of the dispenser. What a success this turned out to be, combining two of kids' favorite things: candy and a toy! This marketing shift proved to be a brilliant move, making PEZ one of the most recognizable commercial names around.

Batman with Cape, from the late 1960s, $75-$120. Photo courtesy Steve Warner

It is hard to say how many different heads have graced the top of a PEZ dispenser. Conservative estimates put the number between 250-300 different heads.

The dispenser itself has seen a few modest changes over the years. One of the biggest changes happened in the late 1980s when "feet" were added to the bottom of the dispenser base to give it more stability when standing upright.

PEZ collecting has been gathering steam since the early 1990s when the first guidebook appeared. In 1993, Christie's auction house in New York took notice of this evolving hobby and held its first ever pop culture auction featuring PEZ. The auction realized record prices, taking the hobby to a new level.

At present, this hobby has two things in its favor: demand far surpasses the supply of vintage dispensers, and PEZ is still produced today and can be found in almost any grocery or discount store, making it available to a whole new generation of collectors.

I have used several sources to determine what I feel is an accurate price range for each dispenser. Therefore, a price quoted will not reflect the top or bottom dollar

Elephant with Flat Hat, $100-$125. Photo courtesy Steve Warner

that a dispenser has sold for. The pricing information should be used for dispensers that are complete and void of any missing pieces, cracks, chips, or melt marks, and have working spring mechanisms.

Generally the value of a dispenser is in the head. Exceptions to this regarding the stems are features such as die-cuts, advertising, or pictures.

The dispensers listed here are divided into subject categories. The common name of the dispenser is listed first, followed by any alternate names. Next you will find a date — this is when production of the dispenser started. Notes on whether the dispenser was made with or without feet (or both) are also included. Finally, a value will be given for the dispenser as well as for known variations.

Shawn Peterson is the author of the Collector's Guide to PEZ® Identification & Price Guide, *second edition, published by Krause Publications, Iola, Wis.*

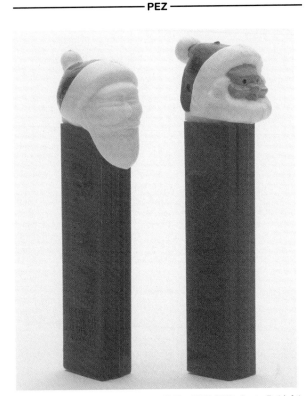

Santa A (on the left), from the late 1950s, $120-$150; Santa B (right), from the 1960s, $125-$160. Photo courtesy Steve Warner

PEZ

Elephant (also known as Circus Elephant or Big Top Elephant)

Early 1970s, No Feet

There are three different variations to the elephant regarding its head gear—flat hat, pointy hat, and hair. The elephant came in many different color combinations, some of which, such as the pink head variation, are tough to find.

Flat hat:..$100-$125
Pointy hat:..$125-$150
Hair:...$150-$175

Mickey Mouse

Early 1960s-Present, No Feet and With Feet

Mickey Mouse has been one of the most popular PEZ® dispensers over the years and has gone through many variations.

Die-cut stem with painted face, early 1960s: ....$300-$400
Die-cut face, early 1960s, No Feet: ....$100-$140
Version A, removable nose, early 1970s, No Feet:.. ....$20-$30
Version B, molded nose, early 1980s, No Feet: ....$15-$25
Version B, With Feet: ....$10-$15
Version C, stencil eyes, 1990s: ....$2-$3
Mickey and Minnie Mouse, 1990s edition: ....$1-$2
Softhead version (rare): ....$3000+

Santa

1950s-Present, No Feet and With Feet

Santa is one of the most popular PEZ® dispensers ever produced. Most commonly found is Santa C, which has been produced since the 1970s.

Santa A, No Feet, face and beard are the same color: ....$120-$150
Santa B, No Feet, flesh-colored face with white beard: ....$125-$160

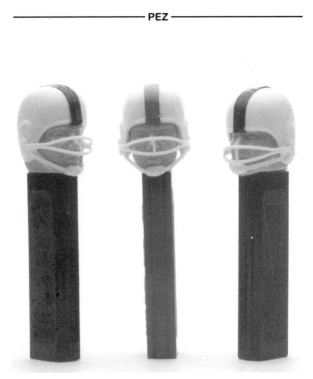

Football Player, from the mid-1960s, $150-$250+. Notice the unique stem—the blank side with the triangle allowed kids to customize the dispenser with a pennant-shaped sticker of their favorite team. Photo courtesy Steve Warner

Santa C, No Feet: .... $5-$10

Santa C, With loop for ornament: .... $35-$50

Santa C, With Feet: .... $2-$3

Santa D, With Feet: .... $1-$2

Santa E, (Current): .... $1-$2

Full Body Santa (1950s): .... $150-$200

Football Player

Mid-1960s, No Feet

This dispenser can be found in either red or blue and will either have
a tape strip on the helmet (as shown) or a plastic strip that snaps
on the front and back of the helmet. This version is very tough
to find. The blank side of the stem with the triangle allowed kids
to customize the dispenser with a pennant-shaped sticker of their
favorite team.

Tape-strip Helmet: .... $150-$175

Snap-on Strip: .... $250+

Bullwinkle

Early 1960s, No Feet

Bullwinkle can be found with either a yellow or a brown stem—the
brown is much harder to find.

Yellow Stem: .... $250-$275

Brown Stem: .... $275-$325

Boy and Boy with Cap

Mid-1960s-current, No Feet and With Feet

Many versions of the PEZ® Pal Boy have been produced through the
years. One of the rarest is the brown-hair boy without hat used in
a mid-1980s promotion for the movie Stand By Me. The dispenser
is packaged with one pack of multi-flavor candy and a miniature
version of the movie poster announcing the videocassette release

Bullwinkle from the early 1960s. The brown stem version on the right ($275-$325) is much harder to find than the yellow stem version ($250-$275). Photo courtesy Steve Warner

and the quote "If I could only have one food to eat for the rest of my life? That's easy, PEZ®. Cherry flavored PEZ®. No question about it." This dispenser must be sealed in original bag to be considered complete.

Boy with blue cap, blonde hair: ....$100-$125

Boy with red cap, blonde hair: ....$250-$300

Boy with blue cap, brown hair: ....$75-$100

Blonde Hair: .... $50-$75

Brown Hair: .... $25-$35

Stand By Me (sealed in bag with mini-poster): ....$200-$250

Boy with blonde hair, $50-$75; boy with blonde hair and blue cap, $100-$125; boy with brown hair, $25-$35; and boy with brown hair and blue cap, $75-$100. Both the blonde- and brown-hair versions can also be found with a red hat.

Batman

Late 1960s, No Feet and With Feet

Batman has gone through several different looks and can still be found today. Batman with Cape is the earliest version and collectors should be aware that reproductions of the cape have been made. The original cape is somewhat translucent whereas reproduction capes are much thicker.

Batman with Cape: ....$75-$120

Short Ears, No Feet: .... $20-$30

Short Ears, With Feet: .... $10-$15

Short Ears, With Feet, Black (available for a very short time in the mid-1990s): .... $10-$15

Pointy Ear Dark Knight: ....$3-$6

Rounded Ear Dark Knight (Current): ....$1-$2

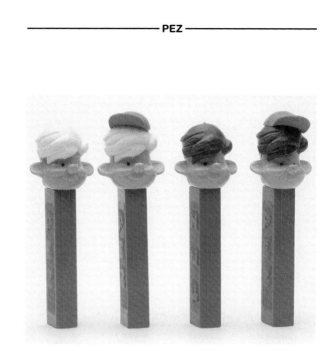

Boy with blonde hair, $50-$75; boy with blonde hair and blue cap, $100-$125; boy with brown hair, $25-$35; and boy with brown hair and blue cap, $75-$100. Both the blonde- and brown-hair versions can also be found with a red hat. Photo courtesy Steve Warner

Robots

Take several hunks of metal, fashion them into a barrel-chested automaton with a blank stare, and you've got a robot.

The style, look, composition, and purpose of robots has changed quite a bit throughout the past 60 years, since the time when the earliest toy robots were made. But collectors have remained enamored of the artistry, design, and function of these otherworldly pieces of pop culture.

Think of a toy robot, and it's likely you'll think of Japan. As early as the 1940s, Japan was making somewhat crude walking robots.

The 1950s was the true golden age of robots and space toys. Science fiction exploded into the pop culture sensibilities with television shows and movies catering to space themes. Makers of lithographed tin toys in Japan responded accordingly, setting the world awash in a sea of spacemen robots.

According to Jim Bunte's book, *Vintage Toys* (Krause Publications, 1999), "Japan had dominated the 1950s robot and space toy category with innovation, creativity, and perhaps most important, low price points.

This Radar Robot toy from the 1950s tops off at a whopping $7,000 MIP value.

"Yet their success was also their undoing, because as the Japanese saw their standard of living grow, the costs associated with their successful industries also rose, reducing their marketplace competitiveness…Most Japanese toymakers fought this losing battle well into the decade, but by the end of the 1960s, most had either vanished or constricted precipitously. In fact, as the 1970s dawned, it was becoming difficult to find playthings on American toy shelves marked 'Made in Japan.'"

By the mid-1970s, interest in robots and space toys had waned. Japan's reign in the space toys arena had fallen. Items made in Hong Kong and Taiwan were more readily available. By the late 1970s, however, the space toy world would turn its focus from robots and space men to Star Wars and other licensed realms.

The exciting historic and artistic world of robot toys would be gone, but those toys remain valuable vintage icons.

The Big Loo Moon Robot from Marx was only manufactured for one year in 1962. Standing 38 inches tall, it speaks, its eyes light up, and it shoots ping-pong balls. $2,600 MIP.

Robots

Advance Toys

	EX	NM	MIP

Mr. Atom, 1960s, Advance Toys, 18", red and silver plastic, battery-operated. "The Electronic Walking Robot... Completely Harmless," according to the box

.... $125.............. $300..................... $650

ALPS

Cragstan Great Astronaut, 1960s, ALPS, 11", red tin, battery-operated, w/video scene, key in head

.... $500.............. $1250.................... $2000

Door Robot, 1950s, ALPS, 9-1/2", tin, battery-operated, remote control, revolving head .... $725.............. $1700.................... $3350

Mechanical Television Spaceman, 1960s, ALPS, 7", tin and plastic, wind-up, w/chest scene and antenna

.... $95.............. $185..................... $325

Television Space Man, 1950s, ALPS, 11", tin and plastic, battery-operated, chest video, key in head operates as

antenna .... $125.............. $350..................... $800

AN-Japan

Astronaut Robot, 1950s, AN-Japan, 8", tin, wind-up, tanks on back, gun in hand .... $500.............. $1250.................... $2000

Arco

Ro-Gun "It's A Robot," 1984, Arco, robot changes

into a rifle .... $11.............. $16..................... $25

Asak

Space Guard Pilot, 1975, Asak, 8"

.... $20.............. $30..................... $45

Left to right: Moon Creature, Marx, 1968, $275 MIP; Lost in Space robot, K-Mart/AHI, 1977, $650 MIP; and Attacking Martian, Horikawa-SH, 1964, $425 MIP.

	EX	NM	MIP

Asakusa-Japan

Thunder Robot, 1950s, Asakusa-Japan, 11", tin and plastic, battery-operated, w/antenna and guns in palms of hands .... $1500 .... $5000.................... $9000

ASC Japan

Radar Robot, 1950s, ASC Japan, 11", orange tin, wind-up, rotating antenna, chest sparks $1500 .... $4000.................... $7000

Cragstan

Countdown-Y, 1960s, Cragstan, 9" .... $100 .... $145 .... $225

Cragstan's Mr. Robot, 1960s, Cragstan, 10-1/2" tin, battery-operated, red or white body, clear dome head .... $300 .... $500 .... $900

Magnor, 1975, Cragstan, 9", plastic .... $23 .... $35 .... $50

Mr. Atomic, 1960s, Cragstan, rare, 8", tin and plastic, battery-operated, bump and go action ..... n/a .... n/a $15000

Mr. LEM Astronaut Robot, 1970, Cragstan, 13", all plastic, battery-operated, rotates .... $150 .... $310 .... $475

Talking Robot, 1960s, Cragstan, 10-1/2", battery-operated, tin and plastic, three functions $375 .... $650 .... $1000

Daiya

Astro Captain, 1970s, Daiya, 6", red/white/ blue tin wind-up sparker, NASA on helmet .... $35 .... $65 .... $100

Durham

Robot 2500, 1970s, Durham, 10", tin/ plastic, battery-operated, "cyclops" .... $25 .... $45 .... $65

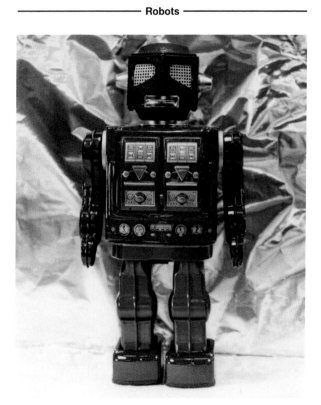

Slot machine-style Attacking Martian, tin, rotating action, 11 inches tall, Horikawa, 1964, $425 MIP.

	EX	NM	MIP

Hong Kong

Action Robot, 1970s, Hong-Kong, 10", yellow/blue plastic, battery-operated, multiple functions .... $15................. $35......................... $55

Radar Hunter, 1970s, Hong-Kong, 5", plastic, wind-up, red/silver or orange .... $15................. $35......................... $55

Robbie Robot, 1970s, Hong-Kong, 9", blue/red/yellow, all plastic, battery-operated, blinks $25................. $45......................... $85

Sounding Robot, 1970s, Hong-Kong, 8", plastic, battery-operated, three push buttons on head .. $25................. $50......................... $75

Sparking Robot, 1970s, Hong-Kong, 6", black plastic, wind-up...................... $20................. $35......................... $50

Star Robot, 1970s, Hong-Kong, 10", plastic, battery-operated, Star Wars Trooper head.............. $25................. $45......................... $70

Horikawa

Cosmic Fighter Robot, 1970s, Horikawa, 11-1/2", plastic, head opens to reveal gunner inside while body spins .... $50................. $85......................... $125

Piston Robot, 1960s, Horikawa, 10", tin/plastic, battery-operated, lighted pistons in square head.............. $200............... $450...................... $750

Space Capsule, 1960s, Horikawa, Blinking nosecone on top, opening panels with astronaut, rolling action .... $220................ $375...................... $600

Space Explorer Robot, 1960s, Horikawa, 11", tin and plastic, battery-operated, drop down chest cover reveals video.............. $95............... $200...................... $325

Ideal

Maxx Steele Robot, 1984, Ideal, 30", plastic, programmable servant, w/charger .... $100............... $250...................... $425

Atlaus (small robot), Velarios (lion with a missile launcher on its back), and Gunper (spaceship) are part of the 10-inch Daltanias robot from Bandai America, 1982, $150 MIP.

	EX	NM	MIP

Mighty Zogg the Leader Zeroid, 1960s, Ideal, 6", plastic, battery-operated, w/Motorific motors .... $60............... $110...................... $225

Mr. Machine, 1961, Ideal, 18", plastic, wind-up, w/bell and key, disassembles .... $85................ $210...................... $425

Mr. Machine, 1977, Ideal, 18", plastic, wind-up, whistles, does not disassemble .... $10................. $25........................ $55

Robert the Robot, 1954, Ideal, 14", plastic, battery-operated, remote "laser gun" styled control attached to toy.......... $100............... $195...................... $425

Robot Commando, 1960s, Ideal, 19", blue/red plastic, battery-operated, remote control, fires rockets and balls................... $150............... $450...................... $800

Zerak the Blue Destroyer Zeroid, 1968, Ideal, 6", plastic, battery-operated, w/Motorific motors...................... $50............... $100...................... $200

Zintar the Silver Explorer Zeroid, 1960s, Ideal, 6", plastic, battery-operated, w/Motorific motors...................... $50............... $100...................... $200

Zobor the Bronze Transporter Zeroid, 1960s, Ideal, 6", plastic, battery-operated, w/Motorific motors...................... $50............... $100...................... $200

Irwin

Man From Mars, 1950s, Irwin, 11", red w/yellow body tin, wind-up, shooting "space boy" $275................. $750...................... $1500

Man from Mars, 1950s, Irwin, 11", red tin, wind-up, "space boy" .... $125............... $275...................... $500

Japan

Answer Game Machine, 1960s, Japan, 14", tin, battery-operated, performs math tricks . $350............... $675...................... $950

Sparky Robot's eyes light up with sparks. All-tin, wind-up, KO-Japan, 1950s, $500 MIP.

	EX	NM	MIP
Apollo 2000 Robot, 1960s, Japan, 12", tin, battery-operated, red and blue, w/chest guns	$95	$175	$300
Apollo 2000X, 1970s, Japan, 6", blue and red tin wind-up w/spark	$45	$95	$165
Atomic Robot Man, 1948, Japan, 6", all tin, wind-up	$325	$900	$1550
Blink-A-Gear Robot, 1960s, Japan, 14", black tin, clear plastic front w/gears, battery-operated	$250	$600	$1150
Construction Robot, 1960s, Japan, 12", yellow tin, battery-operated, with forklift	$450	$1000	$1650
High-Wheel Robot, 1950s, Japan, 9", blue, tin and plastic, battery-operated, remote control	$325	$750	$1250
High-Wheel Ronot, 1950s, Japan, 9", black, tin and plastic, wind-up, w/chest gears	$175	$425	$700
Machine Robot, 1960s, Japan, 11", tin and plastic, battery-operated, w/shoulder antennae	$145	$325	$600
Mars Explorer, 1950s, Japan, 9-1/2", red tin, battery-operated, w/ wheels, face doors open	$450	$1000	$1750
Mars King, 1960s, Japan, 9", tin and plastic, battery-operated, w/video, siren and treads	$125	$350	$650
Mr. Chief, 1960s, Japan, 11-1/2", tin and plastic, battery-operated, smoking action	$475	$1000	$1950
Mr. Patrol, 1960s, Japan, 11" tin and plastic, battery-operated, meter in chest	$150	$350	$575
New Astronaut Robot, 1970s, Japan, 9", tin and plastic, battery-operated, w/three firing chest guns	$45	$85	$135
Piston Robot, 1970s, Japan, 10", tin and plastic, battery-operated, lighted chest pistons	$60	$110	$225

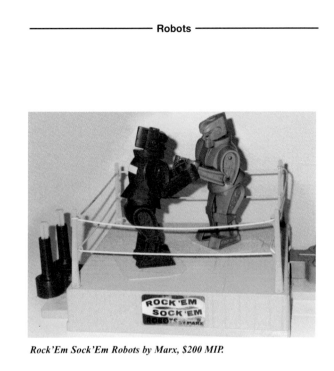

Rock'Em Sock'Em Robots by Marx, $200 MIP.

	EX	NM	MIP

Piston Robot, 1980s, Japan, 10", plastic, battery-operated, lighted chest pistons .... $35................. $65...................... $125

Robot Mighty 8, 1960s, Japan, dark-blue metal body, red feet, electric color display on chest $100............... $225...................... $400

Robot Tank - Mini, Japan, 5-1/2" tall, tin and plastic, battery-operated, w/two guns .... $85................. $160...................... $275

Roto-Robot, 1960s, Japan, 9", tin and plastic, battery-operated, w/chest guns, rotates 360 degrees
.... $95................. $185...................... $325

RX-008 Robot, 1960s, Japan, 5", tin and plastic, wind-up, w/sparking chest .... $150............... $400...................... $700

Singing Robot, 1970s, Japan, 10", plastic, battery-operated, missiles in head.......................... $35................. $75...................... $100

Space Explorer Robot, 1950s, Japan, 9", tin, wind-up, w/02 gauge on chest .... $450............... $1000.................... $1650

Space Explorer Robot, 1960s, Japan, 12", tin and plastic, battery-operated, rotating shoulder antenna .... $450............... $1000.................... $1650

Space Ranger, 1970s, Japan, 10", battery-operated, all plastic, R/C, fires balls from chest.......... $50................. $110...................... $165

Space Robot X-70, 1960s, Japan, 12", tin and plastic, battery-operated, lights, noise, and "Tulip Head"............. $450............... $1000.................... $1650

Sparky Robot, 1960s, Japan, 7", green cylindrical body, tin wind-up .... $45................. $65...................... $100

Super Astronaut, 1960s, Japan, 10", battery-operated, mostly tin, man's face, w/chest guns ...... $65............... $145...................... $250

Zoomer Robot, 1950s, Japan, 7", blue or silver wired, tin, battery-operated, w/wrench... $295............... $525...................... $900

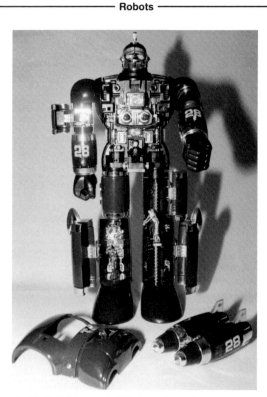

Tetsujin 28, Godaikin, stands 10 inches tall and is covered with removable, magnetic metal armor, 1982, $1,500 MIP.

	EX	NM	MIP

KO-Japan

Chief Robotman, 1960s, KO-Japan, 12", tin and plastic, battery-
operated, bump and go $450 .... $900 .... $1550

Jupiter Robot, 1970s, KO-Japan, 6-1/2", red plastic, wind-up, w/two
antennae .... $85 .... $175 .... $310

Sparky Robot, 1950s, KO-Japan, 8-1/2", silver and red, all tin, wind-up,
w/head spring .... $150 .... $295 .... $500

Venus Robot, 1960s, KO-Japan, 8", blue/red, tin and plastic,
battery-operated, remote
control .... $95 .... $200 .... $325

KTA-Japan

Lilliput Robot, 1940s, KTA-Japan, one of the oldest "6," tin wind-up,
square head w/yellow litho $1500 ..... $5000 .... $9000

Marx

Big Loo, 1960s, Marx, 36", plastic, battery-operated, water squirter,
w/rockets and tools ... $450 .... $1300 .... $2600

Colonel Hap Hazard, 1968, Marx, 11", tin and plastic, rotating antenna
on head .... $250 .... $575 .... $1200

Electric Robot, 1950s, Marx, 15", black and red plastic, battery-
operated, w/Morse code $125 .... $250 .... $500

Frankenstein, 1960s, Marx, 6", metal and plastic,
wind-up walker .... $100 .... $250 .... $450

Frankenstein Robot, 1960s, Marx, 14", tin and plastic, battery-operated,
wired remote control. $575 .... $1250 .... $2000

Moon Creature, 1960s, Marx, 5-1/2", Bug-eyed, mechanical, tin,
wind-up .... $95 .... $165 .... $275

Moon Scout, 1968, Marx, 11", tin and plastic, shoots balls
from chest .... $500 .... $1050 .... $2000

As shown on the box, Daimos transforms from a 9-1/2-inch fist-firing robot to a 9-inch 24-wheeler truck. Bandai America, $275.

	EX	NM	MIP

Mr. Mercury, 1960s, Marx, 14", tin and plastic, battery-operated, bending action .... $175............. $450.................... $1000

Mr. Smash, 1970s, Marx, 6", red plastic, wind-up, Martian Mashed Potato promo .... $45............. $95.................... $150

Rock 'Em, Sock 'Em Robots, 1970s, Marx, two plastic robots in boxing ring controlled by handles, when one is punched just right his head flies upward on a spring
.... $55............. $120.................... $200

Son of Garloo, 1960s, Marx, 6", green metal and plastic, monster wind-up walker................. $100............. $225.................... $425

Masudaya

Forbidden Planet Robby, 1985, Masudaya, 5", plastic, wind-up........................ $10............. $20.................... $35

Forbidden Planet Robby, 1985, Masudaya, 16", plastic, battery-operated, talks............ $65............. $125.................... $200

Giant Sonic Robot (Train Robot), 1950s, Masudaya, red body, black arms and head, robot makes "trainlike" sound as it rolls along
..................................$4000............. $7300...................$16000

Machine Man, 1950s, Masudaya, the rarest robot from Masudaya's "Gang of Five" series, this robot sold for $42,550 at the Sotheby's auction of the Tin Toy Robot Collection of Matt Wyse in 1996 .... n/a................. n/a...................$45000

R-35 Robot, 1950s, Masudaya, 7-1/2", tin litho, battery-operated, remote control-battery box is red, eyes light up .... $150............. $400.................... $650

Robot YM-3, 1985, Masudaya, 5", wind-up, "Lost in Space B9" type .... $10................. $20.........................$35

The Gang of Five, 1997, Masudaya, 5", five mini-robots, Mini Sonic Robot, Mini Target Robot, Mini Machine Man, Mini Non-Stop Lavender Robot, Mini Radicon Robot
.... $50............. $75.................... $110

	EX	NM	MIP

Mego

Gigantor Robot, 1960s, Mego, 17", battery-operated, tin and plastic, silver w/white "hands" and red feet
.... $50............... $100...................... $150

Mego-Japan

Krome-Dome Robot, 1960s, Mego-Japan, 11", plastic, battery-operated, disk-type head opens w/sound
.... $125............... $295...................... $525

Mikes Toy House

Mr. Atomic, 1990s, Mikes Toy House, limited reproduction .. $95............... $200...................... $350

Miscellaneous

Lightning Robot, 1980s, battery-operated, looks like R2D2 w/flashing lights......... $20................. $40........................ $80

Lunar Spaceman, 1978, 12", battery-operated
.... $20................. $30........................ $45

Mechanical Interplanetary Explorer, 1950s, 8", wind-up.................. $180............... $260...................... $400

Mechanized Robot, 1950s, 13", tin and plastic, battery-operated, black body, "Robby the Robot" type
.... $500........... $1200...................... $2000

Myrobo, 1970s, 9", battery-operated
.... $25................. $35........................ $55

Raid "Bug" Robot, Korea, large plastic, battery-operated, remote control, ad promo .... $75............... $150...................... $250

Ranger Robot, Japan, 11", battery-operated, clear body, w/smoke and sound .... $500........... $1200...................... $2250

Space Scout, 1950s, rare 10", tin wind-up, w/radiation meter in chest.................... $1000 .... $2250...................... $5000

	EX	NM	MIP

Zero of Space, 1970s, 14", red and yellow plastic w/visor, battery-operated, w/lights ..... $100 .... $225 .... $350

MTU-Korea

Captain the Robot, 1970s, MTU-Korea, 6", gray plastic wind-up, sparking .... $15 .... $35 .... $50

N-Japan

Walking W Robot, 1960s, N-Japan, 7", tin wind-up sparker, plastic antenna on head .... $100 .... $225 .... $350

Nomura

Musical Drummer Robot R 57, 1950s, Nomura, from the Matt Wyse collection, this robot sold for $17,250 at a Sotheby's auction in 1996 .... n/a .... n/a $20000

Robby Space Patrol, 1957, Nomura, purple and silver metal body, battery-operated with random running action. This is one of the most famous space toys, representing (in an unlicensed way) the robot and his transport from the film, "The Forbidden Planet" .... $7000 .... $17500 ....$37000

Orikawa

Mr. Hustler, 1960s, Orikawa, 11-1/2", tin and plastic, battery-operated, center chest light ...... $100 .... $225 .... $400

Playing Mantis

Robot B-9, Lost In Space, 1990s, Playing Mantis, die-cast metal with rolling wheels under base, sold individually, part of a series of four Lost-In-Space toys made by Playing Mantis Johnny Lightning .... n/a .... n/a $6

R.M.

Astronaut, 1960s, R.M., 7", tin litho, wind-up, arms move back and forth, red body, human face
.... $50 .... $85 .... $125

	EX	NM	MIP

Remco

Big Max & His Electronic Conveyor, 1958, Remco, 8 x 7", battery-operated, plastic, w/truck and coins
.... $100.............. $185..................... $300

Lost in Space Motorized Robot, 1966, Remco, 14", black upper body, red lower body .... $125.............. $250..................... $400

Mr. Brain, 1970, Remco, 13", plastic, battery-operated, programmable memory...................... $75.............. $150..................... $250

Rudy the Robot, 1967, Remco, 16", orange plastic, battery-operated. "He Walks Like a Man!" $50............. $165..................... $375

S.J.M.

Super Astronaut, 1981, S.J.M., 10", battery-operated, tin and plastic, man's face, w/chest guns $12............... $20........................ $30

Saunders

Marvelous Mike, 1950s, Saunders, battery-operated, plastic robot on tin bulldozer .... $110.............. $225..................... $395

Schaper

Tobor, 1978, Schaper, 7", black plastic, battery-operated, radio control
.... $15................. $30........................ $45

SH-Japan

Attacking Martian, 1960s, SH-Japan, 12", tin, battery-operated, green lens on chest doors,
black body............... $100.............. $250..................... $425

Attacking Martian, 1970s, SH-Japan, 10", tin/plastic, battery-operated, guns in chest .... $85............... $150..................... $250

Dino Robot, 1960s, SH-Japan, 11", tin, battery-operated, head opens to reveal dinosaur......... $450............... $950..................... $1600

	EX	NM	MIP
Engine Robot, 1960s, SH-Japan, 9", tin and plastic, battery-operated, w/chest gears	$125	$250	$500
Engine Robot, 1970s, SH-Japan, 10", plastic, battery-operated	$75	$150	$300
Excavator Robot, 1960s, SH-Japan, 10", tin and plastic, battery-operated, w/drill type hands	$275	$550	$875
Excavator Robot, 1970s, SH-Japan, 10", plastic, battery-operated, w/drill-type hands	$60	$125	$250
Fighting Robot, 1960s, SH-Japan, 11", tin and plastic, battery-operated, single chest gun, flashing light on head, "Sounding and lighted rapid fire gun" on box	$125	$350	$600
Gear Robot, 1960s, SH-Japan, 11-1/2", battery-operated, tin w/plastic gears in chest, antennae on shoulders	$225	$500	$850
Gear Robot, 1960s, SH-Japan, 9", wind-up, visible gears	$125	$275	$450
Giant Robot, 1960s, SH-Japan, 17", battery-operated, tin and plastic, yellow legs, red feet and head	n/a	n/a	n/a
Golden Gear Robot, 1960s, SH-Japan, 9", gold tin, battery-operated, w/chest gears and lit dome	$225	$500	$850
Launching Robot, 1975, SH-Japan, 10"	$25	$35	$55
Mr. Zerox, 1960s, SH-Japan, 9", tin and plastic, battery-operated, w/blinking, shooting actions	$100	$210	$350

	EX	NM	MIP
Radar Robot, 1970s, SH-Japan, 6.5", plastic, wind-up, red body, yellow arms, radar rotates	$25	$50	$75
Radar Scope Space Scout, 1960s, SH-Japan, 10", tin and plastic, battery-operated, TV screen w/noise	$65	$125	$210
Sky Robot, 1970s, SH-Japan, 8", yellow/red plastic, battery-operated	$20	$45	$65
Smoking Engine Robot, 1970s, SH-Japan, 10", plastic, battery-operated, piston action, w/sound and smoke	$45	$85	$135
Space Commander Robot, 1960s, SH-Japan, 10", tin and plastic, tank type base, bumpandgo, w/guns	$500	$1200	$2000
Space Fighter, 1960s, SH-Japan, 9", tin and plastic, battery-operated, w/chest doors and guns	$95	$200	$325
Super Giant (Rotate-a-Matic) Robot, 1970s, SH-Japan, 16", battery-operated, plastic, w/chest guns	$85	$150	$250
Super Robot Tank, 1950s, SH-Japan, 9" long, tin, friction powered w/ two guns	$80	$175	$295
Super Space Commander, 1970s, SH-Japan, 10", blue plastic, battery-operated, chest video	$20	$40	$60
Swivel-O-Matic Astronaut, 1960s, SH-Japan, 12", tin and plastic, battery-operated, black body	$75	$150	$250
Video Robot, 1960s, SH-Japan, 9", blue tin and plastic, battery-operated, w/chest video	$75	$155	$250

Straco-Japan

	EX	NM	MIP
Hysterical Robot, 1970s, Straco-Japan, 13", black plastic, battery-operated, bump and go and laughing actions	$100	$250	$400

	EX	NM	MIP

SY Japan

Space Man Robot, 1950s, SY Japan, 7-1/2" tin litho wind-up, w/floppy arms........................ $150.............. $400...................... $700

Sparking Robot, 1960s, SY Japan, 7", all tin, silver w/litho, keywound .... $125.............. $275...................... $450

Taiyo

Wheel-A-Gear Robot, 1950s, Taiyo, 15", black, tin and plastic, battery-operated, w/multi-chest gears and pullies .... $425.............. $1000.................... $1850

TN-Japan

Earthman Robot, 1950s, TN-Japan, 9", tin, battery-operated, remote control, w/sound and blinking gun .... $550.............. $1450.................... $2500

Piston Action Robot, 1950s, TN-Japan, 8-1/2", tin and plastic, battery-operated, remote cont, "Robby" type .... $500.............. $1200.................... $2000

Robot Tank-Z, 1960s, TN-Japan, 10", battery-operated, tin and plastic, bump and go .... $200.............. $425...................... $700

Space Command Robot, 1950s, TN-Japan, 7-1/2", all tin, wind-up, w/gun in hand .... $375.............. $1000.................... $1650

Tomy

Omnibot 2000,1980s, Tomy, 2 ft., plastic, battery-operated, remote control, programmable servant .... $175.............. $400...................... $675

Verbot, 1984, Tomy, 8", plastic, battery-operated, radio control, programmable .... $15.................. $35........................ $60

Topper

King-Ding Robot, 1970, Topper, 12", plastic, battery-operated, separate brain robot goes in head .... $110.............. $275...................... $500

	EX	NM	MIP

Waco-Japan

Laughing Robot, 1960s, Waco-Japan, 13", plastic, battery-operated,
mouth opens, laughs loudly
.... $125 .... $275 .... $500

Yanoman

Rendezvous 7.8, Yanoman,
15" .... $170 .... $245 .... $375

Yonezawa

Directional Robot, 1950s, Yonezawa, 10", blue tin, battery-operated,
rotates, bump and go action
.... $225 .... $650 .... $1200
Lunar Robot, 1960s, Yonezawa, 7", wind-up, sparks, companion to
Thunder Robot .... $225 .... $550 .... $800
Scare Mighty Robot, 1960s, Yonezawa, 10", red and white metal and
plastic, wind-up, sparking action
.... $175 .... $550 .... $900
Smoking Spaceman, 1960s, Yonezawa, dark-gray metal body, smoke
puffs from mouth as robot walks
.... $1250 .... $1900 .... $3750

Yoshiya

Moon Explorer, 1960s, Yoshiya, 12", tin, battery-operated, w/clock in
chest .... $475 .... $1000 .... $1850

Science Fiction and Space Toys

Some would trace the modern age of science fiction to 1956 and *Forbidden Planet*. Undoubtedly, the toy world would be poorer for the lack of the movie's Robby the Robot. But through one medium or another, science fiction has enthralled millions for many years, right back to Jonathan Swift's *Gulliver's Travels*.

Even with its classical pedigree, science fiction is almost exclusively a product of the 20th century as the hard foundation of science had to exist before fiction writers could extrapolate upon it.

Just as science fiction has captivated readers of all ages, so have toys. Space toys have been made continuously for most of the 20th century. The 1930s and 1940s saw Buck Rogers and Flash Gordon. The 1950s saw fiction become reality with the growth of television. Captain Video was the first space series on television, appearing in the summer of 1949. Buzz Correy and his Space Patrol and Tom Corbett, Space Cadet would feed the appetite for adventure until 1956 when the heavens took on a visual scale and grandeur never see before – in the panoramic wonder of *Forbidden Planet*.

In 1966, when the low-budget Star Trek went on the air, few dreamed that for millions of people, life would never be the same. Even though the original show ran only three seasons, its impact and legacy are undeniable.

The Outer Limits Game, Milton Bradley, 1964, $275 MIP.

Marx's tin litho wind-up Tom Corbett Space Cadet rocket ship based on the television series of the 1950s, $600 MIP. Courtesy Don Hultzman. Photo: Ron Chojnacki

Star Trek may be big, but the king of space toys has to be Star Wars. The array of books, models, figures, play sets, and other items released since its debut in 1977 continued unabated until 1988. The license gained a new lease in 1987 with the opening of Star Tours at Disneyland and Disney World, generating still more new merchandise.

In terms of diversity of toys, the universe of Star Wars is easily the most fully realized and diversely populated in all science fiction. Star Wars figures, vehicles and play sets are the most widely traded science fiction toys on the market.

Star Wars longevity and international name recognition are excellent assurances of the continuing popularity of its toys. (See the Star Wars chapter for values.)

Trends

In general, the field of science fiction toys is one with particular growth potential, given the prevalence of science fiction in today's culture and the exceptional strength of franchises like Star Trek and Star Wars. Toys from older nostalgic series such as *Lost in Space* and *Buck Rogers in the 25th Century* continue to top lists of the most sought-after space/science fiction toys, and their values continue to soar, particularly at auction.

Walt Disney Studios' The Black Hole V.I.N.CENT model kit by MPC, 1979, $110 MIP.

Science Fiction and Space Toys

Battlestar Galactica

	EX	NM	MIP
Colorforms Adventure Set, 1978, Colorforms	$12	$25	$35
Cylon Helmet Radio, 1979, Vanity Fair	$25	$50	$85
Cylon Warrior Costume, 1978, boxed	$10	$15	$30
Galactic Cruiser, 1978, Larami, die-cast	$5	$10	$15
Game of Starfighter Combat, 1978, FASA, role-playing game	$10	$17	$30
L.E.M. Lander, 1978, Larami, die-cast	$5	$10	$15
Lasermatic Pistol, 1978, Mattel	$15	$35	$50
Lasermatic Rifle, 1978, Mattel	$25	$50	$75
Muffit the Daggit Halloween Costume, 1978, Collegeville	$7	$15	$35
Poster Art Set, 1978, Craft Master	$6	$12	$20
Puzzles, 1978, Parker Brothers, The Rag-Tag Fleet, Starbuck, Interstellar Battle, price for each	$6	$12	$20
Space Alert Game, 1978, Mattel, hand-held electronic game	$10	$25	$50
Viper Vertibird, 1979, Mattel	$60	$120	$220

Non-Fall Space Patrol X-16, Masudaya, 1955-1960, $175 MIP.

	EX	NM	MIP

Buck Rogers

25th Century Police Patrol Rocket, 1935, Marx, tin wind-up, 12" long . ... $325............... $950 .... $1650

25th Century Scientific Laboratory, 1934, Porter Chemical, w/three manuals................... $800............... $1300 .... $2200

Battle Cruiser Rocket, 1937, Tootsietoy, two grooved wheels to run on string .... $75............... $225...................... $350

Buck Rogers 25th Century Rocket, 1939, Marx, Buck and Wilma in window, 12" long, tin wind-up
.... $250............... $650 .... $1200

Buck Rogers Battlecruiser, 1937, Tootsietoy, with wheels that run on string to simulate flying $75 .... $110...................... $165

Buck Rogers Figure, 1937, Tootsietoy, 1-3/4" tall, cast, gray .... $100............... $150...................... $250

Buck Rogers Flash Blast Attack Cruiser, 1937, Tootsietoy.................. $50............... $90...................... $165

Buck Rogers in the 25th Century Pistol Set, 1930s, Daisy, holster is red, yellow, and blue leather, gun is 9-1/2" pressed steel pop gun .... $210............... $425...................... $750

Buck Rogers in the 25th Century Star Fighter, 1979, Mego, vehicle for 3-3/4" figures .... $20................. $35........................ $60

Buck Rogers in the 25th Century XZ-35 Rocket Pistol, 1934, Daisy, holster is red, yellow, and blue leather, gun is 9-1/2" pressed steel Rocket Pistol w/single cooling fin at barrel base .... $180............... $400...................... $725

Buck Rogers Rubber Band Gun, 1930s, unknown, cut-out paper gun, on card, advertising premium item .... $30................. $60...................... $100

Buck Rogers Sonic Ray Flashlight Gun, 1955, Norton-Honer, 7-1/4" black, green and yellow plastic w/code signal screw .... $70............... $150...................... $300

Robot Commando stands 15 inches tall and moves, fires missiles, and rotates its eyes. Ideal, 1961, $800 MIP.

	EX	**NM**	**MIP**

Buck Rogers U-235 Atomic Pistol, 1946, Daisy, 9-1/2" long, pressed steel, makes pop noise and flash in window when trigger is pulled...................... $125............... $275...................... $550

Buck Rogers XZ-31 Rocket Pistol, 1934, Daisy, 10-1/2" long, heavy-blued metal, grip pumps the action, gun pops when trigger is pulled...................... $140............... $375...................... $650

Buck Rogers XZ-35 Space Gun, 1934, Daisy, 7" long, heavy-blued metal ray gun, the grip pumps the action and the gun pops when trigger is pulled, single cooling fin at barrel base, also called "Wilma Gun" . $125............... $275...................... $550

Buck Rogers XZ-38 Disintegrator Pistol, 1936, Daisy, 10-1/2" long, polished copper or blued finish, four flutes on barrel, spark is produced in the window on top of the gun when the trigger is pulled...................... $115............... $400...................... $600

Buck Rogers XZ-44 Liquid Helium Water Gun, 1936, Daisy, 7-1/2" long, red and yellow lightning bolt design stamped metal body w/a leather bladder to hold water; a later version was available in copper finish .... $175............... $500...................... $800

Electric Caster Rocket, 1930s, Marx........................ $125............... $210...................... $350

Flash Blast Attack Ship Rocket, 1937, Tootsietoy, Flash Blast Attack Ship 4-1/2", Venus Duo-Destroyer w/two grooved wheels to run on string .... $90............... $150...................... $250

Galactic Play Set, 1980s, HG Toys .... $17............... $30........................ $55

Helmet and Rocket Pistol Set, 1933, Einson-Freeman, set of paper partial-face "helmet" mask and paper pop gun, in envelope.................. $115............... $275...................... $550

Interplanetary Games Set, 1934, three game boards in box: Cosmic Rocket Wars, Secrets of Atlantis, Siege of Gigantica, set............................ $235............... $425...................... $700

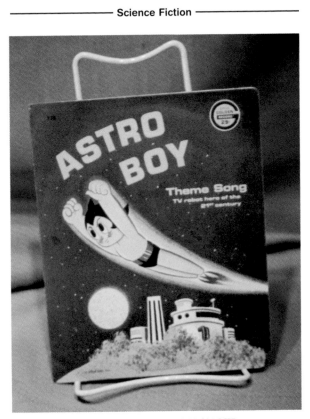

Astro Boy from Little Golden Records, 1964, $35 MIP.

	EX	NM	MIP
Interplanetary Space Fleet Model Kit, 1935, six different kits, including instructions and poster, in box, each	$100	$200	$350
Martian Wars Game, 1980s, TSR, role-playing game	$15	$25	$50
Puzzle, 1945, Puzzle Craft, Buck Rogers and His Atomic Bomber, three different each	$75	$150	$300
Puzzle, 1979, Milton Bradley, two versions showing TV scenes, each	$6	$15	$30
Puzzle with sleeve, 1952, Milton Bradley, space station scene, 14" x 10"	$75	$150	$200
Rocket Ship, 1934, Marx, 12" tall, wind-up	$250	$500	$750
Rubber Band Gun, 1930s, cut-out paper gun, on card	$35	$85	$150
Space Ranger Kit, 1952, Sylvania, 11"x15" premium, envelope w/six punch-out sheets	$50	$100	$200
Strato-Kite, 1946, Aero-Kite	$20	$35	$75
Superdreadnought SD51X Model Kit, 1936, 6-1/2" long, balsa wood, one of Interplanetary Space Fleet kit set	$100	$200	$350
Two-Way Transceiver, 1948, DA Myco	$80	$130	$200
View-Master Set, 1979, View-Master, three-reel set, in envelope or on blister card	$5	$10	$20
Walkie Talkies, 1950s, Remco	$60	$150	$200
Wilma Deering Figure, 1937, Tootsietoy, 1-3/4" tall, cast, gold	$70	$125	$185

Mint-in-box battery-operated Cragstan Mystery Action Satellite with original batteries, $375 MIP.

	EX	NM	MIP

Defenders of the Universe

Battling Black Lion Voltron Vehicle,
1986, LJN .... $9 .... $13 .... $20

Coffin of Darkness Voltron Vehicle,
1986, LJN .... $7 .... $10 .... $15

Doom BlasterVoltron Vehicle, 1986, LJN, mysterious flying
machine .... $9 .... $13 .... $20

Doom Commander Figure, 1985,
Matchbox .... $5 .... $7 .... $10

Green Lion Voltron Vehicle, 1986,
LJN .... $9 .... $13 .... $20

Hagar Figure, 1985,
Matchbox .... $5 .... $7 .... $10

Hunk Figure, 1985,
Matchbox .... $5 .... $7 .... $10

Keith Figure, 1985,
Matchbox .... $5 .... $7 .... $10

King Zarkon Figure, 1985,
Matchbox .... $5 .... $7 .... $10

Lance Figure, 1985,
Matchbox .... $5 .... $7 .... $10

Motorized Lion Force Voltron Vehicle Set, 1986, LJN, black lion
w/blazing sound .... $9 .... $13 .... $20

Pidge Figure, 1985,
Matchbox .... $5 .... $7 .... $10

Prince Lothar Figure, 1985,
Matchbox .... $5 .... $7 .... $10

Princess Allura Figure, 1985,
Matchbox .... $5 .... $7 .... $10

Space Warriors Colorforms Adventure Set, 1960s, $32 MIP.

	EX	NM	MIP
Robeast Mutilor Figure, 1985,			
Matchbox	$5	$7	$10
Robeast Scorpious Figure, 1985,			
Matchbox	$5	$7	$10
Skull Tank Voltron Vehicle, 1986,			
LJN	$9	$13	$20
Vehicle Team Assembler, 1986, LJN, forms			
Voltron	$9	$13	$20
Voltron Lion Force & Vehicle Team Assemblers Gift Set,			
1986, LJN	$9	$13	$20
Voltron Motorized Giant Commander, 1984, LJN, plastic 36", multicolor body w/movable head, arms and wings, wire remote control, battery-operated			
	$15	$25	$40
Zarkon Zapper Voltron Vehicle, 1986, LJN, w/galactic sound			
	$11	$16	$25

Flash Gordon

	EX	NM	MIP
Adventure on the Moons of Mongo Game, 1977,			
House of Games	$15	$25	$40
Arak Figure, 1979, Mattel, 3-3/4",			
carded	$17	$30	$50
Battle Rocket with Space Probing Action,			
1976	$6	$10	$20
Beastman Figure, 1979, Mattel, 3-3/4",			
carded	$15	$25	$45
Book Bag, 1950s, 12" wide, three-color art			
on flap	$17	$35	$75

This battery-operated R-35 from Masudaya, 1950s, moves forward on its feet and swings its arms, $650 MIP.

	EX	NM	MIP
Candy Box, 1970s, eight illustrated boxes, each	$4	$10	$20
Dr. Zarkov Figure, 1979, Mattel, 3-3/4" figure, on card	$15	$35	$50
Flash and Ming Button, 1970s, shows Flash and Ming crossing swords	$4	$10	$20
Flash Gordon Air Ray Gun, 1950s, Budson, 10" unusual air blaster, handle on top cocks mechanism, pressed steel	$215	$350	$700
Flash Gordon and Martian, 1965, Revell, #1450	$60	$125	$175
Flash Gordon and the Ape Men of Mor Book, 1942, Dell, 196 pages, Fast Action Story	$75	$150	$250
Flash Gordon and the Fiery Desert of Mongo Book, 1948, Whitman, Big Little Book	$30	$60	$90
Flash Gordon and the Monsters of Mongo Book, 1935, Whitman, hardback Big Little Book	$50	$90	$135
Flash Gordon and the Perils of Mongo Book, 1940, Whitman, Big Little Book	$35	$70	$100
Flash Gordon and the Power Men of Mongo Book, 1943, Whitman, Big Little Book	$35	$65	$95
Flash Gordon and the Red Sword Invaders Book, 1945, Whitman, Big Little Book	$30	$60	$90
Flash Gordon and the Tournaments of Mongo Book, 1935, Whitman, paperback Big Little Book	$45	$80	$120
Flash Gordon and the Tyrant of Mongo Book, 1941, Whitman, Big Little Book, w/flip pictures	$35	$70	$105

	EX	NM	MIP
Flash Gordon and the Witch Queen of Mongo Book, 1936, Whitman, Big Little Book	$45	$80	$120
Flash Gordon Arresting Ray Gun, 1939, Marx, picture of Flash on handle, 12" long	$200	$500	$1000
Flash Gordon Costume, 1951, Esquire Novelty	$90	$145	$225
Flash Gordon Figure, 1944, wood composition, 5" tall	$115	$195	$300
Flash Gordon Game, 1970s, House of Games	$15	$30	$40
Flash Gordon Hand Puppet, 1950s, rubber head	$90	$145	$250
Flash Gordon in the Forest Kingdom of Mongo Book, 1938, Whitman, Big Little Book	$40	$75	$110
Flash Gordon in the Ice World of Mongo Book, 1942, Whitman, Big Little Book, w/flip pictures	$35	$70	$100
Flash Gordon in the Jungles of Mongo Book, 1947, Whitman, Big Little Book	$35	$65	$95
Flash Gordon in the Water World of Mongo Book, 1937, Whitman, Big Little Book	$35	$70	$105
Flash Gordon Kite, 1950s, 21"x17", paper	$55	$90	$135
Flash Gordon on the Planet Mongo Book, 1934, Whitman, Big Little Book	$55	$105	$155
Flash Gordon Paint Book, 1930s	$60	$125	$200
Flash Gordon Radio Repeater Clicker Pistol, Marx, 10" long, 1930s	$250	$750	$1500
Flash Gordon Signal Pistol, 1930s, Marx, 7", siren sounds when trigger is pulled, tin/pressed steel, green w/red trim	$250	$600	$1200

	EX	NM	MIP

Flash Gordon Space Water Gun, 1976, Nasta, water ray gun on
illustrated card .... $10 .... $25 .... $50

Flash Gordon Three Color Ray Gun, 1976, Nasta, battery-operated
.... $8 .... $35 .... $75

Flash Gordon vs. the Emperor of Mongo Book, 1936, Dell, 244 pages,
Fast Action Story .... $70 .... $140 .... $225

Flash Gordon Water Pistol, 1940s, Marx, plastic w/whistle in handle,
7-1/2" long .... $80 .... $250 .... $500

Flash Gordon Wristwatch, 1979, Bradley, medium chrome case,
back and sweep seconds, Flash in foreground
w/city behind .... $70 .... $115 .... $175

Flash Gordon, The Movie Buttons, 1980,
set of five, each .... $2 .... $4 .... $8

Home Foundry Casting Set, 1935, lead casting set w/molds of Flash and
other characters .... $575 .... $975 .... $1500

Lizard Woman Figure, 1979, Mattel, 3-3/4", carded
.... $15 .... $25 .... $40

Medals and Insignia, 1978, Larami, set of five on blister card
.... $10 .... $25 .... $50

Ming Figure, 1979, Mattel, 3-3/4", carded
.... $12 .... $20 .... $35

Ming's Space Shuttle, Mattel
.... $15 .... $25 .... $40

Pencil Box, 1951 .... $75 .... $150 .... $200

Puzzle, 1930s, Featured Funnies
.... $55 .... $110 .... $160

Puzzle, 1951, Milton Bradley, frame tray
.... $45 .... $80 .... $120

Puzzles, 1951, Milton Bradley, set of three
.... $105 .... $200 .... $300

	EX	NM	MIP
Rocket Fighter, 1939, Marx, tin wind-up, 12" long	$175	$350	$600
Rocket Ship, 1975, 3" die-cast metal	$10	$20	$35
Rocket Ship, 1979, Mattel, inflatable, 3' long, w/plastic nose, rocket, and gondola attachments	$20	$40	$60
Solar Commando Set, 1950s, Premier Products	$65	$115	$175
Space Compass, 1950s, ornately housed compass on illustrated watchband	$25	$40	$75
Space Water Gun, 1976, Nasta, water ray gun on illustrated card	$6	$15	$30
Sunglasses, 1981, Ja-Ru, plastic w/emblem on bridge, carded	$3	$5	$10
Three-Color Ray Gun, 1976, Nasta	$8	$15	$30
Thun, Lion Man Figure, 1979, Mattel, 3-3/4", carded	$15	$25	$45
Two-Way Telephone, 1940s, Marx	$60	$110	$185
View-Master Set, 1963, View-Master, three reels in envelope	$20	$35	$60
View-Master Set, 1976, View-Master, three reels, In the Planet Mongo	$6	$10	$20
Vultan Figure, 1979, Mattel, 3-3/4", carded	$15	$30	$50
Wallet, 1949, w/zipper	$70	$115	$175
Water Pistol, 1950s, Marx, 7-1/2" plastic	$155	$275	$500

	EX	NM	MIP

Lost in Space

Chariot Model Kit, Marusan/Japanese, figures and motor
.... $625.............. $975................... $1500

Chariot Model Kit, 1987, Lunar Models, #SF009, 1:35 scale, w/clear
vacuform canopy and dome, plastic body, treads, roof rack
.... $35................. $50.........................$80

Costume, 1965, Ben Cooper, silver spacesuit w/logo
.... $85................. $150....................... $225

Doll Set, Marusan/Japanese, dressed in spacesuits w/their own freezing
tubes w/a cardboard insert w/color photos and description
.... **$2900** ....$4500 .... $7000

Fan Cards, 1960s, promo cards mailed to fans; color photo
.... $20................. $35.........................$60

Fan Cards, 1960s, promo cards mailed to fans; black/white photo
.... $15................. $25.........................$40

Helmet and Gun Set, 1967, Remco, child size helmet w/blue flashing
light and logo decals, blue and red molded gun
.... $300................. $530..................... $880

Jupiter Model Kit, 1966, Marusan/Japanese, large version
.... $425................. $650..................... $1000

Jupiter-2 Model Kit, Comet/England, 2" diameter, solid metal
.... $8................. $13.........................$25

Jupiter-2 Model Kit, 1966, Marusan/Japanese, 6" molded in green
plastic w/wheels and wind-up motor
.... $425................. $650..................... $1000

Laser Water Pistol, Unknown, 5" long, first season pistol style
.... $30................. $50.........................$80

Lost In Space 3-D Action Fun Game, 1966, Remco, three levels w/
small cardboard figures
.... $530................. $785..................... $1220

	EX	NM	MIP

Puzzles, 1966, Milton Bradley, frame tray; three poses w/Cyclops
.... $40................. $65..................... $100

Robot, 1966, Remco, 12" high, motorized w/blinking lights
.... $180.............. $365..................... $680

Robot, 1968, Aurora, 6" high w/base
.... $150.............. $400 .... $1100

Robot, 1977, Kmart/Ahi, 10", plastic w/green dome, battery-operated
.... $85................. $200..................... $325

Robot YM-3, 1985, Masudaya, 4" high, wind-up
.... $20................. $30......................... $50

Robot YM-3, 1986, Masudaya, 16" high, speaks English and Japanese
.... $85................. $150..................... $250

Roto-Jet Gun Set, 1966, Mattel, TV tie-in, modular gun can be
   reconfigured into different variations, shoots discs
.... $775.............. $1300 .... $2600

Saucer Gun, 1977, AN, disk shooting gun
.... $30................. $60..................... $125

Space Family Robinson Comic Book, 1960s, Gold Key
.... $15................. $25......................... $45

Switch-and-Go Set, 1966, Mattel, figures, Jupiter and chariot that ran
   around track............. $975.............. $1500..................... $2400

Trading Cards, 1966, Topps, 55 black and white cards, no wrappers or
   box .... $175.............. $300..................... $525

Tru-Vue Magic Eyes Set, 1967, GAF, rectangular reels
.... $30................. $50......................... $80

View-Master Set, 1967, GAF, Condemned of Space
.... $25................. $40......................... $65

Walkie Talkies, 1977, AHI, small card
.... $30................. $50......................... $80

	EX	NM	MIP

Space Guns

Astro Ray Gun, 1960s, Shudo/Japan, 5-7/8" long, silver finish body
w/red, yellow, and black detailing, friction sparkling action, single
large spark window near muzzle, prominent "Astro Ray Gun" in
center of body .... $15 .... $30 .... $60

Atom Bubble Gun, 1940s, unknown, red tubular barrel w/handle
attached, two sets of silver finish fins at barrel base and muzzle,
wire loop projects from muzzle for bubble blowing, handle
embossed "Atom Trade Mark"
.... $75 .... $150 .... $250

Atomic Disintegrator Ray Gun, 1954, Hubley, 8" long, die-cast metal
w/red handles, ornately embellished w/dials and other equipment
outcroppings, shoots caps $150 .... $325 .... $675

Atomic Gun, 1960s, Japan, 5" long, gold, blue, white, and red tin litho,
friction sparkling action, "Atomic Gun" on body sides
.... $20 .... $40 .... $75

Baby Space Gun, 1950s, Daiya/Japan, 6" friction siren and spark
action .... $35 .... $60 .... $135

Batman Ray Gun, 1960s, unknown, cap pistol w/bat symbol
for the sight .... $35 .... $65 .... $140

Battlestar Galactica Lasermatic Pistol, 1978,
Mattel .... $15 .... $30 .... $60

Daisy Rocket Dart Pistol, 1954, Daisy, 7" long, red, blue,
and yellow sheet metal gun w/blue body, blue grips
w/yellow trim, blue and yellow barrel stripes, same body
as Zooka Pop Pistol but w/connecting rod from gun
to barrel .... $80 .... $175 .... $350

Flash-O-Matic, The Safe Gun, 1950s, Royal Plastics, 7" long,
red and yellow plastic battery-operated light beam
gun .... $60 .... $100 .... $160

	EX	NM	MIP

Jack Dan Space Gun, 1959, Metamol/Spain, 7-1/2" long, in black, red, or blue painted die-cast metal cap gun w/"Jack Dan" over trigger .... $105 .... $200 .... $300

Planet Clicker Bubble Gun, 1953, Mercury Toys, 8" long, plastic, red body w/yellow accents, dip the barrel in bubble solution and pull trigger to make bubbles and produce click sound, in illustrated box .... $40 .... $65 .... $110

Ratchet Sound Space Gun, 1950s, Ideal, 7" long, red plastic w/silver trim, flywheel ratchet on top of gun .... $30 .... $50 .... $80

Smoke Ring Gun, 1950s, Nu-Age Products, large, sleek gray finished breakfront pistol w/red barrel and muzzle ring, used rocket shaped matches to produce smoke, trigger fired smoke rings, small engraved "Smoke Ring Gun" logo on gunsight fin .... $175 .... $295 .... $450

Space Gun, 1957, Japan, 9" long, friction sparkling action w/three red-tinted plastic spark windows and clear red plastic barrel, body in metallic blue w/large red "SPACE GUN" letters on yellow background .... $35 .... $65 .... $140

Space Jet Gun, 1957, KO/Japan, 9" long, tin, sparkling action w/black body, orange "Space Jet" on body w/orange and red atomic symbol on grip, clear green plastic finned barrel base, clear blue plastic finned muzzle .. $35 .... $60 .... $120

Star Team Ionization Nebulizer, 1969, Ideal, 9" water gun fires water mist, red, white, blue, and black plastic, Star Team decal .... $30 .... $50 .... $85

Strato Gun, 1950s, Futuristic Products, 9" long, gray finish die-cast, cap firing, internal hammer, top of gun lifts to load .... $70 .... $125 .... $200

	EX	NM	MIP

Super Sonic Space Gun, 1957, Daiya/Japan, 7-1/2" long, tin litho, metallic gray body w/red gunsight fin, friction siren and sparkling action, large oval center art w/outstanding lunar scene of rockets, mountains and Earth in sky, red helmeted spaceman on grip............................ $40................. $80...................... $160

Wham-O Air Blaster, 1960s, Wham-O, 10" long plastic gun uses rubber diaphragm to shoot air; styling is reminiscent of Budson Flash Gordon Air Ray Gun... $70............... $120...................... $185

Star Trek

Controlled Space Flight, 1976, Remco, plastic Enterprise, battery-operated .... $80............... $125...................... $225

Enterprise Model Kit, 1980, Mego/Grand Toys, #91232/B, Canadian issue, ST:TMP .... $90............... $100............... $150

Golden Trivia Game, 1985, Western .... $20................. $30...................... $50

Kirk Doll, ST:TMP, 1979, Knickerbocker, 13" tall, soft body w/plastic head............................ $16................. $23...................... $50

Kirk Puzzle, ST:TMP, 1979, Larami, fifteen-piece sliding puzzle .... $5................. $7...................... $12

Klingon Bird of Prey, ST:III, 1984, Ertl, 3-1/2", die-cast w/black plastic stand .... $7................. $10...................... $30

Phaser, 1975, Remco, black plastic, shaped like pistol, electronic sound, flashlight projects target .... $35................. $65...................... $100

Phaser Battle Game, 1976, Mego, black plastic, 13" high battery-operated electronic target game, LED scoring lights, sound effects and adjustable controls .... $195............... $275...................... $450

	EX	NM	MIP

Pinball Game, ST:TMP, Azrak-Hamway, 12", plastic, Kirk or Spock
.... $23................. $35........................$80

Role Playing Game, 2001 Deluxe Edition, FASA, Star Trek Basic Set
  and the Star Trek III Combat Game
.... $20................. $30........................$50

Space Design Center, ST:TMP, 1979, Avalon, blue plastic tray, paints,
  pens, crayons, project book and crew member cut-outs
.... $70............... $110.......................$175

Star Trek Tracer Gun, 1966, Rayline, 6-1/2" plastic firing tracer gun
.... $40................. $65.......................$125

Vulcan Shuttle Model Kit, 1980, Mego/Grand Toy, #91231, ST:TMP
.... $100............... $120.......................$145

Yo-Yo, 1979, Aviva, ST:TMP, blue sparkle plastic
.... $10................. $20........................$40

Star Wars Toys

By Merry Dudley

It's a good time to be a Star Wars collector.

Ten years go, Star Wars fans had little to gloat about. The Power of the Force figures of the mid-1980s were easy to find, and the second round wouldn't come until the late 1990s.

All we had were the usual rumors that someday George Lucas would go back and make the first three movies. But being a skeptical and cynical toy collector, I believed these rumors were part of a cruel hoax perpetuated by the legions of fans who couldn't bear to see the series die with only the eerie memory of furry Ewoks dancing and singing in our heads. Those were dark times indeed.

But at least we had the vintage market. While the Holy Grails of Star Wars collection were still pricey — think telescoping lightsaber Luke, vinyl cape Jawa, or blue Snaggletooth — there were plenty of bargains to be had.

All that changed by the end of the 1990s with the advent of *The Phantom Menace*.

Return of the Jedi Speeder Bike, 1983, $32 MIP.

Scout Walker from Empire Strikes Back. Another vehicle that has been re-issued many times, $42 MIP.

I'm not complaining. New movies meant new toys to collect. But even today, nearly four years after *Menace* debuted, plenty of collectors are still complaining about the glut of toys produced for Episode I. But I assert that too much product is not a problem. I like variety, and I'm not in the game to make money — I just like toys!

Lucasfilm was much more savvy with its licensing choices for *Attack of the Clones* in 2002. Hasbro and Lego practically cornered the market, and each company produced the most amazing Star Wars product to date. Mace Windu with a magnet in his hand that allows him to hold a lightsaber? Why didn't we have this technology 20 years ago!

For the new or uninitiated collector, I will say only this — if increasing the future value of your collection is your main objective, then save your *Clones* product and pare down your *Menace* items. And keep your eyes open for the sneak preview figures and Yoda items for Episode II. These items are sure to be hard to find as the years go on.

Merry Dudley is the editor of Toy Cars and Models *magazine and the Standard Catalog of 1:18 Scale Die-Cast Cars, both published by Krause Publications, Iola, Wis.*

Anakin's speeder with fly-off panels, about $16 MIP. The Anakin figure is about $7 MIP.

Padme Amidala Arena Escape figure from Attack of the Clones. About $8 MIP.

Star Wars

Action Figures, 3-3/4"
Star Wars

	MNP	MIP
Boba Fett, Series 1, 1978	$22	$700
C-3PO, Series 1, 1977	$5	$165
Chewbacca, Series 1, 1977	$10	$250
Darth Vader, Series 1, 1977	$14	$430
Early Bird Figures—Luke, Leia, R2-D2, Chewbacca, Series 1, 1977	$195	$425
Han Solo, Large Head, Series 1, 1977	$18	$475
Han Solo, Small Head, Series 1, 1977	$24	$525
Luke as X-Wing Pilot, Series 1, 1978	$10	$165
Luke Skywalker, Series 1, 1977	$28	$450
Luke w/Telescoping Saber, Series 1, 1977	$185	$3450
Obi-Wan Kenobi, Series 1, 1977	$17	$300
Princess Leia Organa, Series 1, 1977	$21	$460
R2-D2, Series 1, 1977	$15	$170

Empire Strikes Back

	MNP	MIP
Han in Bespin Outfit, Series 2, 1981, includes blaster pistol	$8	$85
Leia in Bespin Gown, Series 2, 1980, brown outfit with printed plastic cloak, includes blaster pistol	$17	$130
Yoda, Series 2, 1981, with cloth cloak, plastic belt, snake, and walking stick, the plastic accessories were produced in varying colors	$26	$210

The Obi-Wan Kenobi Coruscant Chase figure from Attack of the Clones, $8 MIP.

	MNP	MIP

Action Figures, 3-3/4"

Return of the Jedi

	MNP	MIP
Emperor Palpatine, Series 3, 1983	$8	$37
Han in Trench Coat, Series 3, 1984	$11	$41
Luke as Jedi Knight, Blue Saber, Series 3, 1983	$35	$115

POTF

	MNP	MIP
Anakin Skywalker, w/coin, Series 4, 1985	$22	$1825
Chewbacca, w/coin, Series 4, 1985	$9	$100
Darth Vader, w/coin, Series 4, 1985	$12	$165
Luke as Jedi Knight w/Green Saber, w/coin, Series 4, 1985	$20	$155
Obi-Wan Kenobi, w/coin, Series 4, 1985	$13	$105

Droids

	MNP	MIP
Boba Fett, 1985	$20	$650
C-3PO, 1985, solid, multicolored plastic body (not gold chromed) with painted eyes	$85	$145
R2-D2, 1985, simplified body markings and head—same sculpt and legs as regular (vintage) R2	$40	$120

POTF2

	MNP	MIP
Boba Fett, 1996, Series 2, Variation: half circle one hand, full circle on other hand, scarce $350	$4	$50
Chewbacca as Boushh's Bounty, 1998, Series 15	$3	$15
Darth Vader w/Removable Helmet, 1998, Series 12	$4	$40

C3PO, Protocol Droid with removable outer plating and box, $8 MIP.

Zam Wessell's speeder from Attack of the Clones featured "crush zones" to replicate her rough landing on Coruscant. About $17 MIP. The Zam figure is about $11 MIP.

	MNP	MIP
Han Solo, 1995, Series 1	$3	$15
Luke as X-Wing Pilot, 1996, Series 2, short lightsaber	$3	$15
Luke in Stormtrooper Disguise, 1996, Series 4	$4	$35
TIE Fighter Pilot, 1996, Series 2, equipped with two blaster rifles	$3	$6
Tusken Raider, 1996, Series 4	$3	$25
Yoda 1996, Series 2	$3	$12

The Phantom Menace

Anaking Skywalker, Naboo Pilot, 2000, includes helmet and ship controls	$3	$12
Darth Maul, Jedi Duel, 1999, the first release of a 3-3/4" Darth Maul figure	$3	$18
Darth Sidious, Holograph, 2000, translucent purple figure with Commtech chip	$3	$30
Jar Jar Binks, 1999, figure included Gungan Battle Staff and Commtech chip stand	$3	$20
Padme Naberrie, 1999, figure included viewscreen to watch the pod race	$3	$12
Queen Amidala, Battle, 2000, in dark robe, includes blaster pistol and grappling hook crossbow	$3	$30
Qui-Gon Jinn, Jedi Master, 2000, with lightsaber and Commtech chip	$3	$20

Action Figures, 12"

Star Wars

Boba Fett, Series 1, 1979, Star Wars Box	$160	$400
C-3PO, Series 1, 1979	$30	$210

This classic action figure stand was a mail-order Star Wars item in 1978, $65 MIP.

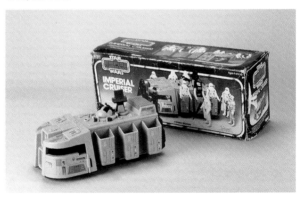

"Imperial Cruiser" vehicle from Empire Strikes Back. This second version doesn't include sounds or any battery-driven features, $75 MIP.

	MNP	MIP
Chewbacca, Series 1, 1979	$50	$200
Darth Vader, Series 1, 1978	$50	$200
Han Solo, Series 1, 1979	$125	$420
Luke Skywalker, Series 1, 1979	$80	$260
Obi-Wan Kenobi, Series 1, 1979	$85	$320
Princess Leia Organa, Series 1, 1979	$80	$220
R2-D2, Series 1, 1979	$42	$165

Empire Strikes Back

Boba Fett, Series 2, 1979, Empire Strikes Back Box		
	$155	$525
IG-88, Series 2, 1980, Empire Strikes Back Box		
	$250	$700

The Phantom Menace

Anakin Skywalker, w/Theed Hangar Droid, 2000		
	$5	$15
Darth Maul, Action Collection, 1999	$5	$35
Jar Jar Binks, Action Collection, 1999	$5	$25
Obi-Wan Kenobi, Action Collection, 1999	$5	$25
Qui-Gon Jinn, Action Collection, 1999	$5	$30
Queen Amidala, Black Travel Dress, Queen Amidala Collection, 1999 Portrait Edition, 1999	$5	$20

Lego Sets

Empire Strikes Back

Bobba Fett's Slave I, 7144	n/a	$20
Twin-Pod Cloud Car w/Lobot, 7119	n/a	$10
Luke Skywalker, Han Solo, Boba Fett, Mini-Figure Sets, 3341	n/a	$5
Yoda, Ultimate Collectors Series, 7194	n/a	$100

Darth Maul Sith Speeder from Phantom Menace includes figure, $25 MIP.

Sneak Preview Clone Trooper figure, 2002, $11 MIP.

	MNP	MIP

Return of the Jedi

B-Wing at Rebel Control Center w/pilot, droid, mechanic,
7180 .... n/a..........................$30

Desert Skiff w/Luke Skywalker,
Han Solo, 7104 .... n/a..........................$6

Ewok Attack w/Biker Scout, Stormtrooper,
two Ewoks, 7139 .... n/a........................$13

Final Duel I w/Emperor, Darth Vader,
7200 .... n/a........................$10

Final Duel II w/Luke Skywalker, Imperial Officer,
Stormtrooper, 7201............................. n/a..........................$7

Imperial AT-ST w/Chewbacca, 7127 .... n/a........................$10

Imperial Shuttle w/Emperor, Pilot, two Royal Guards,
7166 .... n/a........................$35

Chewbacca, two Biker Scouts, Mini-Figure Sets,
3342 .... n/a..........................$5

Star Wars

Darth Vader, 8010.. n/a........................$40

Droid Escape w/R2-D2, C-3PO, 7106............ n/a..........................$7

Landspeeder w/Luke Skywalker, Obi-Wan Kenobi, 1999,
7110 .... n/a..........................$6

Millennium Falcon w/Han Solo, Leia, Luke, Chewbacca,
R2-D2, C-3PO, 7190 .... n/a......................$100

R2-D2, 8009 .... n/a........................$20

Rebel Blockade Runner?Tantive IV Corellian Corvette,
10019.. n/a......................$150

TIE Fighter w/Pilot, Stormtrooper, 7146 .... n/a........................$20

TIE Interceptor, 7181................................... n/a........................$20

X-Wing Fighter, 7140 .... n/a........................$45

Dark Side Developer, Mindstorms, 9754........ n/a......................$100

Sandtrooper figure from 1996, $12 MIP.

Grand Moff Tarkin, a 1997 release, $10 MIP.

	MNP	MIP
Emperor Palpatine, Darth Maul, Darth Vader, Mini-Figure Sets, 3340	n/a	$5
C-3PO, Technic, 8007	n/a	35
Stormtrooper, Technic, 8008	n/a	$35

The Phantom Menace

	MNP	MIP
Darth Maul (bust), 10018	n/a	$125
Droid Fighter, 7111	n/a	$6
Flash Speeder w/Royal Naboo Security Force, 7121	n/a	$10
Gungan Patrol w/Jar Jar Binks, Gungan Warrior, 7115	n/a	$10
Gungan Sub w/Qui-Gon Jinn, Obi-Wan Kenobi, Jar Jar Binks, 1999, 7161	n/a	$45
Jedi Defense I w/Obi-Wan Kenobi, two Destroyer Droids, 7203	n/a	$7
Jedi Defense II w/Qui-Gon Jinn, two Battle Droids, 7204	n/a	$7
Lightsaber Duel w/Qui-Gon Jinn, Darth Maul, 1999, 7101	n/a	$5
Mos Espa Podrace w/Padme, Anakin, R2-D2, Qui-Gon, Jar Jar, Sebulba, Gasgano, 7171	n/a	$85
Naboo Fighter w/Anakin Skywalker, two Battle Droids, 1999, 7141	n/a	$25
Naboo Swamp w/Qui-Gon Jinn, Jar Jar Binks, two Battle Droids, 1999, 7121	n/a	$10
Podracer, 1999, 7131	n/a	$20
Sith Infiltrator w/Darth Maul, 7151	n/a	$30
Trade Federation MTT, 7184	n/a	$45
Command Officer, two Battle Droids, Mini-Figure Sets, 3343	$2	$5

Darth Maul figure by Applause, 1999, $10 MIP.

	MNP	MIP
Battle Droid, Technic, 8001	n/a	$25
Detroyer Droid, Technic, 8002	n/a	$45
Pit Droid, Technic, 8000	n/a	$20

Play Sets

Star Wars

	MNP	MIP
Cantina Adventure Set, Sears Exclusive, 1977	$150	$420
Creature Cantina, 1977	$25	$100
Death Star Space Station, 1977	$75	$320
Droid Factory, 1977	$50	$105
Land of the Jawas, 1977	$41	$85

Empire Strikes Back

	MNP	MIP
Cloud City Play Set, Sears Exclusive, 1981	$90	$250
Dagobah, 1982	$22	$80
Darth Vader's Star Destroyer	$32	$115
Hoth Ice Planet, 1980	$25	$80
Imperial Attack Base, 1980	$17	$60
Rebel Command Center, 1980	$45	$105
Turret and Probot, 1980	$22	$100

Return of the Jedi

	MNP	MIP
Ewok Village, 1983	$38	$80
Jabba the Hutt, 1983	$17	$60
Jabba the Hutt Dungeon, w/EV-9D9, Amanaman, Barada, 1983	$175	$250
Jabba the Hutt Dungeon, w/Nikto, 8D8, Klaatu, 1983	$27	$55

Another Imperial officer, the AT-AT Commander (also known as General Veers figure) was packaged with the vehicle and did not include a weapon. About $10 in mint condition.

R2D2 from Phantom Menace. Mint-in-pack value, $8 MIP.

	MNP	MIP

Ewoks

Ewoks Treehouse, 1985 .... $16 .... $35

Saga

Geonosian Arena, 2002 .... $17 .... $35

Vehicles

Star Wars

Darth Vader's TIE Fighter, 1977, Fly-apart panels, battery-powered laser cannon lights up in front .... $30 .... $80

Imperial Cruiser, 1982, second version of this vehicle. What was once the compartment for a 9-volt battery was now a "weapons storage bin." This vehicle had no battery-powered sounds, but did have opening doors, rotating turret and antenna, and opening tailgate. .... $20 .... $45

Imperial TIE Fighter, 1977, fly-apart panels .... $27 .... $100

Imperial Trooper Transport, 1977, first version was a Sears Exclusive, with battery-powered laser sounds. Later model released with "Empire Strikes Back" didn't include sounds or require battery power. .... $20 .... $65

Jawa Sandcrawler, battery-operated, 1977 .... $220 .... $525

Land Speeder, 1977, retractable hovering wheels, opening hood .... $13 .... $47

Land Speeder, battery-operated, 1977 .... $16 .... $50

Millennium Falcon, 1977 .... $50 .... $310

Sonic Land Speeder, JC Penney Exclusive, 1977 .... $95 .... $400

X-Wing Fighter, 1977, pushing R2 head into vehicle would put foils in "X-wing" position. Opening canopy, light-up laser cannon on front. .... $17 .... $80

The "Epic Force" series figures featured great detail and rotated on a plastic base, $15 MIP.

	MNP	MIP

Vehicles

Empire Strikes Back

AT-AT, 1980, All-Terrain Armored Transport.. $85...................... $160

Rebel Transport, 1980 .... $35........................ $80

Scout Walker, 1982, two-legged vehicle with "walking" legs operated by button behind cockpit. A lever allowed the legs to remain locked so the vehicle could stand in place. Opening flip-up top to place figures, and opening turret allowing stormtroopers to fire weapons. .... $22.........................$42

Slave I, 1980.. $30........................ $70

Snowspeeder, 1980 .... $28........................ $70

Twin-Pod Cloud Car, 1980 .... $26........................ $65

Return of the Jedi

B-Wing Fighter, 1984 .... $60...................... $150

Ewok Combat Glider, 1984 .... $10........................ $22

Imperial Shuttle, 1984................................. $150...................... $420

Speeder Bike, 1983...................................... $10........................ $32

TIE Interceptor, 1984................................... $42........................ $90

Y-Wing Fighter, 1983 .... $55...................... $150

POTF

Ewok Battle Wagon, 1985 .... $75...................... $190

Imperial Sniper Vehicle, 1985 .... $35........................ $55

One-Man Sand Skimmer, 1985 .... $20........................ $45

Security Scout Vehicle, 1985 .... $32........................ $75

Tatooine Skiff, 1985 .... $190...................... $440

*Super Battle Droid from
Attack of the Clones features
laser blast damage and
interchangeable arms, $8
MIP.*

*Rebel Fleet Trooper, 1997,
$14 MIP.*

	MNP	MIP

Droids

ATL Interceptor, 1985	$25	$65
A-Wing Fighter, 1983	$165	$360
Imperial Side Gunner, 1985	$14	$55

Ewoks

Ewoks Fire Cart, 1985	$6	$17
Ewoks Woodland Wagon, 1985	$7	$30

POTF2

Speeder Bike, 1997, includes Scout Trooper figure. Bike pieces and trooper fall off when "battle damage" button is pushed on bike.
.... $10 .... $25

POTJ

TIE Interceptor, 2002, includes figure, wings pop off simulating battle damage. A Toys R Us exclusive, these toys are now exclusively found in the secondary market, doubling the price collectors pay to get their hands on one .... $15 .... $30

Die-Cast

Darth Vader's TIE Fighter, 1979	$14	$50
Land Speeder, 1979	$14	$65
Millennium Falcon, 1979	$20	$105
Naboo Starfighter, 1999	$4	$10
Slave I, 1979	$25	$75
Snowspeeder, 1979	$17	$65
Star Destroyer, 1979	$25	$110
TIE Bomber, 1979	$150	$410
TIE Fighter, 1979	$12	$45

	MNP	MIP
Twin-Pod Cloud Car, 1979	$17	$70
X-Wing Fighter, 1979	$15	$70
Y-Wing Fighter, 1979	$22	$90

The Phantom Menace

	MNP	MIP
Anakin Skywalker's Podracer, 1999	$10	$20
Flash Speeder, 1999, Hovercraft much in the style of other Star Wars speeders.	$5	$15
Naboo Starfighter, 1999	$5	$25
Sebulba's Pod Racer w/Sebulba, 1999	$10	$25
Sith Speeder w/Darth Maul, 1999	$8	$25
STAP w/Battle Droid, 1999	$5	$15
Trade Federation Droid Fighter, 1999	$5	$20
Trade Federation Tank, 1999	$5	$30
Armored Scout Tank w/Battle Droid, Invasion Force, 1999	$5	$25
Gungan Assault Cannon w/Jar Jar Binks, Invasion Force, 1999	$5	$15
Gungan Mini-Sub w/Obi-Wan Kenobi, Invasion Force, 1999	$5	$25
Ammo Wagon and Falumpaset, Wal-Mart Exclusive, 1999	$5	$25

Saga

	MNP	MIP
Anakin Skywalker Speeder, 2002, with blast-off panels. Apparently, Lucas made a last-minute color change to this model (for the movie) making the speeder yellow in homage to Bob Milner's '32 Ford coupe in the movie "American Graffiti."	$3	$16
Anakin Skywalker's Swoop Bike, 2003, w/Anakin figure (showing a lot of teeth)	$10	$20
A-Wing Fighter w/Rebel Pilot, 2003, Target Exclusive	$10	$20

	MNP	MIP

Darth Tyranus' Geonosian Speeder Bike, 2003, w/Darth Tyranus figure .... $10.........................$20

Imperial Dogfight TIE Fighter w/TIE Pilot, 2003, KB Toys exclusive .... $10.........................$25

Imperial Shuttle, 2003, FAO Schwarz exclusive .... $75.........................$125

Jango Fett's Slave I, 2002, launches four missiles, has more vibrant color as a new ship than it does by the time Boba inherits it. .... $10.........................$25

Jedi Starfighter w/Obi-Wan Kenobi, 2002, KB Toys exclusive .... $10.........................$25

Jedi Starfighter, Obi-Wan Kenobi, 2002, no figure .... $10.........................$25

Landspeeder, 2002, TRU exclusive .... $10.........................$20

Republic Gunship, 2002, fits one pilot, carries troops in main body, pivoting laser cannon .... $10.........................$30

TIE Bomber, 2003, w/pilot .... $10.........................$25

X-Wing Fighter, 2002, TRU Exclusive .... $10.........................$25

Zam Wessell Coruscant Speeder, 2002, with flexible "crush zones" to emulate Zam's rough landing on Coruscant .... $3.........................$17

Clone Wars

Anakin Skywalker's Jedi Starfighter, 2003, one missile, red Droid .... $15.........................$22

Armored Assault Tank (AAT), 2003, four missiles .... $15.........................$22

Command Gunship, 2003 .... $15.........................$22

Geonosian Starfighter w/pilot, 2003, exclusive Geonosian pilot, one missile .... $15.........................$22

Hailfire Droid, 2003, thirty-two red missiles .... $15.........................$22

Jedi Starfighter, 2003, blue w/yellow droid .... $15.........................$22

Tin Toys

Yesterday's tin creations are some of today's priciest collectible toys. Many of the metal toys produced before World War I can be considered true works of art, especially since tin toys were often painstakingly hand painted.

The advent of chromolithography changed all that. The technology was actually developed late in the 19th century, but first applied to tin toys in the 1920s. The technique allowed multicolor illustrations to be printed on flat tin plates which were molded into toys. American manufacturers could produce these colorful toys more inexpensively than the classic European toys that had dominated the toy market until this time.

With mass production came mass appeal, and these new tin mechanical toys were often based on the characters and celebrities that were popular at the time. Comic strip characters and Walt Disney movies provided most of the already-popular subject matter for toy marketers.

Among the most well-known makers of mechanical tin toys were Marx, Chein, Lehmann, and Strauss. Others included Courtland, Girard, Ohio Art, Schuco, Unique Art, and Wolverine.

One of the advantages of lithography was that it allowed old toys to be recycled in many ways. When a character's public appeal began to wane, a new image could be printed on the same body to produce a new toy. Or when a toy company was absorbed by another, older models could be dusted off and dressed up with new lithography. Many of the mechanical tin wind-up toys show up in surprisingly similar versions with another manufacturer's name on them.

Of the companies listed here, Marx was no doubt the most prolific. The company's founder, Louis Marx, at one time was employed by another leading toy maker, Ferdinand Strauss. He left Strauss in 1918 to start his own company. Some of his first successes were new versions of old Strauss toys like the (still reproduced and quite famous) Climbing Monkey.

Many of the popular Marx tin wind-ups were also based on popular characters. Not surprisingly, some of the other highly valued character toys are the Amos 'N Andy Walkers, the Donald Duck Duet, Popeye the Champ, Li'l Abner and his Dogpatch Band, and the Superman Rollover Airplane.

Other companies, such as Chein, specialized in inexpensive lithographed tin. Like Marx, Chein also capitalized on popular cartoon characters, producing

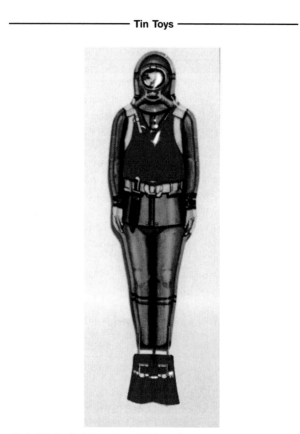

Chein Mechanical Frog Man, 11" long, $200.

several Popeye toys, among others. J. Chein and Company, which was founded in 1903, was best known for its carnival-themed mechanical toys. Its Ferris wheel is fairly well known among toy collectors and was made in several lithographed versions, including one with a Disneyland theme. Chein also produced a number of affordable tin banks.

Prices listed are for toys in good, excellent and mint conditions. Toys will usually command a premium over the listed price if they are in their original boxes.

Tin toys have kept their values over the years, but there doesn't seem to be the demand there once was. It may come down to the simple premise that everyone who wants one has one. Plus, there are a number of quality reproductions for fairly low prices for the collector who just wants the toy without it being an investment.

T.P.S. Bear Playing Ball, $375 MIP. Photo courtesy Don Hultzman

Bobo the Mechanical Juggling Clown, T.P.S., $700.

Tin Toys

Miscellaneous Toys

	EX	NM	MIP
1917 Ford	$50	$80	$125
Aha Truck, 1907-1935, delivery van, 5-1/2"			
	$500	$650	$900
Airplane and Pilot, 1930s, friction toy, oversized pilot			
	$135	$225	$350
Airplane Carousel, 1930s			
	$100	$200	$375
Ajax Acrobat, does somersaults, 10" tall			
	$850	$1425	$2200
Alabama Jigger, 1920s, No. 685, wind-up tap dancer on square base			
	$500	$700	$900
Arithmetic Quiz Toy, 1950s, math quiz machine			
	$30	$50	$75
Army Code Sender, pressed steel			
	$20	$35	$50
Army Drummer, 1930s, plunger-activated, 7" high			
	$125	$200	$250
Artie the Clown in his Crazy Car			
	$300	$400	$500
Automatic Airport, 1940s, two planes circle tower, 9" high			
	$90	$135	$180
Auton Boy & Cart	$200	$325	$495
Baby Grand Piano, w/piano-shaped music books			
	$50	$100	$250
Battleship, 1930s, 14" long..	$75	$125	$200

T.P.S. Gay 90s Cyclist, 7" high, $375. Photo courtesy Scott Smiles

	EX	NM	MIP
Bavarian Boy, 1950s, tin and cloth boy w/beer mug, 5" tall	$100	$200	$300
Bavarian Dancing Couple, tin and cloth, 5" high	$105	$180	$275
Big Shot,	$75	$100	$150
Black Man, tin and cloth, 5" high	$250	$425	$650
Bombo the Monk, 1930s, two pieces, tree and monkey, 9-1/2" tree, 5-1/2" monkey	$125	$150	$225
Capitol Hill Racer, 1930s, 17-1/2" long	$100	$150	$200
Captain of Kopenick, early 1900s	$625	$1050	$1600
Carnival Set, 1930s, diorama w/several rides on tin base	$300	$500	$1000
Casey the Cop	$600	$800	$1000
Cat Pushing Ball, 1938, lever action, wooden ball	$75	$100	$150
Circus Shooting Gallery, 1950s, w/gun and darts, 12" high, 17" long	$60	$90	$150
Clown Playing Violin, 1950s, tin and cloth, 4-1/2" tall	$135	$225	$350
Coast Guard Plane, 1950s, 10" wingspan	$75	$125	$175
Combinato Convertible, 1950s, 7-1/2" long	$100	$175	$250
Coney Island Roller Coaster, 1950s,	$125	$200	$300

Handstand Clown tin wind-up, 5 inches tall, Chein, $125 MIP.

	EX	NM	MIP
Crane, red and blue, 18" high	$40	$65	$100
Crocodile, 1940s, walks, mouth opens	$350	$475	$600
Curvo Motorcycle, 1950s, 5" long	$150	$225	$350
Dancing Boy and Girl, 1930s, tin and cloth	$125	$200	$300
Dancing Mice, 1950s, large and small mouse, tin and cloth	$135	$225	$350
Dancing Monkey with Mouse, 1950s, tin and cloth	$125	$210	$325
Dancing Sailor, 1904-1948, No. 535, 7-1/2" high	$600	$800	$1000
Dandy Jim Dancer, 1921	$500	$700	$900
Daredevil Motor Cop, 1940s, 8-1/2" long	$300	$450	$600
Delivery Van, "Huntley & Palmers Biscuits"	$650	$1075	$1650
Disneyland Tea Set, 1954, fifteen-piece set featuring Disney characters	$100	$175	$500
Doll Stroller, 1950s, teddy bear design	$40	$60	$80
Dolly's Washer, 1930s, washing machine	$65	$100	$300
Donald Duck Carpet Sweeper, 1940s, red w/Disney litho	$60	$100	$250

Rare tin Ferris wheel, Chein, $525 MIP. Photo courtesy Carol Perry

	EX	NM	MIP
Drum Major, round base, 13"			
	$100	$175	$250
Drum Major, 1950	$100	$150	$300
Drummer, 1930s, tin and cloth, 5" tall			
	$125	$210	$325
Easter Basket, nursery rhyme figures			
	$35	$55	$100
Easter Egg, 1938, tin, chicken on top, opens to hold candy, 5-1/2"			
	$35	$55	$85
Examico 4001 Convertible, 5-1/2", maroon tin wind-up			
	$175	$250	$375
Express Bus	$125	$210	$325
Express Man & Cart, 1888-1918, No. 140, porter pulls striped cart,			
6" long	$450	$600	$700
Finnegan the Porter, 1930s, w/cardboard luggage,			
14" long	$200	$300	$400
Flic 4520, traffic cop-type figure			
	$135	$225	$350
Flying Bird	$300	$475	$750
Flying Circus, elephant supports plane and clown			
	$450	$650	$850
Fox And Goose, 1950s, tin and cloth, fox holding goose in cage,			
4-1/4" high	$800	$1200	$1600
G.I. Joe and His Jouncing Jeep, 1940s, wind-up, 7"			
	$175	$250	$350
G.I. Joe and His K-9 Pups, 1940s			
	$150	$225	$300
Galop Race Car, 1920s	$250	$400	$600

Tin wind-up version of Maggie & Jigs, 1924, $850 MIP.

Dottie the Driver tin toy, 6-1/2 inches long, Marx, 1950s, $200 MIP.

	EX	NM	MIP
Gertie the Galloping Goose, 1930s, 9-1/2" long	$125	$175	$225
Gustav The Climbing Miller	$400	$650	$1000
Hee Haw, donkey pulling milk cart, 10" long	$150	$225	$300
Helicopter, Toy Town Airways, 1950s, friction drive, 13" long	$55	$90	$135
Hillbilly Express, 1930s, 18" long	$100	$150	$200
Hobo Train, 1920s, dog biting pants of hobo atop train, 8-1/2"	$300	$450	$650
Hoky Poky, 1930s, clowns on railcar	$200	$300	$400
Hopping Rabbit, 1950s, metal and plastic, 4" tall	$40	$65	$100
Hott and Trott Musical Band, 1920s	$500	$750	$1000
Howdy Doody & Buffalo Bob at Piano	$750	$1300	$2000
Indian in Headdress, 1930s, 5-1/2" high	$125	$175	$225
Ito Sedan and Driver, 1914-1935, No. 679, 6-1/2"	$500	$700	$900
Jazzbo Jim-The Dancer on the Roof, 1920s, 10" high	$250	$375	$500
Jet Roller Coaster, 21" long	$175	$250	$325

Tin wind-up Li'l Abner & His Dogpatch Band, Unique Art, 1930s, $1,000 MIP.

Scottie Dog 5-1/2-inch wind-up toy, Lehmann, 1930s, $600.

	EX	NM	MIP
Juggling Clown, tin and cloth, 4-1/2" tall			
	$135	$225	$350
Jumping Frog	$40	$65	$100
Jungle Eyes Shooting Gallery, 1950s, w/gun and darts, 14" high,			
18" long	$90	$135	$180
Jungle Man Spear,	$100	$150	$200
KADI, 1917-1927, No. 723, Chinese men carrying box			
	$1000	$1700	$2500
Kiddy Go-Round	$175	$250	$400
Kid-Go-Round, plastic horsemen and boat			
	$150	$225	$300
King Kong, on wheels, w/spring-loaded arms,			
6-1/2" tall	$35	$60	$95
Krazy Kar, 1921,	$275	$425	$550
Lehmann's Autobus, 1907-1945,			
No. 590	$1000	$1800	$2400
Li'l Abner and His Dogpatch			
Band	$400	$700	$1000
Li-La Car, 1903-1935, driver in rear, women passengers,			
5-1/2"	$1000	$1500	$2000
Lincoln Tunnel, 1935,			
24" long	$200	$300	$400
Little Red Riding Hood Tea Set, 1920s			
seven-piece set	$100	$200	$350
Marine, 1950s, hand on belt,			
6" high	$125	$150	$200
Mauswagen, tin and cloth mice and			
wagon	$200	$325	$500

Farmer in the Dell tin crank music box, Mattel, 1951, $110 MIP.

	EX	NM	MIP
Melody Organ Player	$75	$125	$175
Mercer Car No. 1225, 1950s, 7-1/2" long	$100	$150	$225
Merry-Go-Round, 1930s, No. 31, 11" diameter, 12" high	$275	$400	$525
Mexican Boy Tea Set, 1940s, nine-piece set	$75	$100	$200
Mickey & Minnie Dancing, tin and cloth	$700	$1200	$1800
Mickey Mouse Tray, 1930s	$50	$100	$200
Mikado Family, 1894-1918, No. 350, 6-1/2"	$650	$1100	$1500
Minstrel Man, early 1900s	$350	$550	$1000
Model Shooting Gallery, 1930s	$85	$200	$300
Monk Drinking Beer, tin and cloth, 5" high	$125	$200	$300
Monkey Drummer, 1950s, tin and cloth	$125	$200	$300
Monkey in Car, 1930s	$335	$550	$850
Monkey on Scooter, 1930s, tin and cloth	$125	$200	$300
Monkey Playing Violin, 1950s, tin and cloth	$125	$210	$325
Mother Duck with Baby Ducks, 1950s, two baby ducks on wheels pulled behind mother ducks	$50	$100	$125

The Happy Warrior tin wind-up, T.P.S., stands 6 inches tall, $450.

	EX	NM	MIP
Mother Goose Tea Set, 1931, seven-piece set	$90	$150	$250
Motorcycle Cop, 1930s, 9" long	$300	$400	$500
Musical Sail-Way Carousel, three kids spin in plastic boats, 9" tall	$175	$250	$350
Musical Top Clown, 1950s, clown head handle, 7" high	$75	$125	$195
Mysterious Woodpecker	$50	$80	$125
Mystery Car	$100	$165	$250
New Century Cycle, 1895-1938, No. 345, driver and black man w/umbrella, 5"	$400	$600	$900
Ostrich Cart	$380	$650	$975
Paddy and the Pig, 1903-1935, No. 500, 6"	$1250	$1750	$2300
Pathe Movie Camera, 1930s, 6" tall	$55	$90	$135
Pecking Goose, Witch and Cat	$350	$525	$700
Player Piano, eight rolls	$195	$325	$500
Quack Quack, duck pulling babies	$300	$450	$600
Rabbit in shirt and pants, 1938, red pants, yellow feet, hands in pockets	$50	$75	$95
Rodeo Joe Crazy Car, 1950s	$150	$225	$325
Rollover Motorcycle Cop, 1935	$300	$400	$500

	EX	NM	MIP
Rooster and Rabbit, rooster pulls rabbit on cart	$400	$625	$975
Rooster Pulling Wagon, 1930s	$60	$90	$120
Sand Toy, monkey bends and twists, 7" high	$30	$50	$75
Sand Toy Set, duck mold, sifter, frog on card	$30	$45	$70
Sandy Andy Fullback, kicking fullback, 8" tall	$175	$295	$450
Schuco Turn Monkey on Suitcase, 1950s, tin and cloth	$125	$195	$300
Scuba Diver, 10" long	$70	$120	$185
Sea Lion	$150	$250	$375
Searchlight, 3-1/2" tall	$40	$65	$100
Sedan and Garage	$350	$550	$750
See-Saw Sand Toy, 1930s, bright colors, boy and girl on see-saw move	$55	$90	$135
See-Saw Sand Toy, 1930s, pastel colors, boy and girl on see-saw move	$70	$120	$185
Shenandoah Zeppelin	$155	$255	$395
Skier, 1920s, wind-up	$500	$850	$1300
Sky Rangers, plane and	$300	$400	$625
Snow White Stove, 1960s	$20	$35	$50
Space Ride, 1940s, tin litho, boxed, lever action w/music, 9" high	$425	$650	$850
Sparkler Toy, on original card, 5"	$30	$50	$75

	EX	NM	MIP
Studio No. 1050 Race Car, 1950s, 5-1/2" long	$125	$180	$250
Submarine, 13" long	$100	$165	$250
Sunny and Tank, yellow and green, 14-1/2" long	$75	$130	$200
Sunny Suzy Deluxe Washing Machine, 1930s	$50	$95	$200
Taxi, 1920s, 10" long	$450	$750	$1150
Ten Little Indians Spinning Top	$15	$25	$35
Three Little Pigs Spinning Top	$15	$25	$35
Three Little Pigs Wind-Up Toy, 1930s, 4-1/2" pigs playing fiddle, fife and drum	$250	$500	$775
Toto the Acrobat	$100	$150	$200
Trapeze Artist, 1930s	$125	$200	$325
Tumbling Boy, 1950s, tin and cloth	$100	$165	$250
Tut-Tut Car, 1903-1935, No 490, driver has horn, 6-3/4" long	$700	$1200	$1700
Watering Cans, many variations, value is for each	$25	$30	$40
Wild West Bucking Bronco	$575	$900	$1400
Yellow Taxi, 1940s, 13" long	$150	$225	$350
Yes-No Monkey	$175	$275	$425
Zebra Cart "Dare Devil," 1920s	$400	$600	$800

	EX	NM	MIP

Zig-Zag, 1910-1945, handcar-type vehicle on oversized wheels,
5" long .... $900 .... $1400 .... $1900

Zilotone, 1920s, clown on xylophone, w/three
musical discs .... $450 .... $700 .... $925

Wind-Up Toys

Acrobatic Marvel Money, 1930s, balances on
two chairs .... $100 .... $175 .... $250

Airplane, square-winged, early tin, 7"
wingspan .... $100 .... $150 .... $225

Amos 'n Andy Fresh Air Taxi, 1930s, 5"x8"
long .... $550 .... $1200 .... $1800

Army Cargo Truck, 1920s, 8" long
.... $235 .... $390 .... $600

Army Plane, 11" wingspan
.... $135 .... $230 .... $350

Army Sergeant .... $70 .... $120 .... $185

Army Truck, open bed, 8-1/2" long
.... $50 .... $75 .... $100

Army Truck, cannon on back,
8-1/2" long .... $50 .... $80 .... $125

Barnacle Bill, 1930s, looks like Popeye, waddles
.... $300 .... $450 .... $600

Barney Rubble Riding Dino,
1960s, 8" long .... $185 .... $310 .... $475

Bear Cyclist, 1934,
5-3/4" tall .... $175 .... $250 .... $325

Busy Miners, 1930s, with miner's car,
16-1/2" long .... $200 .... $300 .... $375

	EX	NM	MIP
Carter Climbing Money, 1921, 8-1/2" tall	$115	$190	$290
Charleston Trio, 1926, man, boy and dog dancers on roof, 9" tall	$500	$750	$950
Charlie McCarthy Bass Drummer, 1939	$450	$750	$1150
Climbing Fireman, 1950s, tin and plastic	$135	$225	$350
Clown Boxing, 8" tall	$300	$485	$600
Dapper Dan Coon Jigger, 1922, 10" tall	$500	$800	$1100
Disneyland Ferris Wheel, 1940s	$425	$650	$1100
Donald Duck Duet, 1946, Donald and Goofy, 10-1/2" tall	$500	$800	$1100
Dopey, 1938, walker, 8" tall	$310	$525	$1000
Doughboy, 1920s, tin litho, WWI soldier w/rifle, 6" high	$175	$250	$325
Duck, 1930, waddles, 6" high	$125	$175	$225
Ferris Wheel, The Giant Ride, 16" high	$100	$250	$500
Fireman on Ladder, 24" tall	$200	$300	$450
Goofy the Walking Gardener, 1960, holds a wheelbarrow, 9" tall	$250	$425	$650
Handstand Clown, 1930s, 5" tall	$75	$125	$200

	EX	NM	MIP

Harold Lloyd Funny Face, 1928, walker, 11" tall
.... $275............. $475.................... $600

Hi-Yo Silver and the Lone Ranger, 1938, 8" tall
.... $200............. $325.................... $575

Jumping Rabbit, 1925, 5"
.... $100............. $125.................... $150

Knockout Champs Boxing Toy, 1930s
.... $175............. $300.................... $450

Little Orphan Annie and Sandy, 1930s
.... $275............. $475.................... $725

Mack Hercules Motor Express, tin litho,
19-1/2" long............. $235............. $385.................... $595

Main Street, 1929, street scene w/moving cars,
traffic cop .... $275............. $425.................... $575

Mammy's Boy, 1929, wind-up walker, 11" tall
.... $500............. $750.................... $1000

Mark 1 Cabin Cruiser, 1957,
9" long .... $50................. $75.................... $100

Mechanical Aquaplane, No. 39, 1932, boat-like pontoons,
8-1/2" long .... $200............. $300.................... $400

Merrymakers Band, 1931, without marquee, mouse band
w/violinist .... $750............. $1000.................... $1400

Mickey Mouse, 7" tall....... $200............. $400.................... $600

Minnie Mouse, 7" tall ...... $200............. $400.................... $600

Mother Goose, 1920s, 7-1/2" tall $150........ $250.................... $400

Musical Aero Swing, 1940s,
10" high .... $250............. $375.................... $500

Musical Circus Horse, 1939, pull toy, metal drum rolls w/chimes,
10-1/2" long............... $80............. $130.................... $200

	EX	NM	MIP
Pinocchio, 1938, 9" tall	$275	$450	$700
Playland Merry-Go-Round, 1930s, 9-1/2" high	$375	$550	$675
Pluto Watch Me Roll-Over, 1939, 8" long	$165	$275	$425
Popeye and Olive Oyl Jiggers, 1936, 10" tall	$700	$1175	$1800
Porky Pig with Rotating Umbrella, 1939, w/or without top hat, 8" tall	$300	$525	$800
Stop, Look and Listen, 1927, circular track toy	$300	$500	$750
Subway Express, 1954, 9-3/8"	$125	$175	$225
Superman Holding Airplane, 1940, 6" wingspan on airplane	$875	$1450	$2250
Touring Car, 7" long	$60	$100	$150
Woody Car, 1940s, red, 5" long	$100	$165	$250

Buddy L Baby Ruth/Butterfinger Curtiss Candies Tandem Truck, $2,000. Photo courtesy John Taylor

Top to bottom: Buddy L Large Trucks Hydraulic Dump Truck (Vehicles), No. 201A, $1,700; Buddy L Large Trucks Dump Truck, No. 201, 25", $1,250. Photo courtesy Tim Oei

Vehicles

By Merry Dudley

I'm always amazed by the way today's pugnacious "realism is king" collector reacts to the sight of a pressed steel truck, particularly a dump truck, tow truck, or car carrier.

First of all, they have to touch it, regardless of condition. The truck could be rusted through and full of dirt, but the person will still touch it with an astounding air of reverence.

The phenomenon changes slightly with a tow truck or car carrier. The hook and pulley assembly gets the most attention on the tow truck, and deservedly so. Car carriers serve a dual purpose. The nostalgia of the car carrier is only slightly eclipsed by the way it has become the perfect piece on which to display other cars of similar scale.

Perhaps it's a response to today's very different market. Stores are flooded with die-cast, a market driven by the flawed idea that licensing is imperative and increased realism is the only feature/technological advancement that matters. In smaller scales, the charm of opening features has been eclipsed by the desire for realistic shut lines. Larger scales suffer from the licensing disease: If it's not licensed by a movie studio, manufacturers reason, why will it sell? And why should it be manufactured in the first place?

The old days may be gone, but the memories of a simpler time remain to come flooding back whenever we encounter those pressed-steel treasures.

Hobby Trends

The affect of Internet auction giant eBay on the toy vehicle hobby is impossible to underestimate. Toys that were once reasonably hard to find at regional toy shows are now available to anyone with Internet access. This makes it easier for those collectors who would rather surf the net than make a cross-country trek to find that elusive toy.

But with every good comes some bad. Smaller toy shows have been hit hard, although it seems that things are picking up on this front while eBay is showing signs of saturation.

Merry Dudley is the editor of Toy Cars and Models *magazine and the* Standard Catalog of 1:18 Scale Die-Cast Cars, *both published by Krause Publications, Iola, Wis.*

Vehicles

Buddy L

Airplanes

	EX	NM	MIP

Army Tank Transport Plane, Buddy L, low-wing monoplane, two small four-wheel tanks that clip beneath wings, 27" wingspan; 1941 .... $250............... $350...................... $400

Four-Engine Transport, Buddy L, green wings, white engine cowlings, yellow fuselage and twin tails, four engine monoplane, 27" wingspan; 1949 .... $205............... $300...................... $405

Cars

Buddywagen (VW), Buddy L, 10-3/4" long; red body with white roof, no chrome "V" on front; 1967 .... $30............... $60......................... $90

Flivver Roadster, Buddy L, black w/red eight-spoke wheels, black hubs, aluminum tires, simulated soft, folding top, 11" long; 1924 .... $650............... $950.................... $1350

Station Wagon, Buddy L, light blue/green body and roof, 15-1/2" long; 1963 .... $75............... $115...................... $150

Town and Country Convertible, Buddy L, maroon front, hood, rear deck and fenders, gray top retracts into rumble seat, 19" long; 1947 .... $300............... $450.................... $600

Emergency Vehicles

Aerial Ladder and Emergency Truck, Buddy L, red w/white ladders, bumper and steel disc wheels, three eight-rung steel ladders, 22-1/4" long; 1952.... $200............... $300...................... $400

Extension Ladder Rider Fire Truck, Buddy L, duo-tone slant design, tractor has white front, lower hood sides and lower doors, red hood top, cab and frame, red semi-trailer, white ten-rung and eight-rung ladders, 32-1/2" long; 1949 .... $150............... $225...................... $300

1950s Buddy L Army truck, missing fabric cover, $225.

1940s Buddy L baggage truck, 17 inches long, wooden wheels, $350 MIP.

	EX	NM	MIP

GMC Red Cross Ambulance, Buddy L, all white, removable fabric canopy w/a red cross and "Ambulance" in red, 14-1/2" long; 1960 .... $150.............. $250...................... $400

Texaco Fire Chief American LaFrance Pumper, Buddy L, promotional piece, red rounded-front enclosed cab and body, white one-piece underbody, running boards and rear step, 25" long; 1962 .... $210.............. $305...................... $410

Farm and Construction Equipment

Cement Mixer on Wheels, Buddy L, medium-gray w/black cast steel wheels and water tank, 14-1/2" tall; 1926-29 .... $700.............. $900.................... $1500

Dandy Digger, Buddy L, red main frame, operators, seat and boom, black shovel, arm, under frame and twin skids, 27" long; 1931 .... $100.............. $160...................... $215

Improved Steam Shovel, Buddy L, black w/red roof and base, 14" tall, 1927-29.................... $100.............. $150...................... $200

Mechanical Crane, Buddy L, orange removable roof, boom and wheels in black cleated rubber crawler treads, olive green enclosed cab and base, hand crank w/rattat motor noise, 20" tall; 1950 .... $175.............. $265...................... $350

Road Roller, Buddy L, dark green w/red roof and rollers, nickel plated steam cylinders, No. 290, 20" long, 1929-31 .... $1300.............. $2400.................... $3500

Sand Loader, Buddy L, warm gray w/twelve black buckets, 21" long, 18" high; 1924 .... $150.............. $210...................... $450

Steam Shovel, Buddy L, black w/red roof and base, 25-1/2" tall; 1921-22 .... $125.............. $250...................... $500

Sets

Big Brute 4-Piece Freeway, Buddy L, scraper, grader, scooper and dump truck; 1971 ..... $125.............. $185...................... $250

1920s Buddy L fire truck, 26 inches long, $2,100 MIP.

1949 Buddy L chemical fire truck, 22 inches long, $250.

	EX	NM	MIP

Family Camping, Buddy L, Camper/cruiser truck, 15-1/2" long maroon suburban wagon, and brown/light gray/beige folding teepee camping trailer; 1963 .. $60................. $95....................... $130

Fire Department, Buddy L, aerial ladder fire engine, fire pumper w/ action hydrant that squirts water, two plastic hoses, two plastic firemen, fire chief's badge; 1960
.... $250............... $375....................... $505

Highway Construction, Buddy L, orange and black bulldozer and driver, truck w/orange pickup body, orange dump truck; 1962
.... $200............... $300....................... $400

Polysteel Farm, Buddy L, blue milkman truck w/rack and nine milk bottles, red and gray milk tanker, orange farm tractor; 1961
.... $70............... $115....................... $160

Road Builder, Buddy L, green/white cement mixer truck, yellow/black bulldozer, red dump truck, husky dumper; 1963
.... $200............... $300....................... $400

Western Roundup, Buddy L, turquoise fenders, hood, cab and frame, white flatbed cargo section, six sections of rail fencing w/swinging gate, rearing and standing horse, cowboys, calf, steer; 1960
.... $175............... $250....................... $400

Trucks

Allied Moving Van, Buddy L, tractor and semi-trailer van, duo-tone slant design, black front and lower sides, orange hood top, cab and van body, 29-1/2" long; 1941
.... $600............... $900.................... $1200

Army Transport with Howitzer, Buddy L, olive drab steel, 17" truck, 9-3/4" gun, overall 27" long; 1955
.... $150............... $250....................... $350

Buddy L Western Auto semi truck, 25 inches long, $195.

1950s Buddy L highway truck, 17 inches long, $200 MIP.

	EX	NM	MIP

Big Fella Hydraulic Rider Dumper, Buddy L, duo-tone slant design, yellow front and lower hood, red upper cab, dump body and upper hood, rider seat has large yellow sunburst-style decal, 26-1/2" long; 1950 .... $110............... $175....................... $225

Boat Transport, Buddy L, blue flatbed truck carrying 8" litho metal boat, boat deck white, hull red, truck 15" long; 1959 .... $300............... $550....................... $750

Borden's Milk Delivery Van, Buddy L, 11-1/2" long, white body sliding side doors, opening rear doors, yellow tray with six white fillable polyethylene milk bottles with yellow caps; 1965-67 .... $90............... $185....................... $275

Brute Sanitation Truck, Buddy L, lime green cabover-engine and frame, white open-top body; wide chrome wraparound bumper, 5-1/4" long; 1969 .... $50................. $75....................... $100

Buddy L Milk Farms Truck, Buddy L, light cream body, red roof, nickel glide headlights, sliding doors, 13" long; 1949 .... $170............... $300....................... $500

Camper, Buddy L, bright medium-blue steel truck and camper body, 14-1/2" long; 1964...... $60................. $95....................... $125

Cattle Transport Truck, Buddy L, red w/yellow stake sides, 15" long; 1956 .... $75................. $115....................... $150

City Baggage Dray, Buddy L, cream w/aluminum-finish grille, no bumper, black rubber wheels, 20-3/4" long; 1940 .... $100............... $200....................... $300

Coal Truck, Buddy L, black front, hood, fenders, doorless cab, red chassis and disc sheels, No. 202, 25" long; 1926 .... $3700............... $7500....................$11500

Coca-Cola Bottling Route Truck, Buddy L, bright yellow, w/small metal hand truck, six or eight yellow cases of miniature green Coke bottles, 14-3/4" long; 1955 .... $125............... $175....................... $250

1940s Buddy L excavation and construction truck and shovel set, 30 inches long, $350.

	EX	NM	MIP

Dump Body Truck, Buddy L, black front, hood, open driver's seat and dump section, red chassis, chain drive dump mechanism, 25" long; 1923 .... $1200.............. $1800.................... $2500

Dump Truck, Buddy L, duo-tone slant design, yellow enclosed cab and hood, red front and dump body, no bumper, bright-metal headlights, 20" long; 1936 $250......... $375...................... $500

Dumper with Shovel, Buddy L, medium-green body, frame and dump section, white one-piece bumper and grille guard, no side mirror, large white steel scoop shovel, spring suspension on front axle only, 15" long; 1964.... $75............... $115...................... $150

Fast Delivery Pickup, Buddy L, yellow hood and cab, red open cargo body, removable chain across open back, 13-1/2" long; 1949 .... $105............... $155...................... $200

Fisherman, Buddy L, sage gray/green and white pickup truck w/steel trailer carrying plastic 8-1/2" long sport cruiser, overall 25" long; 1965 .... $65............... $100...................... $135

GMC Self-Loading Auto Carrier, Buddy L, yellow tractor and double-deck semi trailer, three plastic cars, overall 33-1/4" long; 1959 .... $200............... $300...................... $410

Hi-Lift Scoop-n-Dump Truck, Buddy L, orange truck w/deeply fluted sides, dark green scoop on front rises to empty load into hi-lift cream/yellow dump body, 16" long; 1952 .... $85............... $130...................... $175

Husky Dumper, Buddy L, yellow hood, cab, fram and tiltback dump section w/cab shield, crome one-piece wraparound bumper, 14-1/2" long; 1969...... $55................. $75...................... $105

Hydraulic Auto Hauler with Four GMC Cars, Buddy L, powder blue GMC tractor, 7" long plastic cars, overall 33-1/2" long including loading ramp; 1958... $250............... $350...................... $450

Pre-1932 Buddy L road roller, $3,500 MIP. Courtesy Bill Bertoia Auctions. Photo courtesy Jeanne Bertoia

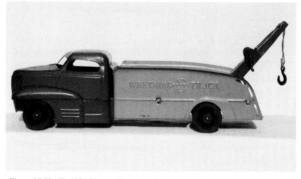

Circa 1940s Buddy L wrecking truck, 19-1/2 inches long, wooden wheels, $300.

	EX	NM	MIP

Hydraulic Highway Dumper with Scraper Blade, Buddy L, orange w/ row of black square across scraper edges, one-piece chrome eight-hole grille and double headlights, 17-3/4" long over blade and raised dump body; 1958 $75.............. $105...................... $155

Hydraulic Rider Dumper, Buddy L, duo-tone slant design, yellow front and lower hood, red upper cab, dump body and upper hood, 26-1/2" long; 1949.... $175............... $265...................... $360

IHC "Red Baby" Express Truck, Buddy L, red doorless roofed cab, open pickup body, chassis and fenders, 24 1/4" long; 1928 .... $750............... $1000...................... $2000

International Delivery Truck, Buddy L, red w/removable black rider saddle, black-edged yellow horizontal strip on cargo body, 24-1/2" long; 1935 .... $225............... $350...................... $450

Jolly Joe Popsicle Truck, Buddy L, white w/black roof, black tires and wooden wheels, 17-1/2" long; 1948 .... $275............... $430...................... $555

Jr. Beach Buggy, Buddy L, yellow hood, fenders and topless Jeep body, red plastic seats, white plastic surfboard that clips to roll bar and windshield, truck 6" long; 1969 .... $45................. $65...................... $90

Jr. Cement Mixer Truck, Buddy L, blue cabover-engine body, frame and hopper, white plastic mixing drum, white plastic seats, 7-1/2" long; 1968 .... $60................. $85...................... $120

Kennel Truck, Buddy L, bright-blue pickup body and cab, clear plastic twelve-section kennel w/twelve plastic dogs fits in cargo box, 13 -1/4" long; 1966..... $95............... $145...................... $190

Mammoth Hydraulic Quarry Dumper, Buddy L, deep-green hood, cab and chassis, red tiltback dump section, black plastic bumper, 23" long; 1962 .... $60............... $105...................... $175

	EX	NM	MIP

Milkman Truck, Buddy L, medium-blue hood, cab and flatbed body, white side rails, eight 3" white plastic milk bottles, 14-1/4" long; 1961 .... $110............... $175...................... $225

Moving Van, Buddy L, black front, hood and seat, red chassis and disc wheels w/black hubs, green van body, roof extends forward above open driver's seat, 25" long; 1924 .... $1200.............. $2000.................... $3000

Overland Trailer Truck, Buddy L, duo-tone horizontal design, red and white tractor has red front, lower half chassis, chassis, enclosed cab, 40"; 1939 .... $350............... $560...................... $710

Polysteel Dumper, Buddy L, green soft-molded plastic front, cab and frame, yellow steel dump body w/sides rounded at back, hinged tailgate, 13" long; 1959 .... $100............... $150...................... $200

Polysteel Supermarket Delivery, Buddy L, medium-blue soft-molded plastic front, hood, cab and frame, steel off-white open cargo section, 13" long; 1959 $75............... $115...................... $150

Railway Express Truck, Buddy L, black front hood, fenders, seat and low body sides, dark-green van body, red chassis, 25" long; 1926 .... $400............... $800.................... $1600

REA Express Truck, Buddy L, dark-green cabover-engine van body, sliding side doors, double rear doors, white plastic one-piece bumper, 11-1/2" long; 1964 .... $200............... $300...................... $400

Ryder Van Lines Trailer, Buddy L, duo-tone slant design, black front and lower hood sides and doors, deep-red hood top, enclosed cab and chassis, 35-1/2" long; 1949 .... $350............... $525...................... $700

	EX	NM	MIP

Saddle Dump Truck, Buddy L, duo-tone slant design, yellow front, fenders and removable rider seat, red enclosed square cab and dump body, no bumper, 19-1/2" long; 1937 .... $200............... $300..................... $400

Sand and Gravel Truck, Buddy L, duo-tone horizontal design, red front, bumper, lower hood, cab sides, chassis and lower dump body sides, white hood top, enclosed cab and upper dump body, 23-3/4" long; 1949 .... $350............... $525..................... $700

Sanitation Service Truck, Buddy L, blue front fenders, hood, cab and chassis, white enclosed dump section and hinged loading hopper, one-piece chrome bumper, no plastic windows in garbage section, 16-1/2" long; 1968...... $75............... $115..................... $150

Shell Pickup and Delivery, Buddy L, yellow/orange hood and body, open cargo section, three curved slots toward rear in sides, chains across back, red coin-slot oil drum w/Shell emblem and lettering, 13-1/4" long; 1952.... $125............... $185..................... $250

Standard Oil Tank Truck, Buddy L, duo-tone slant design, white upper cab and hood, red lower cab, grille, fenders and tank, rubber wheels, electric headlights, 26" long; 1936-37 .... $350............... $500..................... $1000

Texaco Tank Truck, Buddy L, red steel GMC 550-series blunt-nose tractor and semi-trailer tank, 25" long; 1959 .... $175............... $250..................... $400

Traveling Zoo, Buddy L, red high side pickup w/yellow plastic triple-cage unit, six compartments w/plastic animals, 13-1/4" long; 1967 .... $70............... $115..................... $150

U.S. Mail Truck, Buddy L, shiny olive-green body and bumper, yellow-cream removable van roof, enclosed cab, 22-1/2" long; 1953 .... $215............... $410..................... $580

Wrecker Truck, Buddy L, black open cab, red chassis and bed, disc wheels, 26-1/2" long; 1928-29 .... $700............... $1000..................... $2000

Corgi James Bond Aston-Martin, $180 mint.

Chipperfields Circus vehicle and accessory gift set No. 23 from Corgi, $1,300 MIP.

	EX	NM	MIP

Zoo-A-Rama, Buddy L, sand-yellow four-wheel trailer cage, matching
Colt Sports-liner w/white top, three plastic animals, 20-3/4" long;
1968 .... $100............... $155....................... $205

Corgi

Agricultural Vehicles

Agricultural Set, 1967-72, Massey-Ferguson, No. 69 Massey-Ferguson
tractor, No. 62 trailer, No. 438 Land Rover, No. 484 livestock
truck w/pigs, No. 71 harrow, No. 1490 skip and churns; w/
accessories: four calves, farmhand, dog and six sacks, Model No.
5-B .... $120............... $180...................... $400

Country Farm Set, 1974-75, Massey-Ferguson, No. 50 Massey Ferguson
tractor, red No. 62 hay trailer w/load, fences, figures,
Model No. 4-B .... $30................. $45....................... $75

Fordson Tractor and Plow, 1961-64, Fordson, No. 55 Fordson tractor
and No. 56 four furrow plow, Model No. 18-A
.... $55................. $85....................... $140

Massey-Ferguson Combine, 1959-63, Massey-Ferguson, red body w/
yellow metal blades, metal tines, black/white decals, yellow metal
wheels, Model No. 1111-A
.... $70................. $105...................... $175

Silo & Conveyor Belt, 1978-80, w/yellow conveyor and Corgi
Harvesting Co. label on silo, Model No. 43-A
.... $35................. $50....................... $85

Automobiles

Aston Martin D84, 1960-65, Aston Martin, red or yellow body w/
working hood, detailed engine, clear windows, plastic interior,
silver lights, grille, license plate and bumpers, red taillights,
rubber tires, smooth or cast spoked wheels; working scoop on
early models, Model No. 218-A
.... $45................. $65....................... $110

Batman Batmobile & Batboat Gift Set 3 from Corgi, 1973-1981, $350 MIP.

Dinky Unic Auto Transporter. Photo from Christie's South Kensington, $300 mint.

	EX	NM	MIP

Chevrolet Impala, 1960-62, Chevrolet, pink, body, yellow plastic interior, clear windows, silver headlights, bumpers, grille and trim, suspension, die-cast base w/rubber tires; a second version has a blue body w/red or yellow interior and smooth or shaped hubs, Model No. 220-A $50 .... $75...................... $125

Ford Consul, 1956-61, Ford, one-piece body in several colors, clear windows, silver grille, lights and bumpers, smooth wheels, rubber tires, Model No. 200-A $45................ $65...................... $120

Jaguar 2.4 Litre, 1957-63, Jaguar, one-piece white body w/no interior 1957-59, or yellow body w/red interior 1960-63, clear windows, smooth hubs, Model No. 208-A

.... $50................. $50...................... $130

Rover 2000, 1963-66, Rover, metallic blue w/red interior or maroon body w/yellow interior, gray steering wheel, clear windshields, Model No. 252-A .... $30................. $45........................ $75

Volkswagen 1500 Karmann-Ghia, 1963-68, Volkswagen, cream, red, or gold body, plastic interior and taillights, front and rear working hoods, clear windshields, silver bumpers; includes spare wheel and plastic suitcase in trunk, Model No. 239-A

.... $35................. $55........................ $90

Character Vehicles

Batmobile, Batboat and Trailer, 1967-72, first and second versions: red bat hubs on wheels, 1967-72; red tires and chrome wheels 1972-73, Model No. 3-B1 .. $240............... $360...................... $650

Chitty Chitty Bang Bang, 1968-72, metallic copper body, dark-red interior and spoked wheels, four figures, black chassis w/silver running boards, silver hood, horn, brake, dash, tail and headlights, gold radiator, red and orange wings, handbrake operates side wings, Model No. 266-A $180........... $270...................... $425

	EX	NM	MIP

James Bond Aston Martin, 1968-77, Aston Martin, metallic-silver body, red interior, two figures, working roof hatch, ejector seat, bullet shield and guns, chrome bumpers, spoked wheels. Originally issued in a rare bubble pack, the subsequent issues were sold in window boxes. On the left, the rare first issue window box; on the right, the more commonly seen version, Model No. 270-A.
.... $100............... $150...................... $325

Spider-Man Set, 1980-81, set of three: No. 266 Spider-Bike, No. 928 Spider-Copter and No. 261 Spider-Buggy, Model No. 23-B
.... $80............... $160...................... $350

Circus Vehicles

Chipperfield Circus Cage Wagon, 1961-68, red body, yellow chassis, smooth or spun hubs; includes lions, tigers, or polar bears, Model No. 1123-A................ $56................. $84...................... $140

Chipperfield Circus Set, 1st Version, 1963-65, vehicle and accessory set in two versions: w/No. 426 Booking Office, Model No. 23-A1
.... $380............... $600..................... $1300

Jean Richard Circus Set, 1978-81, Land Rover, yellow and red Land Rover and cage trailer w/Pinder-Jean Richard decals, No. 426 office van and trailer, No. 1163 Human Cannonball truck, ring and cut-out "Big Top" circus tent, Model No. 48-C
.... $90............... $135...................... $275

Emergency Vehicles

Bedford Fire Tender, 1960-62, Bedford, single windshield version, red body w/either black ladders and smooth wheels or unpainted ladders and shaped wheels, Model No. 423-A
.... $60................. $90...................... $150

Chevrolet Impala Fire Chief Car, 1963-65, Chevrolet, red body, yellow interior, w/four white doors, w/round either shield or rectangular decals on two doors; includes two fireman, Model No. 439-A
.... $55................. $80...................... $130

	EX	NM	MIP

Citroen Alpine Rescue Safari, 1970-72, Citroen, white body, light-blue interior, red roof and rear hatch, yellow roof rack and skis, clear windshield, man and dog, gold die-cast bobsled, Alpine Rescue decals, Model No. 513-A
.... $80.............. $150...................... $375

Emergency Set, 1976-77, three-vehicle set w/figures and accessories, No. 402 Ford Cortina Police car, No. 921 Police Helicopter, No. 481 Range Rover Ambulance, Model No. 18-B
.... $40.............. $60...................... $100

Mercedes-Benz Ambulance, 1981, Mercedes-Benz, white body and base, red stripes and taillights, red cross and black and white ambulance labels, open rear door, white interior, no figures, Model No. 407-B .... $15................. $20........................ $35

Police Land Rover and Horse Box, 1978-80, Land Rover, white No. 421 Land Rover w/police labels and mounted policeman, No. 112 Horse Box, Model No. 44-A
.... $30.............. $45........................ $75

Volkswagen 1200 Police Car, 1966-69, Volkswagen, two different body versions made for Germany, Netherlands and Switzerland, blue dome light in chrome collar, Polizei or Politie decals. Note the opening hood and trunk on this attractive car. The front wheels turn via the roof warning light, Model No. 492-A.
.... $40................. $60...................... $100

Large Trucks

Bedford Milk Tanker, 1966-67, Bedford, light blue "TK" cab and lower semi, white upper tank w/blue/white milk decals, Model No. 1141-A.................... $110.............. $165...................... $375

Car Transporter & Cars, 1970-73, Scammell, Scammell tri-deck transporter w/six cars: Ford Capri, the Saint's Volvo, Pontiac Firebird, Lancia Fulvia, MGC GT, Marcos 3 Litre, each w/ WhizzWheels; value is for complete set, Model No. 20-B
.... $200................. $400...................... $900

	EX	NM	MIP

Ford Holmes Wrecker, 1967-74, Ford, white upper cab, black roof, red rear body and lower cab, mirrors, unpainted or gold booms, Model No. 1142-A................ $60............... $90.................... $200

Transporter and Six Cars, 1966-69, Ford, first issue: No. 1138 Ford 'H' Series Transporter w/six cars, No. 252 Rover 2000, blue No. 251 Hillman Imp, No. 440 Ford Cortina Estate, No. 180 Mini w/ 'wickerwork' metallic maroon, No. 204 Mini, and No. 321 Mini Rally ('1966 Monte Carlo Rally') racing No. 2; second issue: same as first issue except No. 251 Hillman is metallic gold, No. 204 Mini is blue, No. 321 Mini is substituted for No. 333 SUN/ RAC Rally Mini w/autographs on roof. The Car Transporter gift sets were a good way for Corgi to get rid of their excess stock of automobile models, Model No. 48-A.
.... $225............... $365..................... $700

Racing Vehicles

Citroen DS 19 Rally, 1965-66, Citroen, light-blue body, white roof, yellow interior, four jewel headlights, Monte Carlo Rally and No. 75 decals, w/antenna, Model No. 323-A
.... $70............... $105..................... $185

Grand Prix Racing Set, 1968-72, four vehicle set includes: No. 490 Volkswagen breakdown truck w/No. 330 Porsche (1969), Porsche No. 371 (1970-72), No. 155 Lotus, No. 156 Cooper-Maserati, red trailer, Model No. 12-B
.... $135............... $210..................... $425

Land Rover and Ferrari Racer, 1963-67, red and tan No. 438 Land Rover and red No. 154 Ferrari F1 on yellow trailer, Model No. 17-A .... $60................. $90..................... $150

Monte Carlo Rally Set, 1965-67, three vehicle set, No. 326 Citroen, No 318 Mini, and No. 322 Land Rover rally cars, Model No. 38-A
.... $295............... $450..................... $900

	EX	NM	MIP

Sports Cars

Corvette Sting Ray, 1963-68, Chevrolet, metallic silver, bronze or red body, two workiing headlights, clear windshield, yellow interior, silver hood panels, four rotating jewel headlights, suspension, chrome bumpers, w/spoked or shaped wheels, rubber tires. The swivelling jeweled headlights and spoked wheels added real pizzaz to this cool toy, Model No. 310-A.
.... $60................. $90..................... $175

Ford Mustang Fastback, 1965-66, Ford, metallic lilac, metallic dark blue, silver, or light-green body, spoked or detailed cast wheels, Model No. 320-A .... $30................. $45........................$95

Lamborghini Miura P400, 1970-72, Lamborghini, w/red or yellow body, working hood, detailed engine, clear windows, jewel headlights, bull figure, Whizz Wheels, Model No. 342-A
.... $40................. $60..................... $100

Pop Art Mini-Mostest, 1969, Morris, light-red body and base, yellow interior, jewel headlights, orange taillights, yellow-blue-purple pop art and "Mostest" decals; very rare. This rare Mini is one of the Holy Grails of any Corgi collection. Very few of these cars were produced in 1969, possibly due to the fact that psychedelia had already passed its prime, Model No. 349-A.
.... $1000.............. $1500.................... $2700

Dinky

Aircraft

Boeing Flying Fortress, 1945-48, "Long Range Bomber" under wings, Model No. 62g........... $50............... $125......................$225

Clipper III Flying Boat, 1945-49, silver, no registration, Model No. 60w .... $75............... $175......................$250

Douglas DC3, 1938-41, silver, PH-ALI, Model No. 60t.......... $125............... $300......................$650

Left to right: Leyland Cement Wagon, 1956-59, No. 419, $220; Mighty Antar w/Propeller, 1959-64, No. 986, $425; Guy Van, Slumberland, No. 514, $590.

Dinky Lady Penelope's Fab 1, $220.

Dinky Toys Cadillac Ambulance, 1970s. The main body casting had been used for many years by the time this model was released, $65 MIP.

	EX	NM	MIP

Lockheed P-80 Shooting Star, 1947-62, silver, USAF stars,
Model No. 701/733..... $10................. $20......................$30
Spitfire, 1940-41, silver, small canopy, roundels red, white, and blue,
Model No. 62e/62a..... $35............... $150......................$200

Cars

Austin Healey "100", Model No. 109
.... $25................. $60......................$120
Chrysler Airflow, 1935-40, Model No. 32/30A
.... $130............... $250......................$450
Citroen DS-19, 1959-68, Model No. F522/24C
.... $60................. $90......................$135
Ford Thunderbird, South African issue, blue, Model No. F565
.... $120............... $250......................$600
Jaguar XK 120, 1954-62, yellow/gray, Model No. 157
.... $80............... $125......................$250
Plymouth Fury Convertible, Model No. 137G
.... $20................. $60......................$120
Rolls Royce Silver Wraith, Model No. 150
.... $20................. $60......................$120
Triumph TR2, Model No. 111
.... $20............... $100......................$200
Volkswagen VW Beetle, green body, Model No. 181
.... $20................. $50......................$100

Character & TV Related Vehicles

Lady Penelope's Fab 1, 1966-76, shocking-pink version,
Model No. 100......... $115............... $200......................$340
Parsley's Car Morris Oxford, 1970-72, Cut-out stand-up figures of
Parsley's friends were included for additional play,
Model No. 477........... $65............... $115......................$145

Dinky turntable fire escape, $175.

	EX	NM	MIP

Construction Vehicles
Bedford Tipper, orange,
     Model No. 410 .... $20 .... $75 .... $150
Coles Mobile Crane, 1955-66,
     Model No. 971 .... $40 .... $70 .... $110
Euclid Dump Truck, 1955-69, with lever-operated tipping bed.
     Part of the "Dinky Supertoys" range,
     Model No. 965 .... $55 .... $80 .... $125
Salev Crane, 1959-61,
     Model No. F595 .... $65 .... $100 .... $175

Emergency Vehicles
Ambulance, Model No. 30F
     .... $100 .... $160 .... $275
ERF Fire Tender, Red body, removable extending escape ladder with
     wheels, Model No. 266
     .... $15 .... $50 .... $100
Mersey Tunnel Police Land Rover, 1955-61, Land Rover,
     Model No. 255 .... $60 .... $85 .... $135
Superior Criterion Ambulance, 1962-68, The roof beacon warning light
     actually flashed with the aid of a small battery,
     Model No. 277 .... $40 .... $75 .... $110

Trucks
Breakdown Truck "Dinky Service", Model No. 25x
     .... $20 .... $80 .... $160
Citroen Milk Truck, 1961-65, Model No. F586
     .... $145 .... $275 .... $600
Guy Flat Truck, common variations, Model No. 513
     .... $80 .... $250 .... $500

	EX	NM	MIP

Leyland Cement Wagon, 1956-59, Leyland, one of Dinky's foreign
vehicles, this toy was made in Argentina, Model No. 419/933
.... $90.............. $130..................... $220

Mighty Antar With Propeller, 1959-64, the propeller included with this
model is made of plastic, Model No. 986
.... $150.............. $300..................... $425

Panhard Esso Tanker, 1954-59, this toy was a French-made vehicle as
part of the Dinky Supertoys line, Model No. F32C
.... $75.............. $120..................... $170

Vans

Alco Delivery Van, 1935-40, type 3, Model No. 28N
.... $135.............. $200..................... $350

BBC-TV Camera Truck, 1959-64, Model No. 968
.... $60.............. $125..................... $185

Bedford 10 cwt Van, Ovaltine, Model No. 481
.... $25.............. $100..................... $200

Hot Wheels

❏ **9638** — '57 Chevy — 1977, red, yellow & white tampo, "57 Chevy"
.... $85

❑ **6451** — Ambulance — 1970, met. blue, white back with red cross & blue light on top $130

❑ **9089** — American Tipper — 1976, red metal cab, white plastic tipper bed, American flag tampo, "American Tipper"..................... $65

❑ **7662** — American Victory — 1975, light blue, American flag tampo, "9" on sides, silver interior, exposed silver engine $45

❑ **7670** — Backwoods Bomb — 1975 blue body w/green & yellow tampo, plastic camper, "Keep On Camping," $100

❏ **8258** — Baja Bruiser — 1974, orange, stars & stripes on side tampo, "Firestone", "Cragar", and "Ford" $90

❏ **6256** — Chaparral 2G — 1969, white, back opens to expose metal engine $140

❑ **7671** — Chevy Monza 2+2 — 1975, orange enamel finish, "Monza" rally stripes on hood and roof $110

❑ **6267** — Custom AMX — 1969, met. green, hood lifts to expose engine $225

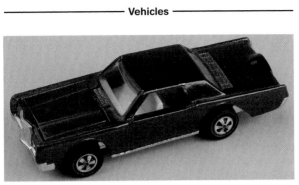

❏ **6266** — Custom Continental Mark III — 1969, met. pink, opening hood, metal engine $400

❏ **6215** — Custom Corvette — 1968, met. orange, opening hood, assorted interior color $400

❏ **6205** — Custom Cougar — 1968, met. green, opening hood, black interior $400

❏ **6212** — Custom Firebird — 1968, met. orange, metal engine, opening hood $280

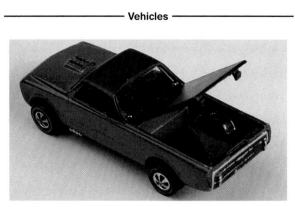

❏ **6213** — Custom Fleetside — 1968, met. purple, black roof, opening bed cover.. $250

❏ **8273** — El Rey Special — 1974, green, yellow & red "Dunlop", number "1" tampos, silver metal base... $120

❑ **7650** — Emergency Squad — 1975, red body, yellow & white side tampos, silver plastic base $75

❑ **6454** — Fire Engine — 1970, met. red cab, black ladder, rear is red plastic, white hoses... $140

❏ **6214** — Ford J-Car — 1968, met. aqua, back opens to reveal metal engine $70

❏ **6408** — Heavy Chevy — 1970, met. blue, exposed engine, black "8" on side $200

❏ **7619** — Heavy Chevy — 1974, yellow, exposed engine, orange & red side tampo, "7" $200

❏ **6175** — Hood, The — 1971, met. light green, exposed engine, black interior $150

❑ **6219** — Hot Heap — 1968, met. white interior, exposed engine
.... $100

❑ **6255** — McLaren M6A — 1969, orange, blue-tint windshield $65

❑ **6275** — Mercedes 280SL — 1969, red, opening hood, metal engine, blue-tint windows..$85

❑ **7660** — Monte Carlo Stocker — 1975, yellow, blue-tint windows, black interior $120

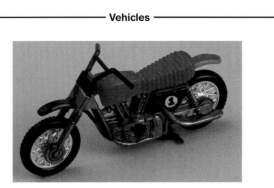

❑ **7668** — Motocross I — 1975, red plastic seat and tank, unpainted gray die-cast body $200

❑ **6981** — Odd Job — 1973, red, white topper, exposed engine $600

❑ **9642** — Odd Rod — 1977, yellow plastic bucket around seats, clear plastic hood with flame graphics..$100

❑ **6963** — Police Cruiser — 1973, white Olds 442, "Police" labels on doors, opening hood & red dome light on roof $110

❑ **9206** — Porsche 911 — 1976, chrome, red & green tampo, black interior $40

❑ **7616** — Rash 1 — 1974, green, blue-tint windshield, yellow & white tampo, exposed engine $140

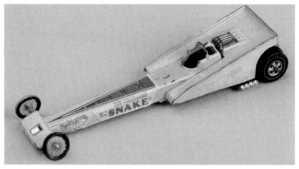

❑ **5856** — Rear Engine Snake — 1972, yellow, blue w/red stars tampo
.... $600

❑ **6186** — Rocket-Bye-Baby — 1971, met. yellow, metal rocket on top
.... $280

❏ **8259** — Rodger Dodger — 1974, plum Dodge Charger, flame tampos on hood & roof, exposed silver engine, red plastic exhaust pipes $125

❏ **6468** — S'Cool Bus — 1971, yellow, lift-up funny car body, silver chassis $750

❑ **6403** — Sand Crab — 1970, red, black interior, clear windshield . $75

❑ **6003** — Six Shooter — 1971, met. blue, exposed engines, six wheels, blue-tinted windshield.. $225

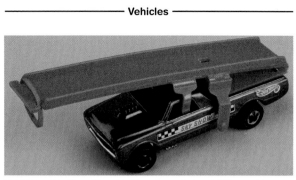

❑ **6436** — Sky Show Fleetside (Aero Launcher) — 1970, met. blue, orange plastic ramp $850

❑ **9641** — Spoiler Sport — 1977, light green van, tropical island scene on side panels $50

❑ **8260** — Steam Roller — 1974, white body, stars & stripes tampo, three stars reversed out of red stripe on hood...................................... $70

❑ **7647** — Torino Stocker — 1975, red, blue-tinted windshield, black interior $95

❏ **7655** — Tough Customer — 1975, olive, with rotating turret and
white numbering turret and white numbering tampos $60

Japanese Tin Cars

Friction-powered Japanese police car, 1960s, $150 mint value.

Japanese Tin Cadillac Sedan, Bandai, 12", $185. Photo courtesy Ron Smith

Marx Linemar NAR Television Truck, 1950s, battery-operated, $600.

	EX	NM	MIP

Japanese Tin Cars

Aston-Martin DB6, 1960s, friction, Asahi Toy Co., 11" (J2)
.... $200............... $400...................... $600

Atom Car, 1950s, Yonezawa, 17" (J284)
.... $300............... $600, ... $1200

Buick, 1959, friction, T.N., 11" (J8)
.... $90............... $150...................... $300

Buick Futuristic LeSabre, 1950s, friction, Yonezawa, 7-1/2" (J276)
.... $200............... $300...................... $500

Buick Roadmaster, 1955, friction, Yoshiya, 11" (J5)
.... $125............... $250...................... $500

Buick Wildcat, 1963, friction, Ichiko, 15" (J13)
.... $250............... $500...................... $900

Cadillac, 1950, battery-op, Marusan, 11" (J18)
.... $400............... $800...................... $1800

Cadillac Convertible, 1959, friction, Bandai, 12" (J25)
.... $60............... $110...................... $220

Cadillac Fleetwood, 1961, friction, SSS, 17-1/2" (J29)
.... $100............... $200...................... $350

Chevrolet Camaro, 1967, battery-op, T.N., 14" (J46)
.... $125............... $175...................... $350

Chevrolet Corvette, 1958, friction, Yonezawa, 9-1/2" (J38)
.... $200............... $300...................... $600

Chevrolet Station Wagon, 1958, friction, Bandai, 8" (J57)
.... $50............... $65...................... $125

Chrysler Imperial, 1962, 16", friction, black, red (white: add
20% to value)........... $600............... $1200 .... $2200

Chrysler New Yorker, 1957, friction, Alps, 14" (J72)
.... $600............... $1200...................... $1800

	EX	NM	MIP

Citroen 2 CV, 1960, friction, Daiya 8" (J269A)
.... $100............... $150...................... $225

Dodge Pickup, 1959, friction, unknown manufacturer, 18-1/2"
(J84) .... $400............... $600................... $1200

Dodge Sedan, 1958, friction, T.N. 11" (J82)
.... $300............... $400...................... $800

Dream Car, friction, "Y" Co., 17" (J278A)
.... $400............... $600................... $1200

Edsel Convertible/Sedan, 1958, friction, Haji, 10-1/2" (J86)
.... $300............... $500...................... $900

Edsel Wagon, 1958, friction, Haji, 10-1/2" (J87)
.... $200............... $300...................... $400

Ford Convertible, 1955, friction, Bandai, 12" (J100)
.... $200............... $400...................... $600

Ford Mustang Hardtop/Convertible, 1965, friction/battery-op, Bandai, 11" (J140)................... $75............... $125...................... $150

Ford Pickup, 1955, friction, Bandai, 12" (J96)
.... $150............... $250...................... $300

Ford Sedan, 1949, wind-up, Guntherman, 11" (J93)
.... $150............... $300...................... $400

Ford Thunderbird, 1955, friction, Bandai, 7" (J126A)
.... $75............... $100...................... $150

Ford Thunderbird Retractable, 1963, battery-op, Yonezawa, 11" (J134)....................... $80............... $150...................... $200

Ford Torino, 1968, friction, S.T. 16" (J126)
.... $200............... $350...................... $800

Ford Wagon, 1956, friction, Nomura, 10-1/2" (J104)
.... $125............... $225...................... $300

	EX	NM	MIP
Jaguar XKE Convertible, 1960s, friction, T.T., 10-1/2" (J155)	$75	$150	$250
Lincoln, 1956, friction, Ichiko, 16-1/2" (J165)	$150	$250	$375
Lincoln, 1964, friction, unknown manufacturer, 10-1/2" (J169)	$90	$175	$275
Lincoln Continental Mark II, 1956, friction, Linemar, 12" (J164)	$600	$1200	$2500
Mercury Cougar Hardtop, 1967, friction, Asakusa Toys, 15" (J197)	$200	$400	$800
Mercury Hardtop, 1956, friction, Alps, 9-1/2" (J193)	$600	$800	$1500
Midget Special No. 6, friction, "Y" Co., 7" (J291)	$200	$350	$700
Oldsmobile, 1952, friction, "Y" Co., 11" (J207A)	$150	$350	$500
Oldsmobile Sedan, 1956, friction, (Ichiko/Kanto, 10-1/2" (J208)	$200	$400	$700
Oldsmobile Toronado, 1966, battery-op, Bandai, 11" (J215)	$65	$110	$150
Packard Convertible/Sedan, 1953, friction, Alps, 16" (J222)	$500	$800	$1600
Packard Hawk Convertible, 1957, battery-op, Schuco, 10-3/4" (J223)	$300	$400	$800
Plymouth Sedan, 1961, friction, Ichiko, 12" (J230)	$150	$300	$550
Pontiac, 1954, Minister, friction, Minister, 11" (J218A)	$10	$20	$30

Marx Milton Berle Crazy Car, tin windup, 1950s, $595 mint.

Marx made several G-Man Pursuit Cars in the 1930s, $750 mint.

	EX	NM	MIP

Pontiac Firebird, 1967, friction, Akasura, 15-1/2" (J219)
.... $200.............. $400..................... $900

Porsche Speedster, 1950s, battery-op, Distler, 10-1/2" (J235)
.... $200.............. $300..................... $600

Renault, 1960, friction, Bandai, 7-1/2" (J241)
.... $60.............. $90..................... $120

Rolls Royce, 1960, friction, T.N. 10-1/2" (J239)
.... $200.............. $300..................... $500

Studebaker, 1954, friction, Yoshiya, 9" (J243)
.... $150.............. $200..................... $375

Studebaker Avanti, 1960s, friction, Bandai, 8" (J242)
.... $90.............. $150..................... $225

Volkswagen Convertible, 1950, friction, T.N., 9-1/2" (J258)
.... $100.............. $150..................... $225

Volvo, 1950s, wind-up, Sweden, 11" (J265A)
.... $600.............. $1000..................... $2000

Marx

Cars

Charlie McCarthy "Benzine Buggy" Car, Marx, w/white wheels, tin
wind-up, 7" long, 1938
.... $450.............. $625..................... $950

G-Man Pursuit Car, Marx, sparks, 14-1/2" long, 1935
.... $190.............. $285..................... $750

Milton Berle Crazy Car, Marx, tin litho, wind-up, 6" long, 1950s
.... $250.............. $375..................... $595

Mortimer Snerd's Tricky Auto, Marx, tin litho, wind-up, 7-1/2" long,
1939 .... $400.............. $660..................... $750

Queen of the Campus, Marx, w/four college students' heads, 1950
.... $250.............. $400..................... $525

Marx Mortimer Snerd's Tricky Auto, 1939, tin windup, $750 mint.

Marx Hi-Way Express Truck, $225 mint. Photo from Calvin L.
Chaussee.

	EX	NM	MIP

Racer #5, Marx, miniature car, tin wind-up, 5" long, 1948
.... $75............... $125...................... $195

Sheriff Sam and His Whoopee Car, Marx, plastic, tin wind-up, 5-3/4"
long, 1949 .... $200............... $300.................... $475

Snoopy Gus Wild Fireman, Marx, 7" long, 1926
.... $500............... $750.................... $1150

Sportster, Marx, 20" long; 1950s
.... $50................. $80...................... $125

Station Wagon, Marx, friction, 11" long; 1950
.... $125............... $200...................... $325

Emergency Vehicles

Ambulance, Marx, 13-1/2" long, 1937
.... $225............... $350...................... $650

City Hospital Mack Ambulance, Marx, tin litho, wind-up, 10" long,
1927 .... $190............... $280...................... $500

Fire Engine, Marx, sheet iron, 9" long,
1920s .... $100............... $175...................... $335

Farm and Construction Equipment

Caterpillar Climbing Tractor, Marx, orange tractor, tin wind-up,
9-1/2" long, 1942 ..... $100............... $175...................... $325

Climbing Tractor, Marx, tin wind-up, 8-1/4" long,
1930 .... $100............... $150...................... $325

Farm Tractor Set, Marx, 40 pieces, tin wind-up,
1939 .... $325............... $500...................... $650

Midget Tractor and Plow, Marx, tin wind-up,
1937 .... $70............... $100...................... $225

Super Power Tractor and Trailer Set, Marx, tin wind-up, 8-1/2" tractor,
1937 .... $125............... $200...................... $375

Marx Queen of the Campus tin windup with college boy passengers, $525 mint.

Marx Charlie McCarthy in his Benzine Buggy, tin windup, $950 mint.

	EX	NM	MIP

Tractor Set, Marx, two-pieces, tin wind-up, 19" long steel tractor;

    1950 .... $65.............. $100...................... $215

Tractor Train with Tractor Shed, Marx, tin wind-up, 8-1/2" long,

    1936 .... $100.............. $150...................... $220

Trucks

Armored Trucking Co. Truck, Marx, tin litho, wind-up, 10" long,

    1927 .... $100.............. $150...................... $325

Army Truck with Rear Benches and Canopy, Marx, olive-drab paint,

    10" long .... $75.............. $125...................... $225

Auto Transport Mack Truck and Trailer, Marx, dark-blue cab,

    dark-green trailer, wind-up, 11-1/2" long,

    1932 .... $150.............. $225...................... $375

Auto Transwalk Truck, Marx, w/three cars,

    1930s .... $175.............. $250...................... $395

Cement Mixer Truck, Marx, red cab, tin finish mixing barrel,

    6" long, 1930s.......... $100.............. $150...................... $300

City Sanitation Dept. "Help Keep Your City Clean" Truck, Marx,

    12-3/4" long, 1940...... $60.............. $90...................... $250

Coca-Cola Truck, Marx, yellow, 20" long;

    1950 .... $150.............. $225...................... $300

Dump Truck, Marx, red cab, gray bumper, yellow bed, 18" long;

    1950 .... $100.............. $150...................... $200

Hi Way Express Truck, Marx, tin, tin tires, 16" long; 1940s

    .... $65.............. $125...................... $190

Miniature Mayflower Moving Van, Marx, operating lights

    .... $60.............. $90...................... $125

Pet Shop Truck, Marx, plastic, six compartments w/six vinyl dogs,

    11" long .... $125.............. $200...................... $250

Matchbox regular wheels, BRM racer, 1965, $25 MIP.

Cadillac 60 Special by Matchbox, 1960, $90 MIP.

	EX	NM	MIP

Sand and Gravel Truck, Marx, "Builder's Supply Co.", tin wind-up, 1920 .... $150............... $225...................... $400

Stake Bed Truck, Marx, rubber-stamped chicken on one side of truck, bunny on other .... $100............... $150...................... $200

Matchbox

Regular Wheels

2-1RW, Dumper, 1953, This first version featured a gold-painted front grille on a green body with red dump bed, 1-1/2" .... $22.................. $40........................ $90

3-2RW, Bedford Tipper Truck, 1961, Available in red and maroon dumper variations, as well as gray and black plastic wheels, 2-1/2". Gray plastic wheeled version harder to find, about $120 MIP .... $10.................. $20........................ $45

6-4RW, Ford Pickup, 1969, Red, with white plastic camper top and white or silver plastic front grill. Featured "Autosteer", a Matchbox innovation making its appearance in the 1969 catalog, that "turns the front wheels in either direction by simple pressue." 2-3/4" .... $10.................. $20........................ $30

7-2RW, Ford Anglia, 1961, Light-blue body, no interior, gray, silver or black plastic wheels, silver painted grille, bumper and headlights, 2-5/8", black painted baseplate, tow hook. Gray plastic wheel versions, about $90 MIP; silver plastic wheel versions, about $55 MIP .... $15.................. $22........................ $45

8-1RW, Caterpillar Tractor, 1955, Yellow or orange with cast driver, silver painted grille. Unpainted roller wheels for treads, 1-1/2". Fully exposed engine under hood. Note: Orange variation harder to find, MIP value can reach over $200; yellow versions with painted drivers also about $200 MIP .... $20.................. $40...................... $85

Matchbox regular wheels Compressor Lorry, 1959. Nicely detailed casting, $60 MIP.

Matchbox Mack Dump Truck, 1969, $25 MIP.

	EX	**NM**	**MIP**

9-2RW, Fire Escape, 1957, Red, cast with driver, metal wheels most common, versions with gray plastic wheels about $400 MIP, front bumper included in casting, 2-1/4"
.... $20................. $45........................ $80

10-2RW, Mechanical Horse and Trailer, 1957, Second casting of Scammell Scarab, red three-wheeled cab and light-tan stake-style trailer with fenders. Grille can be painted or unpainted, metal wheels, 3". Appears first in 1957 catalog/flyer
.... $40................. $60........................ $95

10-4RW, Pipe Truck, 1967, Red Leyland die-cast body, silver grille and baseplate, gray plastic pipes. "Ergomatic Cab" written on baseplate, 3". The Ergomatic cab was a new feature on large British trucks, including Leyland and AEC, beginning in the mid-sixties, so this model reflected the latest advance at time of release
.... $6................. $12........................ $20

12-1RW, Land Rover, 1957, Dark-green body with tan driver, metal wheels. No real windshield, just a low flat piece of the casting appearing where the base of a windshield would be. Slight casting variations, some 1-5/8" length, later editions, 1-3/4" length. Silver-painted grille
.... $8................. $40........................ $80

13-1RW, Wreck Truck, 1955, Tan Bedford truck with red tow hook and scaffold, metal wheels, silver-painted grille and bumper, 2-1/4"
.... $35................. $50........................ $75

13-3RW, Wrect Truck, 1961, Red body with metal or plastic tow hook, and gray or black plastic wheels, decal on side of truck says "A.A. & R.A.C. Matchbox Garages Breakdown Service." Silver trim on front grille .... $18................. $45........................ $110

14-2RW, Ambulance, 1958, Daimler with cream or off-white body with metal or gray plastic wheels. Red Cross decal, slightly larger casting at 2-1/4", word "Ambulance" case in raised letters
.... $18................. $60........................ $90

Bedford Coach by Matchbox, 1958, $95 MIP.

Volkswagen No. 67 1600 TL by Matchbox, 1967, $25 MIP.

	EX	NM	MIP

16-2RW, Atlantic Transporter, 1960, Orange trailer body, black plastic wheels, 4 axles; two at front near drawbar, two at back near ramp, non-skid tire tracks on trailer, pictured here with 15-2RW Atlantic Prime Mover .... $17 .... $40 .... $75

17-3RW, Metropolitan Taxi, 1960, Dark red with gray or silver plastic wheels, gray more common, silver can have $130+ MIP value, gray-wheel values shown

.... $25 .... $40 .... $75

20-1RW, Heavy Lorry, 1956, Dark red ERF truck body, metal or gray plastic wheels, no interior, dropside stake bed appearance with fuel tanks along sides. Can have silver-painted grille, some casting variations, 2-1/4" and 2-5/8"

.... $18 .... $40 .... $100

21-2RW, Bedford Coach, 1958, Light pea-green body with red and yellow "London to Glasgow" decal above windows, metal or gray plastic wheels, "Bedford Duple Luxury Coach" on black base, 2-1/2", silver-painted grille and front bumper, no interior

.... $25 .... $60 .... $95

23-3RW, Bluebird Dauphine Trailer, 1960, metallic tan or green body, opening door, no interior or plastic windows, black or gray plastic wheels. Variations with green bodies are hard to find, and can be quite valuable. More common tan variation prices given below

.... $25 .... $40 .... $85

24-1RW, Hydraulic Excavator, 1956, Yellow or orange body with metal wheels; larger two at rear and smaller at front, figure cast as part of body, front dumping bucket

.... $18 .... $40 .... $75

25-2RW, Volkswagen Sedan, 1960, Volkswagen 1200 Sedan, blue-silver body, gray plastic wheels, opening rear engine hood, green or clear plastic windows, black base

.... $45 .... $65 .... $100

Matchbox Y-05 1907 Peugeot, 1968, $33 mint.

Matchbox Y-11 1912 Packard Landaulet, 1963, $42 mint.

	EX	NM	MIP

26-1RW, Ready Mixed Concrete Lorry, 1957, Orange ERF cab and body with silver-painted grille and side gas tanks, metal or gray plastic wheels, 1-3/4", metal mixer section, four wheels .... $18.................. $45........................ $88

27-3RW, Cadillac Sixty Special, 1960, Silver-gray or silver-purple Cadillac body with cream- or pink-colored roof, plastic windows, no interior and gray or black plastic wheels, red base, tow hook, red-painted taillights and silver-painted trim .... $28.................. $45........................ $90

28-2RW, Ford Thames Compressor Lorry, 1959, Yellow Ford Thames truck cab and chassis with black plastic wheels, no interior or window plastic, silver headlights and grille .... $25.................. $40........................ $60

29-1RW, Bedford Milk Delivery Van, 1956, Tan body with white plastic milk bottles and boxes, silver trim, metal or gray plastic wheels, no interior or window plastic, 2-1/4" .... $18.................. $30........................ $80

30-1RW, Ford Prefect, 1956, Light sage-green or light-brown body with metal or gray plastic wheels, (light blue harder to find, $200 or more MIP). No window plastic or interior, silver-painted grille, headlights and bumpers, red-painted taillights. Tow hook, black-painted base, 2-3/8" ... $15.................. $40........................ $80

31-2RW, Ford Fairlane Station Wagon, 1960, Mint green with pink-white roof, gray or black plastic wheels, silver-painted trim, tow hook. Yellow-painted versions are harder to find, and can bring higher MIP values (up to $300). Two box variations shown .... $22.................. $55........................ $78

33-1RW, Ford Zodiac, 1957, a variety of body colors exist for this model: blue, dark-green, blue-green, silver, tan & orange and turquoise. Dark green and tan and orange models more common, with around $80-$90 MIP values, 2-5/8" .... $20.................. $40........................ $80

Matchbox No. 48 Dodge Dumper Truck, 1967, $26 mint.

Matchbox No. 68 Mercedes Coach, 1965, $18 mint.

	EX	NM	MIP

34-1RW, Volkswagen Microvan, 1957, Blue panel van body, no interior, "Matchbox International Express" yellow type decal on sides, with silver-painted bumper and headlights, 2-1/4". Mostly found with metal or gray plastic wheels, decal on side with "Matchbox International Express" in yellow lettering.
.... $30................. $50......................... $95

34-3RW, Volkswagen Camper, 1967, silver body with opening camper section doors, orange plastic interior, yellow window plastic, raised roof with windows and top window plastic, black plastic wheels, 2-5/8" .... $10................. $18......................... $45

35-1RW, Marshall Horse Box, 1957, Red ERF cab with silver-painted grille and headlights, brown horse box with opening side door, metal and gray plastic wheels most common, 2-1/8". Silver plastic wheel version, about $180 MIP, black plastic wheel version, about $135 MIP .... $15................. $30......................... $80

36-1RW, Austin A50, 1957, Blue-green body, no interior, metal or gray plastic wheels, silver-painted grille, headlights and bumper, tow bar, 2-3/8" .... $20................. $35......................... $75

37-1RW, Coca-Cola Lorry, 1956, Yellow-orange truck with Coca-Cola decals on sides and back of truck, metal or gray plastic wheels, 2-1/4", no step on the running board on cab, silver-painted trim on running boards, grille. Some versions have "uneven" loads of cast Coca-Cola cases (as seen in 1957 flyer) in the bed of the truck. These typically run about $150 MIP. "Even" load versions in gray plastic wheels comparable MIP price. Even-load metal wheel version prices shown below.
.... $30................. $55......................... $95

38-1RW, Refuse Wagon, 1957, Silver-gray or dark-gray cab and almost tanker-truck shaped rounded-top bed and "Cleansing Department" decals. Metal or gray plastic wheels. 1957 flyer shows model painted green and without the decals. Casting variations must account for size difference: 2-1/8" and 2-1/2" lengths
.... $18................. $45......................... $85

Matchbox No. 42 Studebaker Lark Wagonaire, 1965, $19 mint.

Matchbox No. 21 Commer Milk Truck, 1961, $25 mint.

	EX	NM	MIP

38-3RW, Honda Motorcycle with Trailer, 1967, Blue-silver Honda motorcycle with kickstand and orange or yellow trailer. Trailer may or may not included labels or decals, 3". As with many motorcycle-related toys, these fairly common models are increasing in value...... $12................. $25........................$40

40-1RW, Bedford 7-Ton Tipper, 1957, Red Bedford cab and chassis, tan dumper bed, metal or gray plastic wheels, silver painted trim. Casting variations: Size varies between 2-1/8" and 2-1/4". Shown in all-green color in 1957 Flyer .... $15................. $40........................$80

41-1RW, "D" Type Jaguar, 1957, Green D-type body, metal driver in later catalogs, but not in 1957 flyer, "41" decal metal or gray plastic tires, 2-1/4". Photo shows 41-1RW and second release with a larger casting, 41-2R $20................. $45........................$70

42-2RW, Studebaker Station Wagon, 1965, Blue body with blue or light-blue sliding roof, white plastic interior and tow hook, clear window plastic, white plastid dog and hunter figure included with original (often missing), 3" $15............. $30........................$65

43-1RW, Hillman "Minx", 1958, Blue body, light-gray roof, no window plastic or interior, silver-painted grille, metal or gray plastic wheels, 2-1/2", first appears in 1958 catalog .... $12................. $40........................$75

43-3RW, Pony Trailer, 1968, Yellow body with clear window plastic on sides and top, gray/brown plastic door, black plastic wheels, 2 white plastic horses, 2-5/8" $6 .... $11........................$25

44-3RW, Refrigerator Truck, 1967, Red GMC cab and chassis, green refrigerator box, green window plastic, black plastic wheels, opening rear door on box, 3" .... $4................. $7........................$13

45-1RW, Vauxhall "Victor", 1958, Yellow body, silver-painted headlights and grille, can have no windows, clear or green plastic windows. No interior. Metal gray, silver or black plastic wheels, 2-3/8"........................ $18................. $40........................$85

	EX	NM	MIP

47-1RW, Trojan "Brooke Bond" Van, 1958, Red body, metal or gray plastic wheels, decals on van box read "Brooke Bond Tea", tea leaf decal on each door, silver-painted headlights, 2-1/4" .... $18.................... $45........................ $95

48-3RW, Dumper Truck, 1967, Red Dodge cab, chassis and dumper bed, silver plastic baseplate, bumper and front grille, black plastic wheels, 3".................... $3.................... $8........................ $18

55-2RW, Ford Fairlane Police Car, 1963, Dark- or light-blue Ford Fairlane with white plastic interior, clear plastic windows, red dome light, silver-painted grille, black plastic wheels. Dark-blue version is harder to find, about $300 MIP. Light-blue values shown. .... $22.................... $40........................ $85

56-1RW, Trolley Bus, 1958, Red double-decker body with sloped front, no interior; six metal, gray, or black plastic wheels, "Drink Peardrax" Decals on sides, flat trolley poles on roof, "OXO" decal on front, 2-5/8". Note that MIP metal wheel versions have sold for $250. Common prices for gray and black wheel versions shown. .... $20.................... $45........................ $70

59-1RW, Ford "Singer" Van, 1958, Light-green Ford Thames van with "Singer" decals on panel sides and "S" logo decals on doors. No plastic windows, no interior, silver-painted grille, gray plastic wheels, 2-1/8". Dark-green models seem hard to find, about $250 MIP.......................... $35................. $55...................... $100

60-2RW, Site Hut Truck, 1967, Blue Leyland Ergomatic cab and flatbed chassis, silver plastic grille and headlights, blue plastic windows, no interior, black plastic wheels, plastic yellow hut on back with green roof, 2-1/2" .... $3.................... $6........................ $12

61-2, Alvis Stalwart, 1967, white body with green plastic windows and green or yellow wheels with black plastic tires. Plastic canopy over bed (not shown), no interior, 2-5/8". Yellow wheels are less common and have approximately $75 MIP values. .... $9.................... $17........................ $30

	EX	NM	MIP

62-2RW, TV Service Van, 1963, Cream colored body with "Rentaset" or "Radio Rentals" decals on sides, red plastic accessories: antenna, 3 TV sets and ladder. No interior, 2-1/2"
.... $20................. $50...................... $110

62-3RW, Mercury Cougar, 1969, Lime-green Mercury Cougar body with unpainted base, silver wheels with removable black plastic tires (like other Mercury models in the line), opening doors, red plastic interior, "Auto-steer " front wheels, tow hook, 3"
.... $5.................... $8......................... $15

63-3RW, Dodge Crane Truck, 1969, Yellow Dodge cab and chassis, red or yellow plastic hook, black grille and headlights, green plastic windows, 10 interior, six black plastic wheels, swiveling crane section, 3" .... $6................. $10......................... $18

64-2RW, M.G. 1100, 1966, Green car body, white plastic interior with driver in front and dog peeking out of rear window, clear plastic windows, black plastic wheels, unpainted base, white plastic tow hook, 2-5/8"................. $3.................... $7......................... $12

66-1RW, Citroen DS19, 1959, Yellow body, silver-painted grille, no window plastic, no interior, gray plastic wheels
.... $15................. $32......................... $55

66-3RW, Greyhound Bus, 1967, Silver-gray body, "Greyhound" decals or labels, yellow plastic windows, white plastic interior, black plastic wheels, 3".......... $8................. $12......................... $25

67-2RW, Volkswagen 1600 TL, 1967, Red body, white interior, unpainted base running up into headlights, clear window plastic, opening doors 2-11/16". One version with snap-on plastic roof rack was included with Race 'n Rally G-4 gift set, harder to find
.... $11................. $17......................... $25

Nylint Maxi-Mover U-Haul truck and trailer, $30.

Nylint Harley-Davidson trans tanker measures 25 inches long, $20.

	EX	NM	MIP

68-2RW, Mercedes Coach, 1966, White and blue-green or white and orange body, clear window plastic, white plastic interior, black plastic wheels. 2-7/8". Blue-green version harder-to-find with approximately $130 MIP values. More common orange-version values shown .... $7 .... $11 .... $15

69-1RW, Commer 30 CWT Nestle's Van, 1959, Dark-red or red van with Nestle's decals on panel sides, sliding doors, no window plastic, no interior, silver-painted grille, gray plastic wheels .... $22 .... $40 .... $90

Nylint

Cars & Vans

Baja Van, Nylint, black, opening rear doors, 11-1/2" long, late 1970s .... $8 .... $12 .... $17

Howdy Doody Pump Mobile, Nylint, 8-1/2" long .... $255 .... $455 .... $660

Pillsbury Hummer, Nylint, battery-operated, 11" long, 1990s .... $8 .... $12 .... $17

Vacationer Bronco and Travel Trailer, 1960s, Nylint, Blue open-top Ford Bronco with blue and white camper trailer. Bronco featured whitewall tires and fold-down windshield. 20" overall length; 1960s .... $105 .... $155 .... $210

Emergency Vehicles

Aerial Hook-N-Ladder, Nylint, turbine cab, "Nylint Fire Dept.," extra ladders on sides, 29-5/8" long, early 1970s .... $20 .... $30 .... $50

Ladder Truck, Nylint, post war, 30" long .... $100 .... $175 .... $250

Nylint See's Candy truck, $250.

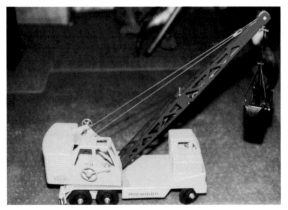

Nylint Michigan shovel is 31 inches long, $280 MIP.

	EX	NM	MIP

Farm and Construction Equipment

Michigan Shovel, Nylint, bright yellow, bucket tips automatically when raised to boom, boom raises and lowers, ten wheels, steerable front wheels, Model No. 2200
.... $150.............. $225..................... $280

Payloader, Nylint, bright red, 3-3/4" rubber tires, 18" long; 1955, Model No. 1600 .... $125.............. $187..................... $250

Road Grader, Nylint, sturdy blade can be raised, lowered, or tilted; tandem-pivoted rear wheels, 3-3/4" steel wheels, 19-1/4" long; 1955, Model No. 1400 $100 .... $180..................... $225

Speed Swing Pettibone, Nylint, orange, raise or lower bucket and tip to dump, steerable wheels, 3-3/4" rubber tires. "Pettibone" decal on sides. 19" long, Model No. 2000
.... $200.............. $300..................... $400

Street Sweep, Nylint, wind-up, 8-1/4" long, Model No. 1100
.... $175.............. $275..................... $350

Tournahopper, Nylint, huge hopper, pull lever at rear opens wide clamshell jaws for bottom dumping, 3-3/4" rubber-tired steel wheels, 22-1/2" long, Model No. 1500
.... $100.............. $150..................... $200

Tournarocker, Nylint, oversize hopper, crank action hoist, 3-3/4" rubber-tired steel wheels, 18" long; 1955, Model No. 1300
.... $75.............. $125..................... $175

Tournatracctor, Nylint, yellow, big, powerful, adjustable blade on front, pivoted tow-bar on rear, 14-3/4" long; 1955, Model No. 1900
.... $100.............. $150..................... $200

Traveloader, Nylint, orange, synchronized feeders, buckets, and rubber conveyor belt, hand crank, steel wheels w/3-3/4" rubber tires, 30" long, Model No. 1800
.... $200.............. $310..................... $400

Smith-Miller Toys Coca-Cola Truck, No. 206-C, 14" long, $900.
Photo courtesy Richard MacNary

Smith-Miller Toys L Mack Army Materials Truck, $925. Photo
courtesy Bob Smith

	EX	NM	MIP

Tractor-Trailers

Bandag, Nylint, display box, "Bandag, Your Tire Resource" on side
.... $5................. $10..................... $20

Case, Nylint, display box..... $17................. $33..................... $48

Cross Country Sears Van, Nylint, blue, 22" long;
1970s......................... $20................. $30..................... $50

Horse Van Truck & Trailer, Nylint, Bronze and white finish,
side and rear tailgates on trailer, includes two plastic horses
and two plastic colts, Model No. 6300
.... $45................. $65..................... $110

Mobile Home, Nylint, turquoise, #6600, 30" long;
1960s........................ $105................. $160..................... $210

Nutrena Feeds: Nylint, Sound Machine Semi series, display box,
20" long..................... $10................. $20..................... $35

Wal-Mart, Nylint, "Wal-Mart/Sam's",
21" long..................... $10................. $20..................... $30

Trucks

Ford Bronco N-8200 w/Sportsman Trailer, Nylint, open-topped Bronco,
blue and white trailer w/"Sportsman" decal
.... $50................. $72..................... $95

Ford Econoline w/camper, Nylint, turquoise, 12-1/2" long 1960s
.... $32................. $62..................... $105

Jumbo Michigan Shovel, Nylint, 20" long, 40" high with boom
extended; 1970s......... $10................. $14.00..................... $20

Missile Launcher, Nylint, rotating radar and launcher, late 1950s,
Model No. 2600......... $80................. $135..................... $180

Pepsi Truck, 1962, Nylint, Red, white and blue Pepsi truck features
plastic cases of Pepsi bottles, steel dolly, whitewall tires; 1962,
Model No. 5500....... $190................. $365..................... $500

Smith-Miller Toys GMC Mobilgas Tanker, No. 409-G, $750. Photo courtesy Tim Oei

Two examples of Structo's Motor Express Stake Truck, No. 601, $110. Photo courtesy Randy Prasse

	EX	**NM**	**MIP**

Ranch Truck, Chase & Sanborn Special, 1961, Nylint, Light blue and white truck with silver hubs, whitewall tires, removable stake sides, Chase & Sanborn boxes; 1961, Model No. 4500
.... $52................ $76.................... $100

Roamer, Nylint, turbine cab pickup w/camper
.... $10................ $15.................... $25

Tournahauler, Nylint, dark green, tractor w/enclosed cab, platform trailer, slid-out ramps, 41-1/2" long w/ramp extended; 1955, Model No. 1700 .... $125............... $150.................... $250

Tow Truck, Nylint, futuristic cab; 1970s
.... $18................ $30.................... $45

True Value Pickup, Nylint, red and white; 1970s
.... $50................ $85.................... $130

U-Haul Chevy Truck, 1975, Nylint, Orange and white cab, silver box, opening rear door; 1975, Model No. 8411
.... $80............... $115.................... $155

U-Haul Ford Truck and Trailer, Nylint, w/twin I-Beam suspension
.... $125............... $190.................... $250

Smith-Miller

Emergency Vehicles

"L" Mack Aerial Ladder, Smith-Miller, red w/gold lettering; polished aluminum surface, SMFD decals on hood and trailer sides, six-wheeler, 1950........... $375............... $475.................... $795

Trucks

"B" Mack Associated Truck Lines, Smith-Miller, red cab, polished aluminum trailer, decals on trailer sides, six-wheel tractor, eight-wheel trailer, 1954 .... $500............... $850.................... $1200

"B" Mack Lumber Truck, Smith-Miller, yellow cab and timber deck, three rollers, loading bar and two chains, six-wheeler, load of nine timbers; 1954........... $450............... $650.................... $1000

	EX	NM	MIP

"B" Mack P.I.E., Smith-Miller, red cab, polished trailer, six-wheel
tractor, eight-wheel trailer; 1954
.... $375.............. $600...................... $850

"L" Mack Army Materials Truck, Smith-Miller, Army green, flatbed
w/dark-green canvas, ten-wheeler, load of three wood barrels, two
boards, large and small crate; 1952
.... $375.............. $500...................... $750

"L" Mack Bekins Van, Smith-Miller, white, covered w/"Bekins" decals,
six-wheel tractor, four-wheel trailer; 1953
.... $1000.............. $1650................... $2000

"L" Mack International Paper Co., Smith-Miller, white tractor cab,
"International Paper Co." decals, six-wheel tractor, four-wheel
trailer; 1952 .... $375.............. $650...................... $900

"L" Mack Material Truck, Smith-Miller, light metallic-green cab, dark-
green fenders and frame, wood flatbed, six-wheeler, load of two
barrels and six timbers; 1950
.... $400.............. $600...................... $875

"L" Mack Mobil Tandem Tanker, Smith-Miller, all red cab, "Mobilgas"
and "Mobiloil" decals on tank sides, six-wheel tractor, six-wheel
trailer; 1952 .... $450.............. $725................... $1000

"L" Mack Orange Hydraulic Dump, Smith-Miller, orange cab, orange
dump bed, hydraulic, ten-wheeler, may or may not have "Blue
Diamond" decals; 1952
.... $850.............. $1500................... $1950

"L" Mack Sibley Van, Smith-Miller, dark-green cab, black fenders and
frame, dark-green van box w/"Sibley's" decal in yellow on both
sides, six-wheeler; 1950
.... $850.............. $1375................... $1850

"L" Mack Telephone Truck, Smith-Miller, all dark or two-tone green
truck, "Bell Telephone System" decals on truck sides, six-wheeler;
1952 .... $475.............. $750...................... $975

	EX	NM	MIP

Chevrolet Arden Milk Truck, Smith-Miller, red cab, white wood body,
four-wheeler; 1945 ... $275............... $465...................... $800

Chevrolet Coca-Cola Truck, Smith-Miller, red cab, wood body painted
red, four-wheeler; 1945
.... $300............... $600...................... $850

Chevrolet Lumber, Smith-Miller, green cab, load of 60 polished boards
and two chains; 1946 $150............... $195...................... $275

Chevrolet Stake, Smith-Miller, yellow tractor cab
.... $185............... $250...................... $425

Chevrolet Transcontinental Vanliner, Smith-Miller, blue tractor cab,
white trailer, "Bekins" logos and decals on trailer sides; 1946
.... $200............... $350...................... $495

Ford Bekins Van, Smith-Miller, red sand-cast tractor, gray sheet metal
trailer, fourteen-wheeler; 1944
.... $275............... $500...................... $750

GMC Arden Milk Truck, Smith-Miller, red cab, white-painted wood
body w/red stakes, four-wheeler; 1947
.... $200............... $425...................... $650

GMC Coca-Cola Truck, Smith-Miller, all yellow truck, red Coca-Cola
decals, five spoke hubs, four-wheeler, load of six cases each
w/24 plastic bottles; 1954
.... $275............... $450...................... $750

GMC Furniture Mart, Smith-Miller, blue cab, off-white body,
"Furniture Mart, Complete Home Furnishings" markings on body
sides, four-wheeler; 1953
.... $135............... $275...................... $295

GMC Kraft Foods, Smith-Miller, yellow cab, yellow steel box, large
"Kraft" decal on both sides, four-wheeler; 1948
.... $200............... $300...................... $450

Structo Package Delivery, No. 603, $200. Photo courtesy Randy Prasse

Structo Livestock Trucking semi truck and trailer, $95.

	EX	NM	MIP
GMC Mobilgas Tank, Smith-Miller, red cab and tanker trailer, large "Mobilgas", "Mobiloil" emblems on sides and rear panel of tanker, fourteen-wheeler; 1949	$135	$225	$400
GMC People's First National Bank and Trust Company, Smith-Miller, dark brownish-green cab and box, "People's First National Bank and Trust Co." decals on box sides; 1951	$165	$250	$385
GMC Rack Truck, Smith-Miller, red or yellow cab, natural finish wood deck, red stake sides, six-wheeler; 1948	$135	$200	$325
GMC Scoop Dump, Smith-Miller, rack and pinion dump w/a scoop, five-spoke wheels, six-wheeler; 1954	$275	$350	$575
GMC Super Cargo Tractor-Trailer, Smith-Miller, silver-gray tractor cab, hardwood bed on trailer w/red wraparound side rails, fourteen-wheeler, load of ten barrels; 1948	$150	$225	$395
GMC Tow Truck, Smith-Miller, white cab, red body and boom, five-spoke cast hubs, "Emergency Towing Service" on body side panels, four-wheeler; 1954 $95	$135		$200
GMC U.S. Treasury Truck, Smith-Miller, gray cab and box, "U.S. Treasury" insignia and markings on box sides, four-wheeler; 1952	$235	$325	$475

Structo

Aerial Fire Truck, 1950, StructoRed, 24Lx6.75Wx6.25H, 1 raising/2 side ladders & bell on hood, Model No. 250	$115	$175	$255
Aerial Hook & Ladder, 1965, StructoRed and red, 30.75Lx6.25Wx6.25H, two metal ladders, crank-operated lift ladder, Model No. 900 $55	$95		$135

Structo road grader measures 18 inches long, $105.

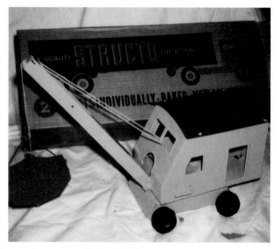

Structo clam crane with box, $175.

	EX	NM	MIP

Air Force Truck, 1958, StructoBlue and red, 17.25Lx7.25Wx8H, includes soldiers and canvas top, spare tires on side, Model No. 212 .... $115.............. $155...................... $195

American Airlines Sky Chef, 1962, StructoBlue and white, 12.5Lx5.25Wx7H, lever lifts cargo box with scissors lift mechanism, Model No. 303
.... $75................. $95...................... $125

Army Troop Tansport, 1959, StructoGreen, 18.75Lx6.75Wx9H, canvas top with "USA" printed. 4 plastic soldiers, Model No. 412
.... $55................. $75...................... $95

Army Troop Transport, 1959, StructoGreen, 18.75Lx6.75Wx9H, canvas top with "USA" printed. 4 plastic soldiers, Model No. 412
.... $55................. $75...................... $95

Auto Haulaway, 1956-57, StructoBlue and orange, 25Lx4.5Wx6.5H, with two cars, loading ramp and "S" grill cab, Model No. 175
.... $105.............. $175...................... $195

Auto Transport, 1963, StructoMet. gold, 22Lx5.5Wx7H, one metal car, one metal truck plus loading ramp, Model No. 402
.... $35................. $55...................... $75

Barrel Truck, 1954, StructoWhite and red, 12.75Lx5.5Wx5H, rare, made only in 1954. Replaced #811, no wind-up, Model No. 609
.... $115.............. $175...................... $205

Boon Dock'r, 1972, StructoRed and green, 23Lx5.5Wx5.25H, sport model design with buggy towing boat & trailer, Model No. 758
.... $25................. $35...................... $45

Bridge Set, 1970, StructoYellow and white, 22.25Lx3.5Wx5.5H, road tow'ds design with stake truck, 2 trailers & 4 pc. Bridge, Model No. 290 .... $15................. $25...................... $35

Bulldozer, 1960, StrucdtoYellow, 11.75Lx7Wx6.75H, black tires and motor, blade tips up, Model No. 210
.... $35................. $55...................... $75

	EX	NM	MIP

Cabin Cruiser, 1960, StructoRed and white, 12Lx4Wx3H, plastic hull, wooden deck and cabin, battery op motor, Model No. 212
.... $55................. $95...................... $125

Camper, 1964, StructoTeal and teal, 10.5Lx4.5Wx6.5H, plastic camper in truck bed, Model No. 203
.... $35................. $65...................... $85

Car Carrier, 1968, StructoRed and yellow, 22.25Lx6Wx7H, 3 plastic cars (Mustangs & T-Birds) loading ramp, Model No. 331
.... $45................. $65...................... $85

Cattle Trailer, 1953, StructoWhite and red, 21.5Lx5.5Wx7.5H, no loading ramp or animals, Model No. 708
.... $95............... $155...................... $205

Cattle Transport, 1960, StructoRed and white, 21.25Lx5.5Wx7.5H, plastic mirrors, windshield wipers and horn, Model No. 403
.... $45................. $65...................... $85

Cement Mixer, 1968, StructoRed and yellow, 16.5Lx6.5Wx7.5H, axle-driven gear operates barrel, Model No. 270
.... $35................. $55...................... $75

Clam Bucket and Machinery Truck, 1956-57, StructoYellow and green, 32Lx7.25Wx13.75H, with plastic fireball motor under the hood, Model No. 404......... $105............... $175...................... $205

Contractor Set, 1967, StructoGrey and orange, 3 pc. set includes #141, #153, #183, Model No. 192
.... $55................. $85...................... $125

Deluxe Auto Transport, 1956-57, StructoChrome and yellow, 27Lx6Wx6.75H, with 4 die-cast cars and loading ramp, Model No. 706 .... $75............... $135...................... $195

Deluxe Camper With Boat & Trailer, 1959, StructoRed and white, 29Lx6Wx6H, red truck with white roof, battery op boat motor, Model No. 601 .... $75............... $125...................... $175

	EX	NM	MIP

Deluxe Earth Mover, 1958, StructoOrange, 22Lx6.5Wx6.5H, with
plastic fireball motor under the hood, Model No. 322
.... $65.............. $105...................... $125

Deluxe Moving Van, 1958, StructoChrome and blue, 31Lx6Wx8.5H,
with loading ramp and mini grocery freight, Model No. 710
.... $105.............. $165...................... $205

Deluxe Transport, 1961, StructoRed and white, 23.5Lx6.5Wx8H, North
American Vanlines decals on trailer, Model No. 504
.... $55.............. $95...................... $155

Dispatch Truck, 1961, StructoMet. green, 13Lx5.25Wx5H, similar to
1950's barrel truck, plastic mirrors, wipers & horns, Model No.
208 .... $55.............. $75........................$95

Dump Truck, 1948, StructoRed 20L x 6.75Wx6.25H
long bullet headlights, Model No. 200
.... $95.............. $155...................... $225

Dump With Front-End Loader, 1958, StructoYellow and blue,
23Lx6.75Wx6.25H, spring loaded dump with front loader bucket,
Model No. 202 .... $105.............. $135...................... $175

Earth Mover, 1955, StructoOrange, 21.5Lx6.5Wx6.5H,
with plastic fireball motor under the hood, Model No. 320
.... $75.............. $105...................... $155

End Loader, 1954, StructoOrange, 15.25Lx6.25Wx6.75H,
with plastic fireball motor under the hood, Model No. 340
.... $65.............. $95...................... $145

Farm Set, 1964, StructoTeal and white, 5 pc. set includes
#314 & trailer, #250 cub pickup & trailer, Model No. 914
.... $95.............. $125...................... $155

Fire Rescue Truck, 1967, StructoRed, 12.75Lx5.75Wx5.75H,
turbine cab, lever operated ladder, Model No. 453
.... $55.............. $75........................$95

	EX	NM	MIP

Fisherman, 1965, StructoTeal and red, 20Lx4.5Wx5H, rampside
pick-up towing plastic boat on trailer, Model No. 204
.... $35................. $65........................ $85

Gasoline Truck, 1951, StructoRed and red, 13.5Lx5.5Wx5H, wind-up
motor, Model No. 866 $135............... $195...................... $255

Giant Bulldozer, 1965, StructoOrange and black, 11.5Lx7Wx5H,
blade raises and lowers with lever controls, Model No. 405
.... $45................. $65........................ $85

Grain Trailer, 1954, StructoWhite and orange, 20.75Lx5.5Wx5.5H,
sliding rear door, Model No. 704
.... $95................. $155...................... $205

Guided Missile Launcher, 1959, StructoRed and silver,
12.25Lx5.25Wx10.25H, plastic missile launcher on bed, metal
"S" grille, Model No. 203
.... $75................. $95........................ $125

Highway Builder Set, 1966, StructoGreen and yellow, 4 pc. set includes
#207, #316, sand hopper & sand loader, Model No. 910
.... $95................. $125...................... $155

Hi-Lift Dump Truck, 1952, StructoRed and blue, 12.5Lx5.5Wx5.25H,
wind-up motor with scissors lift box, Model No. 844
.... $105................. $155...................... $215

Hydraulic Dumper, 1962, StructoGreen, 13.75Lx5.5Wx6.25H,
hydraulic cylinder controls dump box, Model No. 407
.... $35................. $55........................ $75

Hydraulic Sanitation Truck, 1959, StructoBlue and white,
18Lx6Wx7.5H, hydraulic cylinder controls dump box,
Model No. 454 .... $65................. $95........................ $125

Kennel Truck, 1967, StructoYellow, 8.75Lx3.5Wx4H, Kom-pak
design with clear cover and 6 dogs, Model No. 137
.... $15................. $35........................ $55

	EX	NM	MIP

Livestock Truck, 1970, StructoGreen and white 9.5Lx4.25Wx4H, hurricanes design with white stake panels and 5 animals, Model No. 870 .... $15 .... $25 .... $35

Livestock Van, 1968, StructoTeal and white, 21.25Lx7.75Wx5.75H, turbine cab, white panels on side of trailer, Model No. 344 .... $55 .... $75 .... $95

Machinery truck, 1951, StructoOrange and blue, 12.75Lx5.5Wx5H, with loading ramp and chain winch, Model No. 607 .... $95 .... $155 .... $205

Mobile Anti-Missile Unit, 1959, StructoBlue and yellow, 27Lx7.5Wx11.25H, scarce, battery op spotlight & missile launcher on trailer, Model No. 620 .... $85 .... $115 .... $175

Mobile Crane, 1964, StructoOrange, 15.5Lx6.5Wx7.25H, cranks control the boom and clam bucket, swivels, Model No. 801 .... $75 .... $95 .... $125

Mobile Outer Space Launcher, 1959, StructoRed and blue, 19.5Lx6Wx12.75H, scarce, 2 plastic missiles launch. Launcher swivels, Model No. 503 .... $95 .... $135 .... $195

Motor Express Truck, 1951, StructoGrey and orange, 12.75Lx5.5Wx5H, cast cab "Freeport Motor Express" decals, Model No. 601 .... $75 .... $125 .... $195

Package Delivery Truck, 1954, StructoWhite and orange, 13Lx5.5Wx5H, cast cab, tailgate with chain, w/hubcaps, Model No. 603 .... $75 .... $125 .... $195

Pick-Up Truck With Horse Van, 1958, StructoBlue and yellow, 10.5Lx2.5Wx3H, includes 2 plastic horses, Model No. 100 .... $55 .... $85 .... $105

Power Shovel, 1961, StructoYellow, 26.5Lx7.5Wx7H, rubber tracks, Model No. 305 .... $35 .... $55 .... $75

Tonka pickup with update grille and body style from the early 1970s, $50 MIP.

Tonka pickup with grille style used from late 1962 to 1964, $40 MIP.

	EX	NM	MIP

Rampside Pick-Up, 1968, StructoRed, 10.5Lx4.5Wx5H, plastic bed liner and drop-down door in side of bed, Model No. 230 .... $25 .... $45 .... $65

Ready-Mix Concrete Truck, 1961 StructoRed and white, 15.5Lx7.75Wx9H, axle-driven gear operates barrel, Model No. 609 .... $55 .... $95 .... $115

Road Builder Set, 1962, StructoRed and yellow, same as #913 set plus #400, Model No. 915 $125 .... $155 .... $195

Road Grader, 1951, StructoOrange, 18Lx7Wx7.5H, with plastic fireball motor under the hood, Model No. 300
.... $55 .... $85 .... $105

Sand Hopper, 1963, StructoChartreuse, 8.25Lx6Wx12H, goes with construction sets, Model No. 190
.... $15 .... $25 .... $35

Sand Master Set, 1969, StructoYellow, 17.5Lx9Wx15H, plastic sand hopper with rubber conveyor belt, Model No. 580
.... $15 .... $25 .... $35

School Bus, 1962, StructoYellow, 10.5Lx4.75Wx5H, steel body, plastic mirrors, wipers and horn, Model No. 196
.... $55 .... $75 .... $95

SemiTrailer Lumber Truck, 1955, StructoGreen and orange, 17Lx4.5Wx4.5H, with three wooden logs and "S" grill cab, Model No. 156 .... $95 .... $155 .... $175

Shovel Dump Truck, 1951, StructoOrange and blue, 12.75Lx5.5Wx5H, cast cab, dump box, Model No. 605
.... $75 .... $125 .... $195

Speedway Pacer, 1973, StructoGreen, 9.25Lx4Wx4H, same as hurricane design #801 with speedway decals, Model No. 865
.... $25 .... $35 .... $45

Tonka Dump Truck, No. 006, 1961, $250. Photo courtesy Don and Barb DeSalle

	EX	NM	MIP
Steel Cargo Trailer, 1951, StructoBlue and red, 20.75Lx5.5Wx5.5H, blue cast cab with red trailer, no hubcaps, Model No. 702	$95	$135	$195
Stock Farm Set, 1959, StructoRed and white, 15Lx6Wx7.25H, stake truck with cattle loading ramp and 4 plastic horses, Model No. 501	$55	$85	$115
Stock Farm Set, 1959, StructoRed and white, 15Lx6yWx7.25H, stake truck with cattle loading ramp and 4 plastic horses, Model No. 501	$75	$95	$125
Timber Toter, 1955, StructoChrome and green, 21Lx6Wx6H, with six wooden logs and chains, Model No. 714	$65	$135	$175
US Main Truck, 1958, StructoBlue and red, 12.25Lx5.25Wx6.5H, Model No. 943	$95	$125	$175
Vista Dome Horse Van, 1968, StructoMet. gold, 21.75Lx6Wx6H, 2 ramp doors and 2 horses, 2 colts, Model No. 322	$45	$65	$85
Weekender, 1967, StructoTeal, 12Lx5.75Wx6.5H, molded built-in refrigerator & sink detail, Model No. 708	$55	$75	$95
Wrecker Truck, 1951, StructoRed and grey, 12.25Lx5.5Wx5.25H, wind-up motor and chain winch, Model No. 822	$95	$125	$175
Wrecker, 1963, StructoWhite, 13Lx5.25Wx5.5H, door windows and interior detail, black metal boom arm, Model No. 301	$55	$75	$95

Tonka

	EX	NM	MIP
No. 0100 Steam Shovel, 1947, 20-3/4" long	$135	$200	$350

	EX	NM	MIP
No. 0130 Tractor-Carry-All Trailer, 1949, 30-1/2" long	$100	$150	$350
No. 0500 Livestock Hauler Semi, 1952, 22-1/4" long	$100	$150	$350
No. 0550 Grain Hauler Semi, 1952, 22-1/4" long	$125	$180	$350
No. 0750 Carnation Milk Step Van, 1954, 11-3/4" long	$200	$400	$600
Allied Van Lines, 1955, No. 400-5, 23-3/4" long	$100	$200	$300
Dump, 1955, 13" red cab, green dump body	$100	$150	$350
No. 0725 Minute Maid Orange Juice Van, 1955, 14-1/2" long. White truck with Minute Maid graphics and opening rear doors	$275	$650	$950
No. 0575-6 Tonka Logger, 1956, 13-1/2" long. Red cab, logging trailer includes 9 sanded dowel logs. Silver five-hole hubs	$130	$240	$360
Big Mike Dual Hydraulic Dump Truck, 1957, 14" long	$325	$595	$1000
No. 0002 Pickup Truck, 1958 Next Generation Cars, dark-blue body, opening tailgate, trailer hitch	$100	$150	$300
No. 0005 Sportsman Pickup w/Topper, 1958 Next Generation Cars, 12-3/4" long, dark-blue body with camper topper, opening tailgate	$150	$225	$450
No. 0006 Dump Truck, 1958 Next Generation Cars, Red cab, two-position tailgate on dumper bed	$100	$150	$300
No. 0012 Road Grader, 1958 Next Generation Cars. Orange body with rotating and tilting blade, working steering, floating rear wheels	$75	$112	$150

	EX	NM	MIP

No. 0020 Hydraulic Dump Truck, 1958 Next Generation Cars
.... $125.............. $175..................... $275

No. 0028 Pickup with Stake Trailer and Animal, 1958 Next Generation
Cars, Standard dark-blue pickup, red stake trailer, plastic livestock
animal, stake tailgate on trailer lifts for loading and unloading
.... $125.............. $175..................... $350

No. 0035 Farm Stake, 1958 Next Generation Cars, w/two-horse trailer,
21-3/4" long. Trailer includes two plastic horses
.... $125.............. $250..................... $450

No. 0037 Thunderbird Express, 1958 Next Generation Cars, White cab
and freight trailer with fold-down wheels and opening rear doors
.... $150.............. $300..................... $600

No. 0041 Hi-Way Service Truck, 1958 Next Generation Cars, Orange
dump truck with two-position tailgate, drop side bed, scraper
blade and plastic road signs
.... $100.............. $200..................... $400

No. 0001 Service Truck, 1959, 12-3/4" long. Blue body, square box bed
with "Tonka Service" decals, whitewall tires, solid silver hubs,
removeable ladder, plastic windshield
.... $100.............. $150..................... $350

No. 0005 Sportsman, 1959, Tan body, camper top, whitewall tires, solid
silver hubs, white plastic boat attaches to topper with rubber straps
.... $100.............. $175..................... $350

Jolly Green Giant Special, 1960, white, green stake racks
.... $150.............. $300..................... $450

No. 0002 Pickup, 1960, Gold body, whitewall tires, solid silver hubs,
opening tailgate, trailer hitch, plastic windshield
.... $100.............. $200..................... $375

No. 0041 Boat Transport, 1960, 38" long. Blue truck with semi-trailer
that stacks four plastic boats virtually upright, with a bar at the
front for storing the outboard motors
.... $250.............. $450..................... $850

GMC box truck by Tootsietoy. Postwar and Prewar versions are shown here. Prewar models general feature more painted detail and separate castings. About $40 each.

Tootsietoy '48 Buick Super Estate Wagon, postwar, 6" long, $65. Photo courtesy John Gibson

	EX	NM	MIP

No. 0125 Lowboy and Bulldozer, 1960, 26-1/4" long. Light green cab, trailer, and bulldozer. Solid rubber tires without hubs on rear of trailer. Bulldozer with 3-position blade
.... $190.............. $375..................... $675

No. 0118 Giant Dozer, 1961, 12-1/2" long. A king-sized version of the regular dozer.............. $70.............. $100..................... $250

No. 0136 Houseboat Set, 1961, 29" long total. Includes red and white "Fisherman" pickup with red tilt-bed boat trailer and plastic (floating) houseboat .. $200.............. $400..................... $800

No. 0140 Sanitary Truck, 1961, 19-1/2" long. White cab and rounded garbage section. Swinging rear door, hopper bucket raises up to drop garbage in truck $400.............. $700..................... $1500

No. 0145 Tanker, 1961 ...... $100.............. $250..................... $350

No. 0249 Jeep Universal, 1962
.... $75.............. $125..................... $175

No. 840 Car Carrier, 1965, Yellow cabover truck and trailer with three plastic vehicles, 27" long. Makes first appearance in 1965 catalog
.... $80.............. $170..................... $365

No. 1070 Camper, 1968, Jeep Gladiator truck body, magenta, with white camper top. The pattern for these trucks is the same as the No. 70 models dating from 1963, but color changes and line expansion forced Tonka to add more two more digits to the stock number..................... $15................. $30......................... $50

Tootsietoy

Cars

Armored Car, Tootsietoy, "U.S. Army" on sides, camouflage, black tires, 1938-41, Model No. 4635
.... $25.............. $35......................... $65

*Tootsietoy Kayo Ice Wagon, No. 5105, prewar, $300. Photo courtesy
John Gibson*

*Tootsietoy Tow Trucks, the '35 and '34 Wreckers. Note the separately
cast grille and wheels with tires on the earlier model on the right.
Each about $70 MIP.*

	EX	NM	MIP

Auburn Roadster, Tootsietoy, red, white rubber wheels, Model No. 1016
.... $15................. $30........................$45

Buick Coupe, Tootsietoy, blue w/white wheels, 1924, Model No. 4636
.... $30................. $42........................$65

Buick Estate Wagon, Tootsietoy, yellow and maroon w/black wheels,
6" long, 1948 .... $20................. $30........................$50

Cadillac, Tootsietoy, HO series, blue car/white top, 2" long; 1960
.... $10................. $20........................$30

Cadillac 62, Tootsietoy, red-orange w/white top, black wheels, four-
door, 6" long; 1954..... $20................. $35...................... $120

Chevrolet Ambulance, Tootsietoy, 4"
.... $15................. $20........................$35

Chevrolet Bel Air, Tootsietoy, yellow w/black wheels, 3" long; 1955
.... $15................. $30........................$50

Chevrolet Brougham, Tootsietoy, Model No. 6203
.... $40................. $60........................$85

Chevrolet Touring Car, Tootsietoy, Model No. 6205
.... $60............... $150...................... $200

Chrysler New Yorker, Tootsietoy, blue w/black wheels, four-door,
6" long; 1953 .... $25................. $35........................$55

Corvair, Tootsietoy, red, 4" long; 1960s
.... $30................. $55........................$75

Corvette Roadster, Tootsietoy, blue open top, black wheels, 4" long;
1954-55...................... $15................. $20........................$35

DeSoto Airflow, Tootsietoy, green w/white sheels, Model No. 0118
.... $20................. $35........................$60

Ford Convertible Coupe, Tootsietoy, 1934
.... $30................. $50........................$70

	EX	NM	MIP

Ford Fairlane 500 Convertible, Tootsietoy, red w/black wheels, 3" long;
1957 .... $10................. $15........................ $30

Ford Ranch Wagon, Tootsietoy, green w/yellow top, four-door, 4" long;
1954 .... $15................. $25........................ $35

Ford Roadster, Tootsietoy, powder blue w/open top, white wheels,
Model No. 0116 .... $25................. $40........................ $60

Ford Thunderbird, two-door 1955 coupe, 4" long; open wheel wells, fin-
style rear fenders, open wheel wells, patterned plastic tires,
1960-67........................ $6................. $12........................ $18

Ford Tourer, Tootsietoy, open top, red w/silver spoke wheels, Model No.
4570 .... $20................. $30........................ $45

Graham Convertible Coupe, Tootsietoy, rear spare tire, rubber wheels,
1933-35, Model No. 0514
.... $50.............. $125........................ $175

International Station Wagon, Tootsietoy, 4" long, rubber wheels;
1940s .... $25................. $45........................ $50

Jaguar XK 120 Roadster, Tootsietoy, green open top, black wheels,
3" long .... $10................. $15........................ $25

Kaiser Sedan, Tootsietoy, blue w/black wheels, 6" long; 1947
.... $25................. $45........................ $55

LaSalle Convertible, Tootsietoy, rubber wheels,
Model No. 0714 .... $80.............. $200........................ $300

Lincoln, Tootsietoy, prewar; red w/white rubber wheels, four-door
.... $110.............. $400........................ $500

Mercedes 190 SL Coupe, Tootsietoy, powder blue w/black wheels,
6" long; 1956 .... $15................. $25........................ $40

Mercury Fire Chief Car, Tootsietoy, red w/black wheels, 4" long;
1949 .... $25................. $35........................ $50

	EX	NM	MIP
Nash Metropolitan Convertible, Tootsietoy, red w/black tires; 1954	$25	$35	$60
Oldsmobile Roadster, Tootsietoy, orange/black, white wheels, 1924, Model No. 6301	$25	$45	$75
Packard, Tootsietoy, white body w/blue top, black wheels, four-door, 6" long; 1956	$12	$23	$35
Plymouth Belvedere, Plymouth 1957 model, 3" long; two-door hardtop, blue or red, open wheel wells, patterned plastic tires, 1959-69	$6	$12	$18
Pontiac Fire Chief, Tootsietoy, red w/black wheels, 4" long; 1950	$20	$35	$50
Porsche Roadster, Tootsietoy, red w/open top, black wheels, two-door, 6" long; 1956	$20	$25	$40
Studebaker Coupe, Tootsietoy, green w/black wheels, 3" long; 1947	$25	$35	$50

Trucks

	EX	NM	MIP
Army Half Truck, Tootsietoy, 1941	$30	$55	$75
Buick Delivery Van, Tootsie toy, Model No. 6006	$25	$35	$50
Cherry Picker, Super Tootsietoys series, 8" long; Ford Pickup truck with cherry-picker snorkel mounted in truck bed, 1966	$7	$15	$22
Chevrolet Cameo Pickup, Tootsietoy, green w/black wheels, 4" long; 1956	$15	$25	$40
Chevrolet El Camino Camper and Boat, Tootsietoy, blue body w/red camper, black/white boat on top of camper	$25	$35	$45

	EX	NM	MIP

Dodge D100 Panel, Tootsietoy, green and yellow, 6" long
.... $18................. $36........................$55

Ford F6 Pickup, Tootsietoy, red, 4" long; 1949
.... $15................. $25........................$40

Horse Trailer, Road Haulers series tractor-trailer, 8-1/4" long, die-cast cab with white plastic interior and grille, orange plastic horse trailer with lowering gate, six plastic horses, white hub tires; 1970s .... $5............... $10........................$15

International Car Transport Truck, Tootsietoy, red tractor, orange double-deck trailer w/cars
.... $35................. $50........................$70

Mack Transport, Tootsietoy, red, open cab w/flatbed trailer, Model No. 190 .... $60............... $150......................$200

Model T Pickup, Tootsietoy, 3" long, 1914, Model No. 4610
.... $30................. $50........................$75

Sinclair Oil Truck, Tootsietoy, 6" long; green/silver, Model No. 1007
.... $25................. $50........................$75

Tootsietoy Dairy, Tootsietoy, semi-trailer truck, Model No. 0805
.... $75............... $110......................$140

Wrigley's Box Van, Tootsietoy, w/or without decal; 1940s, Model No. 1010 .... $45................. $60........................$75

Resources

200 Years of Dolls Identification and Price Guide, second edition, by Dawn Herlocher, 2002, Krause Publications, Iola, Wisconsin

Collector's Guide to PEZ®, Identification & Price Guide, second edition, by Shawn Peterson, 2003, Krause Publications, Iola, Wisconsin

Fisher-Price Historical, Rarity, and Value Guide, 1931-Present, third edition, by Bruce R. Fox and John J. Murray, 2002, Krause Publications, Iola, Wisconsin

O'Brien's Collecting Toy Cars & Trucks Identification & Value Guide, third edition, edited by Elizabeth A. Stephan, 2000, Krause Publications, Iola, Wisconsin

O'Brien's Collecting Toys Identification & Value Guide, tenth edition, edited by Elizabeth A. Stephan, 2001, Krause Publications, Iola, Wisconsin

Standard Catalog of Farm Toys Identification and Price Guide, edited by Elizabeth A. Stephan and Dan Stearns, 2001, Krause Publications, Iola, Wisconsin

Toy Shop's Action Figure Price Guide, edited by Elizabeth A. Stephan, 2000, Krause Publications, Iola, Wisconsin (out of print)

Toys & Prices, eleventh edition, edited by Karen O'Brien, 2003, Krause Publications, Iola, Wisconsin

Warman's Barbie® Doll Field Guide edited by Paul Kennedy, 2003, Krause Publications, Iola, Wisconsin

Warman's Hot Wheels™ Field Guide, by Michael Zarnock, edited by Tracy Schmidt, 2003, Krause Publications, Iola, Wisconsin